Global Issues in Constitutional Law

By

Brian K. Landsberg
Professor of Law
University of the Pacific, McGeorge School of Law

Leslie Gielow Jacobs
Professor of Law
University of the Pacific, McGeorge School of Law

AMERICAN CASEBOOK SERIES®

Mat #40541669

American Casebook Series and West Group are trademarks
registered in the U.S. Patent and Trademark Office.

© 2007 Thomson/West
  610 Opperman Drive
  P.O. Box 64526
  St. Paul, MN 55164–0526
  1–800–328–9352

Printed in the United States of America

ISBN: 978–0–314–17608–0

TEXT IS PRINTED ON 10% POST
CONSUMER RECYCLED PAPER

Preface

Law schools have begun to recognize the need to provide global perspectives in so-called domestic law courses. *See, e.g.*, Mathias Reimann, *From the Law of Nations to Transnational Law*, 22 Penn. St.Intl.L.R. 397 (2004) and *Making Transnational Law Mandatory: Requirements, Costs, Benefits*, 23 Penn. St. Intl.L.R. 787 (2005); Franklin A. Gevurtz, et al., *Report Regarding the Pacific McGeorge Workshop on Globalizing the Law School Curriculum*, 19 Pac. McGeorge Global Bus. & Dev. L.J. 267 (2006). This recognition extends to Constitutional Law. *See, e.g.*, Neil S. Siegel, *Some Modest Uses of Transnational Legal Perspectives in First-Year Constitutional Law*, 56 J. Legal Ed. 201 (2006); Mark Tushnet, *How (And How Not) to Use Comparative Constitutional Law in Basic Constitutional Law Courses*, 49 St. Louis U.L.J. 671 (2005). Nonetheless, the case books commonly used to teach Constitutional Law in law schools contain almost no comparative or international materials. *But see,* Donald Kommers, *American Constitutional Law: Cases, Essays and Comparative Notes* (2d ed. 2004). The most obvious reason is that the case books already have more pages than a conscientious professor can cover in the time allotted. Faculty must almost always make hard choices as to which material to cover and which material to skip.

So we are torn between the need for coverage of basic domestic concepts and our felt need to also introduce global perspectives. The latter, we feel, can be invaluable in illuminating the U.S. Constitution. In addition, of course, international law is a direct source of constitutional law. Moreover, exposure to foreign constitutional law helps prepare students for practice in a globalized society. Limited exposure will not lead to understanding of other constitutions, but will both whet the interest and create awareness that more study is needed if one engages in a global law practice. Deeper understanding can be fostered in courses in International Law and in the newer discipline of Comparative Constitutional Law. (For very fine case books, *see, e.g.*, Norman Dorsen, Michel Rosenfeld, András Sajó, and Susanne Baer, *Comparative Constitutionalism: Cases and Materials* (2003) and Vicki C. Jackson and Mark Tushnet, *Comparative Constitutional Law* (2d ed. 2006)). Finally, exposure to foreign constitutional cases can help students understand the debate over the use of foreign law as persuasive authority in American constitutional cases.

This book is designed to help constitutional law professors who wish to provide some exposure to global perspectives but are concerned about detracting unduly from core coverage. The amount of comparative and international law material available is overwhelming. Our object was not to write a comprehensive book but to give faculty a modest menu of comparative and international materials from which to choose. We have kept it short, in an effort to minimize the need to cut domestic coverage in order to add comparative and international coverage. The materials are keyed to the major themes of most constitutional law courses. Some professors may feel comfortable assigning the entire book, while others will wish to pick and choose.

We have test run some of the material. In addition, Brannon Denning of Cumberland Law School used some material in his class. Overall student reactions have been positive, even though use of the material may have lengthened some reading assignments. Many students recognize the growing force of globalization in the law and are hungry to learn more.

We wish to thank the participants in two Pacific McGeorge workshops on global issues in the law. Their insights significantly influenced us as we put this book together. Participants in the Constitutional Law portion of the August 2005 workshop at Squaw Valley were Vikram D. Amar, Alan E. Brownstein, Leslie Gielow Jacobs, Michel Rosenfeld, Mark V. Tushnet, and Lorraine Weinreb. Participants in the Constitutional Law breakout session at the January 2007 workshop at Georgetown Law Center were session leaders Mark S. Kende and Brian Landsberg, as well as Lisa Dolak, Sudha Setty, Mirat Guarori, Ettie Ward, John Sims, Brannon Denning, and Rosemary C. Salomone.

We are also grateful to Kim Clarke, Director of the Pacific McGeorge library, and Jessica Rader, student research assistant, for invaluable assistance in gathering materials, guiding us, and formatting and cite-checking. Finally, thanks to Franklin Gevurtz, who spearheaded the globalization project, Louis Higgins and Kathleen Vandergon at Thomson West, and to Dean Elizabeth Rindskopf Parker and Pacific McGeorge, for their support of the project.

Acknowledgments

We gratefully acknowledge receiving permission to reprint the following materials:

Penelope Andrews and Stepehn Ellman, eds., The Post Apartheid Constitutions: Perspectives on South Africa's Basic Law (Johannesberg, South Africa: Witwatersrand University Press Publications, 2001).

Edgar Bodenheimer, John Bilyeu Oakley and Jean C. Love, An Introduction to the Anglo-American Legal System (St. Paul: West Publishing Company, 1980).

Rakesh Chhetri, Bhutan's Sham Constitutionalism, Kathmandu Post, Jan 30, 2002. Reprinted with the permission of the Mercantile Communications Pvt. Ltd., which holds the copyright.

Sarah H. Cleveland, Our International Constitution, 31 Yale J. Int'l L. 1 (2006). Reprinted with the permission of the Yale Journal of International Law, which holds the copyright.

Combating Discrimination in Russia: Strategies for Lawyers and NGO's, Open Society Institute. Copyright © 2003 Open Society Institute. Reprinted with the permission of the Open Society Institute, 400 West 59th Street, New York, NY 10019 USA, www.justiceinitiative.org. or www.soros.org.

Robert J. Cottrel, Brown and the Contemporary Brazilian, 66 U.Pitt.L.Rev. 113 (2004). Reprinted with the permission of the University of Pittsburgh Law Review, which holds the copyright.

Louis F. Del Duca and Patrick Del Duca, An Italian Federalism?—The State, Its Institutions and National Culture as Rule of Law Guarantor, Am'n J. Comp. L., 2007. Reprinted with the permission of the American Journal of Comparative Law, which holds the copyright.

Norman Dorsen, The relevance of foreign legal materials in U.S. constitutional cases: A conversation between Justice Antonin Scalia and Justice Stephen Breyer, 3 Int'l. J. Const. L. 519 (2005). Reprinted with the permission of the International Journal of Constitutional Law, which holds the copyright.

Norman Dorsen et al., Comparative Constitutionalism, Cases and Materials. Reprinted with the permission of Thomson West.

Ter Ellingson, "The Nepal Constitution of 1990: Preliminary Considerations" in Himalayan Research Bulletin, Vol. XI, Nos. 1–3. 1991. Reprinted with the permission of the Himalayan Research Bulletin, which holds the copyright.

Jon Elster, Forces and Mechanisms in the Constitution-Making Process, 45 Duke L.J. 364 (1995). Reprinted with the permission of the Duke Law Journal, which holds the copyright.

European Union, A Constitution for Europe (2004). Luxembourg: Office for Official Publications of the European Communities, 2004.

Richard J. Goldstone, A South African Perspective on Social and Economic Rights, Hum. Rts. Br., Winter 2006. Reprinted with the permission of the Human Rights Brief, which holds the copyright.

Nicholas Haysom, Federal Features of the Final Constitution, in The Post-Apartheid Constitutions: Perspectives on South Africa's Basic Law (Penelope Andrews and Stephen Ellman, eds., 2001).

Louis Henkin, A New Birth of Constitutionalism: Genetic Influences and Genetic Defaults, 14 Cardozo L. Rev. 533 (1993). Reprinted with the permission of the Cardozo Law Review, which holds the copyright.

Steven Holmes and Cass Sunstein, The Politics of Constitutional Revision in Eastern Europe in Responding to Imperfection (1995).

Human Rights Watch, China: A Year after New Regulations Rights Still Restricted (2006).

Donald P. Kommers, Comparative Constitutional Law: Its Increasing Relevance in Defining the Field of Comparative Constitutional Law (Vicki Schultz & Mark Tushnet eds., 2002).

Donald P. Kommers, The Constitutional Jurisprudence of the Federal Republic of Germany (1997).

Ivana Krstic, Affirmative Action in the United States and the European Union: Comparison and Analysis, 1 Law and Politics 825 (2003). Reprinted with the permission of Scientific Journal, Law and Politicas, which holds the copyright.

H. Kwasi Prempeh, Marbury in Africa: Judicial Review and the Challenge of Constitutionalism in Contemporary Africa, 80 Tulane L.Rev. 1239 (2006). Reprinted with the permission of the Tulane Law Review, which holds the copyright.

John M. Maki, Court and Constitution in Japan: Selected Supreme Court Decisions: 1948–60 (1964).

Jonatas E.M. Machado, Freedom of Religion: A View From Europe, 10 Roger Williams U.L. Rev. 451 (2005). Reprinted with the permission of the Roger Williams University Law Review, which holds the copyright.

Magna Carta in ICONS: A Portrait of England.

James T. McHugh, Comparative Constitutional Traditions. New York: Peter Lang Publishing, 2002. Reprinted by permission of the publisher. All rights reserved.

Patrick J. Monahan, Constitutional Law (2d ed., 2002).

Claude Moraes, Race Against Time: The European Union's new directive will enforce the principle of equal treatment regardless of ethnic origin, June 30, 2000. Reprinted with the permission of the Guardian Unlimited, which holds the copyright.

Martha I. Morgan, Emancipatory Equality, Gender Jurisprudence in The Gender of Constitutional Jurisprudence (Beverly Baines & Ruth Rubio-Marin, eds., 2005). Reprinted with the permission of Cambridge University Press.

Makau Wa Mutua, Limitations on Religious Rights: Problematizing Religious Freedom in the African Context in Religious Human Rights, in Global Perspective, Legal Perspectives 417, 439–40 (Johan D. van der Vyver and John Witte, Jr. eds., 1996).

Gerald L. Neuman, Human Rights and Constitutional Rights: Harmony and Dissonance, 55 Stan. L. Rev. 1863 (2003). Reprinted with the permission of the Stanford Law Review, which holds the copyright.

Dullah Omar, Constitutional Development: The African Experience in Defining the Field of Comparative Constitutional Law (Vicki Schultz & Mark Tushnet, eds., 2002).

Frances Raday, Culture, Religion and Gender, 1 Int'l J. Const. L. 663 (2003). Reprinted with the permission of the International Journal of Constitution Law which holds the copyright.

Bjorn Erik Rasch & Roger D. Congleton, "Amendment Procedures and Constitutional Stability", in Democratic Constitutional Design and Public Policy: Analysis and Evidence (Roger D. Congleton and Birgitta Swedenborg, eds., 2006).

Isabelle Rorive, Strategies to Tackle Racism and Xenophobia on the Internet—Where are We in Europe?, Int'l J. Comm. L. & Policy

1 (2002/2003). Reprinted with the permission of the International Journal of Comparative Law and Policy, which holds the copyright.

Herman Schwartz, Building Blocks for a Constitution in Issues of Democracy: Constitutionalism and Emerging Democracies (March 2004).

Shimon Shetreet, State and Religion: Funding of Religious Institutions—The Case of Israel in Comparative Perspective, 13 Notre Dame J.L. Ethics & Pub. Pol'y 421 (1999). Reprinted with the permission of the Notre Dame Journal of Law Ethics and Public Policy, which holds the copyright.

Tad Stahnke & Robert C. Blitt, The Religion-State Relationship and the Right to Freedom of Religion or Belief: A Comparative Textual Analysis of the Constitutions of Predominantly Muslim Countries, 36 Geo. J. Int'l. 947 (2005). Reprinted with authors' permission.

Cass R. Sunstein, Why Does the American Constitution Lack Social and Economic Guarantees? 56 Syracuse L. Rev. 1 (2005). Reprinted with the permission of the Syracuse Law Review, which holds the copyright.

Amin Tarzi, Afghanistan: Apostacy Case Reveals Constitutional Contradictions, Radio Free Europe: Radio Liberty (2006). Copyright © 2007. RFE/RL, Inc. Reprinted with the permission of Radio Free Europe/Radio Liberty, 1201 Connecticut Ave., N.W. Washington DC 20036. www.rferl.org.

Adam Tomkins, Public Law (Oxford University Press, 2003). Reprinted with the permission of Oxford University Press.

Hannibal Travis, Freedom or Theocracy?: Constitutionalism in Afghanistan and Iraq, 3 Nw. U.J. Int'l Hum. Rts. 17 (2005). Reprinted with the permission of the Northwestern University Journal of International Human Rights, which holds the copyright.

UN Office for the Coordination of Humanitarian Affairs, ZIMBABWE: Media monitor condemns radio jamming, 21 March 2005. Reprinted with the permission of IRIN, which holds the copyright.

United States Congressional-Executive Commission on China, Annual Report 2005

United States Department of State, International Religious Freedom Report 2005.

Wil Waluchow, Constitutionalism, in The Stanford Encyclopedia of Philosophy (Spring 2004 Edition) (Edward N. Zalta, ed.). Reprinted with the permission of the Metaphysics Research Lab, CSLI, which holds the copyright.

James Q. Whitman, The Two Western Cultures of Privacy: Dignity Versus Liberty, 113 Yale L.J. 1151 (2004). Reprinted with the permission of the Yale Law Journal, which holds the copyright.

Garret Wilson, The Effect of Legal Tradition on Affirmative Action in the U.S. and Brazil. Reprinted with the permission of the University of San Francisco, Comparative Law, which holds the copyright.

*

WI Waluchow, Constitutionalism, in The Stanford Encyclopedia of Philosophy (Spring 2004 Edition) (Edward N. Zalta, ed.). Reprinted with the permission of the Metaphysics Research Lab, CSLI, which holds the copyright.

James Q. Whitman, The Two Western Cultures of Privacy: Dignity Versus Liberty, 113 Yale L.J. 1151 (2004). Reprinted with the permission of the Yale Law Journal, which holds the copyright.

Carrol Wilson, The Effect of Legal Tradition on Affirmative Action in the U.S. and Brazil. Reprinted with the permission of the University of San Francisco, Comparative Law, which holds the copyright.

Global Issues Series

Series Editor, Franklin A. Gevurtz

Titles Available Now

Global Issues in Civil Procedure by Thomas Main, University of the Pacific, McGeorge School of Law
ISBN 978–0–314–15978–6

Global Issues in Constitutional Law by Brian K. Landsberg, University of the Pacific, McGeorge School of Law and Leslie Gielow Jacobs, University of the Pacific, McGeorge School of Law
ISBN 978–0–314–17608–0

Global Issues in Contract Law by John A. Spanogle, Jr., George Washington University, Michael P. Malloy, University of the Pacific, McGeorge School of Law, Louis F. Del Duca, Pennsylvania State University, Keith A. Rowley, University of Nevada, Las Vegas, and Andrea K. Bjorklund, University of California, Davis
ISBN 978–0–314–16755–2

Global Issues in Corporate Law by Franklin A. Gevurtz, University of the Pacific, McGeorge School of Law
ISBN 978–0–314–15977–9

Global Issues in Criminal Law by Linda Carter, University of the Pacific, McGeorge School of Law, Christopher L. Blakesley, University of Nevada, Las Vegas and Peter Henning, Wayne State University
ISBN 978–0–314–15997–7

Global Issues in Labor Law by Samuel Estreicher, New York University School of Law
ISBN 978–0–314–17163–4

Global Issues in Legal Ethics by James E. Moliterno, College of William & Mary, Marshall-Wythe School of Law and George Harris, University of the Pacific, McGeorge School of Law
ISBN 978–0–314–16935–8

Global Issues in Property Law by John G. Sprankling, University of the Pacific, McGeorge School of Law, Raymond R. Coletta, University of the Pacific, McGeorge School of Law, and M.C. Mirow, Florida International University College of Law
ISBN 978–0–314–16729–3

For Fall 2007 adoption, we also expect to have titles available in Employment Discrimination and Family Law.

*

Summary of Contents

Table of Contents

*

Table of Cases

The principal cases are in bold type. Cases cited or discussed in the text are roman type. References are to pages. Cases cited in principal cases and within other quoted materials are not included.

Global Issues in Constitutional Law

*

Chapter One

INTRODUCTION TO A CONSTITUTION

The United States was the first nation to create a constitution. Now, almost all nations have one. This section asks both what makes a document a "constitution" and looks at why and how one is made.

I. CONSTITUTION-MAKING

What prompts constitution-making? What are the crucial considerations when one is made?

Jon Elster
Essay: Forces and Mechanisms in the Constitution–Making Process

45 Duke L.J. 364, 368–95 (1995)

Modern constitution-making began in the late eighteenth century. Between 1780 and 1791, constitutions were written for the various American states, the United States, Poland, and France.

The next wave occurred in the wake of the 1848 revolutions in Europe. Counting all the small German and Italian states, revolutions took place in more than fifty countries. Many of these also adopted new constitutions—often replaced within a short period by constitutions imposed by the victorious counterrevolutionary forces.

A third wave broke out after the First World War. The newly created or recreated states of Poland and Czechoslovakia wrote their constitutions. The defeated German state adopted the Weimar Constitution.

Next, the fourth wave occurred after the Second World War. The defeated nations—Japan, Germany and Italy—adopted new

1

constitutions under the more or less strict tutelage of the Allied Powers.

A fifth wave was connected with the breakup of the French and British colonial empires. It began in India and Pakistan in the 1940s, but the process did not really gain momentum until the 1960s. In many cases, the new constitutions were modeled closely on those of the former colonial powers. To name only a few examples, the constitution of the Ivory Coast was modeled on that of the Fifth French Republic, whereas those of Ghana and Nigeria followed the British "Westminster model."

The next wave is linked to the fall of the dictatorships in Southern Europe in the mid–1970s. Between 1974 and 1978, Portugal, Greece, and Spain adopted new democratic constitutions.

Finally, a number of former Communist countries in Eastern and Central Europe adopted new constitutions after the fall of communism in 1989. Although I do not have an exact count, there must be a couple of dozen new constitutions in the region.

[A] large fact that may help us understand why constitutions occur in waves ... is that new constitutions almost always are written in the wake of a crisis or exceptional circumstance of some sort....

[The result is] two basic paradoxes of constitution-making. ... The first paradox arises from the fact that the task of constitution-making generally emerges in conditions that are likely to work against good constitution-making. Being written for the indefinite future, constitutions ought to be adopted in maximally calm and undisturbed conditions....

The second paradox stems from the fact that the public will to make major constitutional change is unlikely to be present unless a crisis is impending.... If people find themselves with all the time they need to find a good solution, no solution at all may emerge.

Herman Schwartz
Building Blocks for a Constitution
Issues of Democracy, 12, 12–17 (March 2004)
http://usinfo. state.gov/journals/ itdhr/0304/rjde/ rjde0304.pdf

Those who write constitutions for emerging democracies face daunting challenges. First, they must write a document that enables the society to decide difficult and divisive questions peacefully, often under grave circumstances. At the same time they must establish effective protections for human rights, including the right of the minority to disagree.

Secondly, divisions and conflicts usually begin quickly and resolving these can create long-term problems. When the transformation is negotiated, as in much of the former Soviet bloc, the losers will try to hold on to as much power as they can. If the change involves the complete ouster of a regime, as in Iraq, then the winners will vie for power. The compromises resolving these disputes are often incorporated into the constitution, which can be troublesome in the long run. For example, compromises over slavery in the U.S. Constitution made it possible to get that Constitution adopted but were ultimately not good for the nation.

Moreover, a constitution is written at a specific point in time, usually when the society faces very difficult economic, social and other problems. There is a temptation and often a necessity to deal with these problems quickly. But provisions designed to quickly deal with immediate problems may not be appropriate solutions for the long term.

Overhanging all documents written at a specific time and place is the fact that it is impossible to foretell the future—and the future will always be different from what is anticipated. Thus, drafters of constitutions must give future governments the flexibility to meet unpredictable and unforeseeable challenges.

. . .

PRELIMINARY CONSIDERATIONS

First, should the constitution be written by an ordinary legislative body or by a special constituent assembly? If the decision is to go with the former, incumbent legislators can write a constitution that keeps themselves in office. A special constituent assembly representing as many elements in society as possible is preferable, even though it is more cumbersome and expensive.

Another preliminary decision is about changing or amending the constitution after it is adopted. It should not be easy to do this.

. . .

THE BUILDING BLOCKS

An initial issue is whether to have a presidential or a parliamentary system.

. . .

There is no obvious answer to which system is better. The choice will often depend on history, the needs of the moment, and other factors. All the countries of the former Soviet bloc outside the Soviet Union, as well as the Baltic nations, adopted parliamentary regimes, in large part because they wanted to become a part of Western Europe which is almost entirely parliamentary. All the former non-Baltic components of the Soviet Union however, have adopted presidential systems. . . .

It must also be decided whether to have a unicameral (single house) or a bicameral (upper and lower house) legislature. If the state is to be a federal state with relatively autonomous components, such as the United States or Germany, it may be desirable to have a second (usually upper house such as the U.S. Senate) legislative chamber that represents the interests of the components.

. . .

Whether to have a second chamber raises an additional question: how centralized is the state to be? How much authority and autonomy should be allocated to lower levels of government like regions or national units?

. . .

THE JUDICIARY

History has established the need for an independent judiciary that can keep the other branches from transgressing constitutional limits, and particularly where basic human rights are concerned. This can be either the regular judicial system, as in the United States, or a special tribunal, a constitutional court, limited to deciding constitutional questions and a few other matters, as in Germany.

. . .

Whatever system is chosen, the constitution must explicitly establish the courts' authority to annul laws and other norms and acts inconsistent with the constitution.

. . .

The constitution must also provide that the lower court judges apply the constitution in their decision-making. In many of the new democracies, all too often those judges ignore constitutional issues when making decisions.

. . .

PROTECTION OF HUMAN RIGHTS

Every new constitution now contains a statement of basic human rights. This is not enough. The constitution must create institutions to make those rights enforceable. The constitution must specifically provide that persons who claim that their rights have been violated have ready access to a court, and that if a violation has occurred, the victim can obtain an adequate remedy for that violation.

. . .

ADOPTING THE CONSTITUTION

The final question is how should the constitution be adopted? By the special constituent assembly discussed earlier? By the regular parliament, as in many European countries? By the general public? Should the public's involvement take place before or after the constitution is drafted? If the latter, how should the public's participation be obtained? These and other questions have been answered in different ways, and though many political scientists believe that the approval of a constitution should be by the people, that has not been the universal approach.

Writing a constitution is an experiment, the results of which will always be significantly different from what was intended and anticipated. Moreover, the success of a constitution is usually the result of external factors—the economy, the social forces at work within the society, the nation's foreign relations, natural disasters, and many other factors over which constitutional drafters have no control.

Notes

1–1.   Two recently drafted constitutions are those of Afghanistan and Iraq, pursuant to processes that were heavily covered in the U.S. news. Although they do not fall into any of the waves described in the first excerpt, do they form another, identifiable "wave" of their own? Do those constitutional drafting processes exhibit the paradox described above? How did those countries resolve the many questions of the constitutional drafting process?

1–2.   Does the history of the U.S. Constitution—its drafting and amendment—illustrate the paradox described above? How were the questions confronting the drafters of the U.S. Constitution similar or different from those confronting the constitutional drafters in Afghanistan or Iraq?

II. CONSTITUTIONALISM

What does it mean to have a "constitution"? Is more than simply having a document with that label required?

Stanford Encyclopedia of Philosophy
Constitutionalism
(Spring 2004)
http://plato.stanford.edu/archives/spr2004/entries/
constitutionalism/

In some minimal sense of the term, a "constitution" consists of a set of rules or norms creating, structuring and defining the limits of, government power or authority. Understood in this way, all states have constitutions and all states are constitutional states.

Anything recognisable as a state must have some acknowledged means of constituting and specifying the limits (or lack thereof) placed upon the three basic forms of government power: legislative power (making new laws), executive power (implementing laws) and judicial power (adjudicating disputes under laws). Take the extreme case of an absolute monarch, Rex, who combines unlimited power in all three domains. If it is widely acknowledged that Rex has these powers, as well as the authority to exercise them at his pleasure, then the constitution of this state could be said to contain only one rule, which grants unlimited power to Rex. He is not *legally* answerable for the wisdom or morality of his decrees, nor is he bound by procedures, or any other kinds of limitations or requirements, in exercising his powers. Whatever he decrees is constitutionally valid.

When scholars talk of constitutionalism, however, they normally mean something that rules out Rex's case. They mean not only that there are rules creating legislative, executive and judicial powers, but that these rules impose limits on those powers. Often these limitations are in the form of individual or group rights against government, rights to things like free expression, association, equality and due process of law. But constitutional limits come in a variety of forms. They can concern such things as the *scope* of authority (e.g., in a federal system, provincial or state governments may have authority over health care and education while the federal government's jurisdiction extends to national defence and transportation); the *mechanisms* used in exercising the relevant power (e.g., procedural requirements governing the form and manner of legislation); and of course *civil rights* (e.g., in a Charter or Bill of Rights). Constitutionalism in this richer sense of the term is the idea that government can/should be limited in its powers and that its authority depends on its observing these limitations. In this richer sense of the term, Rex's society has not embraced constitutionalism because the rules defining his authority impose no constitutional limits.

A. ELEMENTS

Scholars have struggled to define the details of "constitutionalism." The attributes of rule of law, separation of powers, popular sovereignty and guarantee of rights are on most lists. Bhutan, a small nation located between China and India, has never had a constitution. In the following opinion piece, a critic of the Bhutan monarch's effort to create a constitution articulates many of the more specific elements that "constitutionalism" is thought to require.[1]

1. The king unveiled the draft constitution in March, 2005, which has yet to be approved by national referendum.

Rakesh Chhetri
Bhutan's Sham Constitutionalism

Kathmandu Post, Jan. 30, 2002, available at
http://www.nepal news.com.np/contents/
englishdaily/ktmpost/2002/jan/
jan30/features.htm

Authoritarian Bhutan does not have a Constitution. Under pressure from Bhutanese activists in exile and international community, the King has commissioned a Constitution drafting committee on November 30, 2001. It is yet another gimmick and 'window dressing' to show democratic credentials of the king to the international community. An authoritarian absolute monarch is hardly expected to write an effective representative democratic Constitution. It is important to discuss the principles of constitutionalism vis-a-vis the authoritarian rule. The basic principle of constitutionalism is to limit powers as against absolutism in Bhutan. A constitution is established to restrict the possibility of abuse of power by the ruler.

Constitution is the basic law and legal authority of a state. All laws are derived from it. It establishes a framework under which law is made and administered. It establishes the three organs of the government—legislature, to make laws; executive or the government to administer and execute the laws-and an independent judiciary to adjudicate on legal disputes between the citizens and the state, and among the citizens. In Bhutan's context, the king is the executive head of all the three organs of the government and exercises absolute power. He, and not the constitution, is the basis of legal authority.

. . .

Constitutionalism: Constitutionalism means limited government. Most of the countries, even those having totalitarian and despotic governments, have constitutions. In a totalitarian and despotic system, constitution confers wider powers and discretion on the government to suppress and oppress their people. They cannot be accepted as a constitutional government. There is a fundamental difference between constitutions which exist at the pleasure of those in power, and constitutions which limit power—absolute power of an individual or a group. How could Bhutan ruled by an absolute monarch and governed by the 'rule of man' suddenly and voluntarily offer constitutionalism or rule of law? This only lends credence to the belief that Bhutan is trying to acquire a sham constitutionalism. True constitutionalism is not at all possible in Bhutan unless the king gives up his powers.

. . .

Rule of law: The rule of law is essential for safeguarding civil liberties and for maintaining social order. The rule of law envisages that if our relationships with each other and with the state are governed by a set of rules, rather than by an individual or a group of individuals' we are less likely to fall victim to the authoritarian rule. The rule of law calls for both individuals and the government to submit to the law's supremacy. It is not possible to establish such rule of law in the present despotic Bhutan. Those close to the king will continue to exercise the law at their whims and fancies.

Democracy: Effective Constitutionalism is not at all possible without a system of representative democracy and a system of checks and balances on those exercising power.... An elected government should be restricted by the constitution and the law. The government is also periodically accountable to the people and the people have the right to criticize. A representative democracy is incomplete without the existence of political parties, civil society, free and fair elections, freedom of expression and real decentralization of power. Thus, Bhutan must establish a representative democracy before drafting the Constitution. How could the constitution become functional without a representative democracy? We often hear the government hawks saying that 'people are not ready for democracy'. Democracy is a system, which offers preferences to people and they do not have to be 'ready' to accept a good system.

Checks and balances: A system of checks and balances checks both corruption as well as improper conduct of the political leaders. The law and the constitution exert various pressures on the representative government. The opposition party, parliament, media, civil society, pressure groups, trade unions, civil society, consumer forums etc., exercise substantial influence on the government, which direct and indirectly restrain government power. These are non-existent in Bhutan. Practice of holding regular elections imposes restrictions on the actions of the politicians and the government. Freedom of speech and expression is one of the most important restrictions. But there is no such freedom in Bhutan. Any criticism of the king and his government is considered treasonable offence. Bhutan must allow freedom of expression before embarking on sham constitutionalism and democracy....

Personal liberty: In a country like Bhutan, individuals live under perennial fear. A knock on the door can mean arrest and imprisonment without trial and even torture and death. People brought to trial are denied a fair hearing and charges often concern acts which are regarded as legitimate conduct in a democratic world. Bhutanese jails are occupied by prisoners of conscience and political dissidents, who are guilty of no criminal offence by democratic standards.

. . .

No Nepali-speaking citizens, who comprise about 45 percent of Bhutan's population, has been included in the drafting Committee. The constitution will not represent the aspiration of all the sections of the Bhutanese society.... Unless, the king gives up his absolute powers, allow the political parties to function and pave the way for the establishment of a true liberal representative democracy, the so-called Constitution will have no meaning. It will be a sham constitution.

Notes

1–3.   In *Marbury v. Madison,* 5 U.S. (1 Cranch) 137, 163, 2 L.Ed. 60 (1803), Justice John Marshall states, "The government of the United States has been emphatically termed a government of laws, and not of men." Does the above excerpt help you to see what a "government ... of men" might mean? As to a more precise definition of the "rule of law," *see* Michel Rosenfeld, *The Rule of Law and the Legitimacy of Constitutional Democracy*, 74 S.Cal. L. Rev. 1307, 1308–13 (2001) ("[T]here is no consensus on what 'the rule of law' stands for.... At a minimum ... the rule of law requires fairly generalized rule through law: a substantial amount of legal predictability (through generally applicable, published and largely prospective laws); a significant separation between the legislative and the adjudicative function; and widespread adherence to the principle that no one is above the law."); Richard H. Fallon, Jr., *"The Rule of Law" as a Concept in Constitutional Discourse*, 97 Colum. L. Rev. 1, 8–9 (1997) ("[L]eading modern accounts generally emphasize five elements that constitute the Rule of Law. (1) The first element is the capacity of legal rules, standards, or principles to guide people in the conduct of their affairs. People must be able to understand the law and comply with it. (2) The second element of the Rule of Law is efficacy. The law should actually guide people, at least for the most part.... (3) The third element is stability.... (4) The fourth element of the Rule of Law is the supremacy of legal authority. The law should rule officials, including judges, as well as ordinary citizens. (5) The final element involves instrumentalities of impartial justice. Courts should be available to enforce the law and should employ fair procedures.").

1–4.   Why is separation of powers so important to make a constitution "real"? Could a king other than the one described as ruling Bhutan exist in a constitutional democracy?

1–5.   What does popular sovereignty as a requirement of constitutionalism mean? Does it apply to the creation of the constitution itself, as the above writer implies? Consider that far fewer than half of the U.S. residents at the time were eligible to vote to ratify the Constitution. Or does popular sovereignty apply to the way current laws are enacted and applied? Does the U.S. constitutional structure meet the demands of popular sovereignty?

1–6. Protection of individual rights is widely viewed as an element necessary to make a constitution "real." But constitutions vary widely in the rights protected. Are there some core individual rights that a constitution must protect to meet the demands of constitutionalism? Was the U.S. Constitution a "sham" before the effective date of the Bill of Rights?

1–7. In 2004, representatives of the nations of the European Union (EU) signed the Treaty establishing a Constitution for Europe. It was in the process of required ratification by member states when, in 2005, both French and Dutch voters rejected it in referendums. These rejections have stalled the ratification process by other nations. Whether a supranational organization such as the EU should or can have a "constitution" has been the subject of extensive debate. The European Union itself describes the document as follows:

> A Constitution is a text which contains the fundamental rules of a State or a group of States. These rules answer several questions. How do the institutions work? How is the division of powers arranged? What means can be used to implement policies? What values are upheld? What are the citizens' fundamental rights?

> In actual fact, the European Constitution is both a treaty subject to the rules of international law and a Constitution in that it contains elements of a constitutional nature.

> The European Constitution replaces the main existing Treaties [which establish the rules of the EU] with a single text.

> The European Constitution does not replace the national Constitutions of the countries of Europe. It coexists with these Constitutions and has its own justification and its own autonomy. The European Constitution defines the contexts within which the European Union is competent to act. Europe also has a distinct institutional system (European Parliament, Council of Ministers, European Commission, Court of Justice of the European Union, etc.). . . .

> The European Constitution is divided into 4 parts. Part I defines the values, objectives, powers, decision-making procedures and institutions of the European Union. It also describes the symbols, citizenship, democratic life and finances of the Union. Part II contains the "Charter of Fundamental Rights." Part III describes the policies, the internal and external action, and the functioning of the European Union. Part IV contains general and final provisions, including the procedures for adopting and revising the constitution.

European Union, *A Constitution for Europe* 3–4 (2004), http://europa. eu.int/constitution/download/brochure_160904_en.pdf. Would the EU Constitution, if ratified, serve the purposes of a national constitution? How would it be different and how the same?

B. STRUCTURE

What should a constitution look like?

1. Written vs. Unwritten

Justice Marshall, again in *Marbury v. Madison*, 5 U.S. at 176–179, lauds the value of a "written" constitution. For a constitution to be "real," is a writing required?

James T. McHugh

Comparative Constitutional Traditions

33 (2002)

The United States Constitution generally is cited as a "written" constitution. However, a more accurate and meaningful designation would be to refer to it as an "entrenched" constitution.

The concept of "entrenchment" refers not to the presence of a written document but to the manner in which it is created and maintained. Constitutions, by their nature, should not be subject to the degree of change possible through the normal legislative process. An entrenched document is created in a manner that imposes certain obstacles, even upon a general expression of the sovereign will, and its amendment or replacement is made equally difficult. Generally, an indication of some form of broad consensus is required to create or alter an entrenched constitutional document, thus raising its status above all other law within a society.

. . . .

Many observers commonly refer to the British constitutional tradition as a prime example of an "unwritten constitution." However, that term is inaccurate. . . . [T]he British constitutional tradition can be identified in terms of numerous written documents, statutes, and other, positive sources that can be read and analyzed. . . .

The British constitutional tradition is more accurately identified as an "unentrenched" constitution. Its interpretation and application depend upon an ability to recognize its presence without the need for a formal document that defines it, succinctly. Furthermore, it is grounded upon expectations that are, while informal in appearance, just as powerful and binding as any formally entrenched constitutional legacy. . . .

One colloquial expression that may be found among some members of modern British society may be a reference to something that is, in practical terms, prohibited, simply because it is considered to be "not the done thing." . . . An unentrenched constitutional tradition absolutely depends upon that sort of attitude in order for it to function with any semblance of feasibility.

An unentrenched constitution does not have a formal structure. Its norms and principles are located in a diversity of sources that are well known to constitutional scholars, legal practitioners, and political elites.

Notes

1–8. Like England, New Zealand and Israel have so-called "unwritten" constitutions, although the Israeli Knesset is in the process of enacting a series of Basic Laws, which have constitutional stature. *See* New Zealand Parliament, *How Parliament Works; Our System of Government*, http://www.parliament.govt.nz/en-NZ/HowPWorks/Our System/1/8/e/18e21b6e2651428bb64fab273c1c4d86.htm (last visited Nov. 27, 2006) ("New Zealand has no single written constitution or any form of law that is higher than laws passed in Parliament. The rules about how our system of government works are contained in a number of Acts of Parliament, documents issued under the authority of the Queen, relevant English and United Kingdom Acts of Parliament, decisions of the court, and unwritten constitutional conventions."); Daniel J. Elazar, *The Constitution of the State of Israel*, Jerusalem Center for Public Affairs, http://www.jcpa.org/dje/articles/const-intro–93.htm (last visited Nov. 27, 2006) ("Israel is, in fact, formally committed to the adoption of a written constitution. The first Knesset was elected as a constituent assembly and spent considerable time debating whether or not to write a constitution. The body was deadlocked as the religious parties opposed the idea of a constitution other than the Torah, while the left-wing socialists were equally opposed because they knew that any constitution that would emerge would not embrace their Marxian vision of what the new state should be. In a classic speech, David Ben–Gurion, Israel's first prime minister, moved that preparation of a comprehensive constitution be set aside in favor of piecemeal development through enacting Basic Laws as consensus was achieved about each subject, that together would ultimately form a constitution. . . . The proposal for piecemeal writing of the constitution was accepted so every Knesset is also a constituent assembly that can enact Basic Laws, usually by a modest special majority of 61, namely, half plus one of its total membership. The Knesset deals with Basic Laws and other constitutional matters through a standing Constitutional, Legislative and Judicial Committee."). Is there a difference between application of an "unwritten" constitution and the U.S. Constitution? Is there a significant unwritten background to the U.S. Constitution as well?

1–9. In constitutional democracies without one formal document, convention acts much like fundamental law, as the following excerpt explains.

Conventions that do not have the force of law

There is a strong element in British constitutional affairs of things happening just because this is the way they have always been done, or at least have been for a very long time. Tradition dictates that the State Opening of Parliament must begin with Black Rod, the monarch's messenger, having the door to the Commons chamber slammed in his face when he comes to summon members to the House of Lords. This symbolises the constitutional supremacy of the elected house, which is able to defy the wishes of peers.

The conventions also cover the code of conduct for ministers of the Crown, who are expected to conform to certain standards of behaviour. A secretary of state who has lost the confidence of the House, particularly of those on his or her own side, is expected to do the decent thing and resign. Similarly, a minister who is found to have told a deliberate untruth has to go. The conventions are not legally enforceable, but have been almost invariably observed throughout history.

ICONS, *A Portrait of England,* http://www.icons.org.uk/theicons/collection/magna-carta/features/the-british-constitution-finished (last visited Nov. 27, 2006). Are there conventions that apply to U.S. constitutional law? *See* Elazar, *supra* page 12 ("[I]n the American constitutional system, the conventions surrounding the Electoral College that morally bind presidential electors to follow the decision of the majority of the voters in their respective states are considered by Americans to be a matter of fundamental law, even though they are merely custom.").

1–10. To the extent that democracies operate without a formal constitution, Parliament is supreme. *See* ICONS, *supra* page 13 ("[In England a]ll executive power resides ultimately with Parliament. No other body is capable in practice of overruling the decisions of Parliament. Laws flow from Parliament, and the House of Lords, as well as being a legislative chamber, is also the highest court in the land. If your case has failed in a normal court of law, and then in the Appeal Court, you have the right finally to have it heard in the upper chamber of Parliament. Parliament has the right to summon anybody to appear before its committees, and acting in contempt of Parliament is a serious offence."). Note that Justice Marshall in *Marbury v. Madison,* 5 U.S. at 178, suggested that such legislative supremacy "would subvert the very foundation of all written constitutions." Does the situation in England prove him right or wrong?

1–11. Why haven't more countries followed the British model? The following excerpt offers some possibilities.

It is noteworthy that in none of the constitutional transformations of the last two decades has the transforming country adopted the British model of parliamentary supremacy coupled with the absence of a single written constitutional document. This model, also represented in New Zealand and Israel but nowhere else among developed countries, has plainly fallen into some disrepute, but the reasons for this are unclear. One possibility is that the American model has won the day in the court of world constitutional opinion. Another is that a functioning government in the absence of a written constitution requires a degree of antecedent political stability that few, if any, transforming societies are likely to have. And still another is that transforming societies believe, perhaps correctly, that the very process of constitution-making serves important political functions independent of the product of that process.

Frederick Schauer, *The Causes and Consequences of Constitutional Form, Discussion Draft* 9 n.8 (1998), http://siteresources.world bank.org/INTLAWJUSTINST/Resources/ConstilReformSchauer.pdf. Why do you think countries opt for a formal, written constitution?

2. *Short or Long*

Herman Schwartz
Building Blocks for a Constitution
Issues of Democracy, 12, 13–14, March 2004,
http://usinfo. state.gov/journals /itdhr/0304/rjde /rjde0304.pdf

[Another] preliminary question [in drafting a constitution] is whether the constitution should be short or long. Many in the United States believe that because our short Constitution has lasted for more than 200 years, short constitutions are the best, even for nascent democracies. I do not share that view. U.S. constitutional law cannot be found within the texts of the thirty-four original and amending articles. It can only be found in the almost 540 volumes of decisions that a powerful and solidly established U.S. Supreme Court has issued over some 215 years. These decisions have established our most fundamental constitutional principles and rights, few of which can be discerned from the bare text of the U.S. Constitution. Democracies that are new, however, do not have the luxury of either the 215 years to develop these rights and few, if any, start out with a powerful judiciary. They can and should build on American and other experience, and write these fundamental rights and principles into their constitutions without having to wait for the courts.

This does not of course mean that the constitution should be very detailed. Constitutions that include too much can block the necessary flexibility. Deciding what should go into a constitution, what should be left to the legislature, and what should not be regulated at all, is one of the most basic and difficult initial questions.

Ter Ellingson
The Nepal Constitution of 1990:
Preliminary Considerations

Himalayan Res. Bull. (1991),
http://inic.utexas. edu/asnic/ countries/nepal/ nepconst analysis.html

With its 133 articles, the Nepal constitution is considerably longer and more complex than the U.S. constitution (1789/1979), with its 7 articles and 26 amendments, and much shorter and simpler in structure than the Indian constitution (1950/1983) with its 395 articles, 10 schedules, and 3 appendices. It closely approximates the constitution of the People's Republic of China (1982/1987) in number of articles (the Chinese constitution has 138); but, owing to greater length and complexity of the articles, the Nepal constitution is perhaps two to three times longer than the Chinese. In overall comparison, the Nepal constitution falls fairly high on the scale of length and complexity, but below some others such as the Sri Lanka constitution (1978), to say nothing of the Indian constitution, which forms a widely-recognized class in itself.

Following a general rule to which the 1990 Nepal constitution is no exception, length and complexity increase with the amount of detail of administrative law and procedures superimposed on the more widespread and basic prescriptions of principles and governing structures shared by all constitutions. Thus, for example, not only do over half of the 24 articles of the section of the Nepal constitution which deal with the legislature (Part 8, Articles 44–67) concern matters of procedure, but also the entire section is followed by two more sections with an additional 16 articles (Parts 9–10, Articles 68–83) devoted entirely to procedural matters. While shorter constitutions leave administrative and procedural details to be worked out by means such as enacted laws, legal challenges and test cases, custom and consensus, longer constitutions with explicit prescriptions of such details embed them in the basic law of the land. It can be expected that in such cases, procedures are more difficult to adjust and adapt to changing circumstances, as a constitutional amendment would theoretically be required in every case. On the other hand, constitutional encoding of such details can provide safeguards against easy abuses and arbitrary changes in procedure at the administrative level. Whether this additional protection is worth the tradeoff in procedural rigidity and resistance to change remains to be seen.

Notes

1–12.   What particular circumstances might dictate whether a constitution should be short or long? How long would you expect the new constitutions of Afghanistan or Iraq to be?

1–13.   The Nepal constitution deals with procedures in detail. What circumstances might cause drafters to opt for this approach? How does the U.S. Constitution, though short, deal with procedure? Why?

III. AMENDMENT

Must a constitution be amendable? Or does it defeat the fundamental, entrenched quality of a constitution that a current majority can change it?

PRIVACY OF COMMUNICATIONS
CASE [THE KLASS CASE]

30 Bverfge 1 (1970) (F.R.G. Fed. Const. Ct.)
Translated in Norman Dorsen et al., *Comparative Constitutionalism,
Cases and Materials* 92 (2003)
Reprinted with permission of Thomson West

[Article 79(3) of the Basic Law provides: "Amendments to this Basic Law affecting the division of the Federation into Lander, their participation in the legislative process, or the principles laid down in Articles 1 and 20 shall be prohibited. Article 1 declares human dignity to be inviolable and Article 20 sets out the elements that define Germany as "a democratic and social federal state." A constitutional amendment to another article of the German Basic Law allowed for a broader range of secret surveillance of individuals than had previously been permitted and altered some aspects of judicial review.]

Judgement of the Second Senate:

.   .   .

2.a.   The purpose of Art. 79, par. 3, as a check on the legislator's amending the Constitution is to prevent both abolition of the substance or basis of the existing constitutional order, by the formal legal means of amendment . . . and abuse of the Constitution to legalize a totalitarian regime. This provision thus prohibits a fundamental abandonment of the principles mentioned therein. . . .

b.   . . . Restriction on the legislator's amending the Constitution . . . must not, however, prevent the legislator from modifying by constitutional amendment even basic constitutional principles in a system-immune manner. From this point of view, the subsidiary principle derived from the rule of law [of which, some of its specifics are set out in Art. 20], that a maximum of judicial protection must be available to the citizen, does not belong among the "principles laid down" in Art. 20....

C. Art. 79, par. 3, does exempt from possible amendment the protection afforded by Art. I to the dignity of man. But whether a constitutional amendment violates human dignity can only be decided in the context of a specific situation....

III. [The amendment] is compatible with Art. 79, par. 3....

Dissenting opinion by Justices Geller, Dr. v. Schlabrendorff, and Prof. Dr. Rupp.

a) Art. 79, par. 3, declares inviolable certain principles laid down in the Constitution. The Basic Law also ... limits constitutional amendments. Such an important, far-reaching, and exceptional provision must certainly not be interpreted in an extensive manner. But it would be a complete misunderstanding of its meaning to assume that its main purpose was only to prevent misuse of the formal legal means of a constitutional amendment to legitimatize a totalitarian regime.... Art. 79, par. 3, means more: Certain fundamental decisions of the Basic Law maker are inviolable.

. . . .

[W]e conclude: the principle based upon Art. 1 that man must not be treated as a mere object of the state and that his rights must not summarily be disposed of by authorities and Art. 20's constitutional call for a maximum of individual legal protection are among the "principles laid down in Arts. 1 and 20." These two principles contain fundamental decisions of the Basic Law that decisively shape the image of a state based upon the rule of law.... Art. 79, par. 3, specifies that these constituent elements shall be irrevocable.

C) The constitutional amendment "affects" the principles laid down in Arts. 1 and 20.

The wording and meaning of Art. 79, par. 3, do not merely forbid complete abolition of all or one of the principles. The word "affect" means less.... The constituent elements are also ... to be protected against a gradual process of disintegration.

Notes

1–14. In the Klass case, the German Constitutional Court recognized the possibility of an "unconstitutional constitutional amendment." Is such a thing possible under the U.S. Constitution? Consider the following:

A constitution, among other things, is a document that is unusually difficult to change. Constitutionalism hinges upon a distinction between the procedures governing ordinary legislation and the more onerous procedural hurdles that must be overcome in order to recast the ground rules of political life. To understand the amending power and its limits, therefore, is to understand the balance of rigidity and flexibility, or permanence and adaptability, that lies at the heart of constitutional government....

. . .

A theory of the amending power must prove the difficult relationship between constitutional limits on power and the limbo-inhabiting power to revise those limits....

Amendability suggests, to put it crudely, that basic rights are ultimately at the mercy of interest-group politics, if some arbitrary electoral threshold is surpassed and amenders play by the book.... Does Article V of the U.S. Constitution imply the triumph of procedure over substance, formal rules over moral norms? Are there no goods that are protected absolutely, rather than depending on a percentage of votes?

This question can be reformulated in practical terms. Does the political system of a specific country, say the United States or Germany, admit judicial review of procedurally correct constitutional amendments? The United States does not, on the ground that the constitution-remaking power is superior to the power of judicial review; but Germany does, on the ground that an amendment, even if passed in the formally correct manner, may be inconsistent with the core or fundamental features of the constitution. Germany entrenches certain rights in the sense that it places them beyond not only politics, but even the kind of revision represented by constitutional amendment.

The form taken by the amending power, in other words, sheds light on the variety of theories underlying different Liberal democracies. It helps us identify the broad norms and basic commitments behind the constitutional fine print. It helps explain how various framers conceived the relationship between procedure and substance, for instance, or the distinction between the core and the periphery of the constitutional order. In the American case, the amending power builds upon a democratic conception of popular sovereignty, of the authorizing democratic will that stands above the constitution and is able to change it in toto. This idea fits well with the self-conscious American revision of the English understanding of sovereignty. The German Constitution, while gesturing in the direction of popular sovereignty, declares many provisions unamendable, allowing the unelected court effectively to block certain attempts by the elected branches to change the constitution.

Stephen Holmes & Cass Sunstein, *The Politics of Constitutional Revision in Eastern Europe, in* Responding to Imperfection 275, 275–79 (Sanford Levinson ed., 1995). Why do you think the German Basic Law makes some provisions unamendable? Is it worrisome that the U.S. Constitution, with two exceptions, does not?

1–15. Constitutions employ a broad range of amendment procedures, as the following excerpt explains.

Almost all constitutions specify procedures for rewriting or replacing the constitutional text, and they are almost always more stringent or demanding than ordinary legislative procedures. However, a wide range of formal amendment procedures potentially satisfy this condition, and, this allows the stringency of amendment processes to vary widely. More stringent amendment procedures help make constitutional commitments stable and thus credible. Such procedures, consequently, help to create a higher legal system that will stand above and limit ordinary legislation (Ferejohn 1997). Less stringent amendment procedures allow constitutional mistakes to be readily corrected and institutional experimentation to be more readily conducted.

The stringency of a formal amendment process reflects a commitment by constitutional designers to *entrench* certain rules and procedures or specific programs and prohibitions. Often formal amendment procedures are quite complex, and in many cases different methods of amendment are stipulated for different provisions in the constitution or allowed in more or less urgent times. Finland, for example, has a main procedure requiring delay and decision by two-thirds of the members of parliament (MPs), as well as an urgency procedure in which the threshold is increased to a five-sixths majority for adoption of an amendment via a single vote. Estonia also has an urgency procedure. All the Baltic States have tried to protect the most important articles of their constitutions by saying that they cannot be amended unless the voters agree (referendum). In Lithuania, no less than a qualified majority of three-fourths is needed to change the first article of the constitution.

Other constitutions rule out particular formal constitutional reforms altogether. For example, Article V of the U.S. Constitution says that "no state, without its Consent, shall be deprived of its equal Suffrage in the Senate." In Germany, the federal system is protected against changes. Similarly, amendments of the basic principles of Articles 1 (on human dignity) and 20 (on basic principles of state order and the right to resist) are inadmissible (see Article 79). A recent example to the same effect is found in the constitutional framework of Bosnia–Herzegovina, based on the Dayton agreement. Paragraph 2 of Article X states that "No amendment to this Constitution may eliminate or diminish any of the rights and freedoms referred to in Article II of this Constitution or alter the present paragraph."

. . .

In general, it becomes more difficult to change a constitution as the number of actors and decision points increase, and as the required degree of consensus increases. To put it differently, the stability of a constitution depends to some extent on the number of veto players, that is, actors whose agreement is necessary for amending the constitution. . . .

Although amending processes are often strikingly complex, usually a relatively small set of devices are actually used in constitutions around the world. . . .

[C]onstitutional stability is typically achieved in two ways. First, some form of *repeated decisions or a series of decisions by multiple actors* may be used. The purpose of these devices could simply be delay in order to ensure that society acts on well-founded and stable expectations about the consequences of reform and sufficient time is provided at the preparatory stages of the decision process. Second, ratification may require a broader consensus than ordinary legislation. Consensus can be broadened through super-majority rules or by including extra-parliamentary actors, such as the voters by means of a referendum or an intervening election, or subnational units of the state by means of a decentralized ratification method in federal systems. In most constitutional systems the elected representatives of the citizenry play a prominent, but not necessarily exclusive, role in amendment processes.

With respect to the Nordic region, constitutional amendments require multiple decisions in parliament in all the countries but Norway. In Norway, it is sufficient to submit the constitutional amendment to parliament one year before the next election, and it is the task of the next parliament to decide on the proposal after the election. Denmark, Sweden, Finland, and Iceland require consent from two different parliaments, that is, those assembled before and after an election. The Baltic states require repeated decisions in parliament, but none of them demands that proposals must rest over an election (as in all the other countries [surveyed]). Denmark is the only Nordic country requiring direct voter involvement as part of any constitutional process, not only with respect to the most important changes.

Bicameral and presidential systems normally require separate approvals by both chambers of the legislature and/or by an independently elected president. Germany illustrates this possibility. The consent of both the Bundestag and the Bundesrat is needed, but not an intervening election. In the Netherlands, both chambers must agree to the constitutional amendment before and after an election, which requires a total of four separate decisions (or perhaps five, if the intervening election is counted). In several countries, separate constitutional referenda are also required, as in Denmark and Switzerland. In federal states, consent of regional governments as in the United States, Canada, and Australia is also required for constitutional reform.

Bjonn Erik Rasch & Roger D. Congleton, *Amendment Procedures and Constitutional Stability, in* Democratic Constitutional Design and Public Policy: Analysis and Evidence 319, 325–31 (Roger D. Congleton and Birgitta Swedenborg eds., 2006).

IV. THE INFLUENCE OF THE UNITED STATES CONSTITUTION ON OTHER NATIONS' LAW

As the first, the U.S. Constitution has always been available as a model for others in drafting their constitutions. What prompts nations to accept or reject the American example?

Louis Henkin
A New Birth of Constitutionalism: Genetic Influences and Genetic Defaults
14 Cardozo L. Rev. 533, 536–39 (1993)

It is neither chauvinistic nor unduly self-congratulatory to claim for the United States major credit for establishing and spreading the constitutionalist ideology. Our Declaration of Independence includes perhaps the most famous articulation of the principles of popular sovereignty, of limited and accountable government, and of individual rights. The United States Constitution also provided essential precedents. Ours was the first written constitution—a prescriptive constitution that is supreme law, that governs the governors, that cannot be suspended, and that is not subject to derogations even in national emergency. The United States Constitution is difficult to amend. The United States, which sought an alternative to the Westminster parliamentary system, developed the "presidential system" as a model of democratic government. The United States adopted the first national, constitutional, lasting Bill of Rights The United States established constitutional review by the judiciary.

The United States Constitution has been an inspiration to others. It spread the idea of inherent human rights, and its Bill of Rights served as a source and a model. The United States concepts of constitutional monitoring and constitutional review have been widely imitated. Above all, the United States has set an example of a successful "culture" of constitutionalism.

. . .

[But i]n light of contemporary constitutionalism, the system of government established by the United States Constitution was deficient in key respects. At its inception, the Constitution did not reflect strong commitment to popular sovereignty, to democracy, or to representative government. "We the People" ordained and established the Constitution, but those who authorized and approved the Constitution represented a small fraction of the inhabitants of the United States. The system of government established by the Constitution was not democratic and not representative. Only one branch of the legislature was representative and was, therefore, called the House of Representatives. The Senate represented states, not people. The President represented no one. Even the House of Representatives was elected by a process that would not satisfy the requirements of constitutionalism today, since only a small proportion of the inhabitants voted for representatives. Women, slaves, most free blacks, and those who did not meet property qualifications did not vote for their representatives.

Today, the United States system would presumably pass the requirements of constitutionalism. Senators are elected by the citizens of their states. All citizens vote for the president in fact if not in theory or in form. As a result of imaginative constitutional construction of the Bill of Rights and of the Equal Protection Clause of the Fourteenth Amendment, all citizens now have the right to vote for representatives, for senators, and for the president.

The ideology of constitutionalism is not sufficiently developed or precise to determine whether our presidential system and our kind of bicameral legislature meet the requirements of "will of the people," "democracy," and "representative government." Our jurisprudence has no coherent view of representative government, and the election of senators by states rather than according to population, and the system of electing the president, need justification and rationalization. As conceived, the presidency was perhaps too weak; now it has perhaps grown too strong. Surely, checks and balances are not working as planned. Does our system satisfy the demands of constitutionalism? Surely, constitutional text, and even the jurisprudence that emanates from the opinions of the Supreme Court, do not tell a whole, coherent constitutionalistic story.

Donald P. Kommers
Comparative Constitutional Law: Its Increasing Relevance

in Defining the Field of Comparative Constitutional Law 61,
62–64 (Vicki Schultz & Mark Tushnet eds., 2002)

Writing in 1996, Giovanni Sartori reported that "[o]f the 170 or so written documents called constitutions in today's world, more than half have been written since 1974," not to mention the remodeling in recent decades of some post–1945 Western European constitutions. These new constitutions include those of Greece

(1975), Portugal (1976), Spain (1978), and Brazil (1988), along with Canada's Charter of Rights and Freedoms, adopted in 1982. Equally notable is the cascade of constitution-making that took place in post-Communist Eastern Europe. A comparison of these documents with the American Constitution reveals a common core of basic rights and liberties, both substantive and procedural. Although many of these constitutions are still on trial, especially those adopted in Eastern Europe's transitional democracies, they nevertheless incorporate an emerging constitutional morality in tension with certain basic precepts of American constitutionalism. Whether this should give Americans pause or disturb their self-certainty is an issue worthy of discussion and debate.

. . .

One finds that many of the constitutions drafted since 1974, particularly those of Eastern Europe and Latin America, not to mention Spain, Greece, Portugal, and South Africa, have been heavily influenced by Germany's Basic Law. Institutional structures such as dual executives, specialized constitutional courts (including abstract judicial review), and systems of proportional representation largely imitate their corresponding German models. They also imitate the Basic Law in combining rights with duties and in their incorporation of state objectives. It is no exaggeration to suggest that Germany's Basic Law is the preferred model of constitutional governance today, a reality that should prompt Americans to take stock of their constitution by assessing its capacity to meet the aspirations and needs of a society of a new millennium.

In recent decades, accordingly, the U.S. Constitution has served mainly as a negative model of constitutional governance around the world, not only with respect to governmental structures and relationships, but also ... with respect to certain guaranteed rights. The positive influence of the United States on the development of constitutionalism abroad during the nineteenth century, especially in Latin America and Europe, has been well documented. American influence was also important in the reconstruction of democracy in Europe and Asia after World War II. Since then, however, the world's constitution makers have been disinclined to follow the lead of American constitutionalism. Rather, as noted, they are more inclined toward the model of constitutional governance and morality represented by Germany's Basic Law.

Three interrelated themes, conspicuous for their absence in the U.S. Constitution, distinguish many of the world's new constitutions. First, they unite liberal constitutionalism with a strong commitment to social solidarity. Second, they speak in the language of individual duties as well as rights. Finally, they impose on government an obligation to foster and protect the dignity of persons. As with Germany's Basic Law, these constitutions celebrate negative liberties against government but qualify them with an overlay of positive rights and institutional guarantees that the state is required to honor, defend and promote.

Dullah Omar
**Constitutional Development:
The African Experience**
in Defining the Field of Comparative Constitutional Law 175,
183–85 (Vicki Schultz & Mark Tushnet eds., 2002)

In our [the drafters of South Africa's post-Apartheid constitution's] survey of constitutions and constitutional systems in different parts of the world, we learned quickly that we could not be mechanical and simply take over, willy-nilly, aspects of constitutions and systems from other parts of the world. Therefore, in our constitution we adopted measures that are not found in any other constitution.

Further, while we learned from many countries, we did not always follow them. Canada, for example, has no property clause in its Bill of Rights. We adopted a bill of rights that did have a property clause in our Interim Constitution, and our final constitution has a property clause. There is still a great deal of debate as to whether we made the right choice, but here it was not only a question of deliberate choice, but also of compromise.

In terms of the core values of our constitution, we had to take into account our history. The system of apartheid built up massive inequalities between the minority, which enjoyed privilege, and the overwhelming majority, which suffered at the hands of apartheid. Hence, an important component of the core values of our constitution is equality. Dignity assumes a central position in our constitution due to the many indignities suffered by our people over such a long period of time. Liberty is not the main core value of our constitution, rather it is equality and dignity. We deliberately chose the word "freedom" rather than liberty because of the connotation of liberty in the American constitution jurisprudence.

We also wanted to ensure that we distanced ourselves from the divisions of the past. Apartheid had divided our country. It fragmented our country and our people. Building the unity of our people, and therefore national unity, was an important component of the liberation struggle. And yet, due to the diversity of our people in terms of religion, language, and culture, we had to take care to develop a constitution that made it possible for us to build that nation, and, at the same time, to respect diversity. That is why our constitution includes a specific provision that the state shall set up a special commission to protect and promote the rights of religious, linguistic, and cultural communities. Of course, our new democracy is only five years old, and it is too early to judge success. But thus far I think we have managed to protect both the right to be the same and the right to be different. We also borrowed from the Indian experience. There was great pressure that South Africa should be declared a religious state. But the view of the ANC prevailed that the state shall be a secular state: not an irreligious state, but a secular state with many religions. There we looked closely at the Indian Constitution and modeled ourselves somewhat on that experience.

Again, while building a nation and building the unity of a single country, we wanted to ensure that there was real democracy for our people and that there was an evolution of power. Therefore, we created nine provinces in our country. But to ensure that the apartheid-based racial fragmentation of the past did not persist, we looked at the way Germany dealt with its problem and modeled the second chamber of our Parliament after the German experience. We have a second chamber called the National Council of Provinces, to which each of the provinces sends ten delegates. There is a strong bond beginning to pull the provinces together, but at the same time each province is able to deal with matters of concern to it.

We also paid a lot of attention to what rights should be entrenched in our Bill of Rights. Our Bill of Rights contains civil and political rights as well as social and economic rights. Because of our history, we chose to include social and economic rights in the Bill of Rights itself, not just as guiding principles.

In sum, I think we benefited from a comparative approach to constitutional drafting. We learned a great deal from the U.S. experience—both positive and negative. For seventy-five years, the United States existed with both a Bill of Rights and slavery. Because we live in a globalized world, South Africa does not have the luxury of time to make our Bill of Rights work. . . .

A classical liberal democratic constitutional framework is inadequate to address the problem of democratic transformation and the renewal of the African continent. Civil and political rights are very important, but they are not enough in the context of our continent. While it had the trappings of the Westminster type of constitution, independence ultimately turned out to mean very little for people in African countries. We need to deal with the legacy of the past and with a cultural of violence that is the result of the repression that went on for many hundreds of years. We need a developmental state in the countries of Africa. We need to promote nation-building and we need to address the massive inequalities and poverty in Africa, and the state has to play a role in this.

Notes

1–16.   Do you think the system of government set out in the U.S. Constitution meets the demands of constitutionalism? What defects do you perceive in the U.S. constitutional guarantees of rule of law, separation of powers, popular sovereignty and individual rights? How might these defects be remedied?

1–17.   Should the fact that nations are choosing the German over the U.S. constitutional model "give Americans pause or disturb their self-certainty"? What about the criticisms implicit in the South African Constitution's drafters' rejection of a U.S.-style Bill of Rights?

Chapter Two

JUDICIAL REVIEW

Judicial review is a core component of the U.S. constitutional system. Some check on the actions of the democratically elected branches exists in all nations that meet the requirements of constitutionalism. The particulars of the structure and scope of this check, or judicial review, differ widely.

I. JUDICIAL SYSTEM

Constitutions typically provide for the maintenance of a judicial system. However, the makeup and powers of courts vary. Some countries have both federal and state courts, while others have only one court system. Some primarily rely on courts of general jurisdiction, while others rely more on specialized courts. Some constitutions provide detailed descriptions of the courts, while others, including the United States, are more general. Some constitutions operate in civil law systems, which had their origins in continental Europe and have spread to some countries in Asia, Africa, and South America. Others operate in common law systems, which originated in England and spread to the former English colonies in America, Africa, Australia and New Zealand.

Edgar Bodenheimer, John Bilyeu Oakley
and Jean C. Love
An Introduction to the Anglo–American
Legal System
9 (1988)
Reprinted with permission of Thomson West

The starting point of legal reasoning in civil law countries is almost always a statute or code provision. Judicial precedents, at least in theory, play a secondary role; their authority is considered to be no greater than that of legal writers. However, in actual practice prior decisions are widely followed by the courts. In the common law orbit legal arguments often center around the interpretation and applicability of earlier judicial decisions, especially those rendered by the highest court of the jurisdiction in question; but statutes and administrative regulations are gaining an ever-increasing importance.

Certain differences also exist in the structure of legal procedure in the two systems.

A. CHINA

The Chinese Constitution, Article 123, provides: "The people's courts in the People's Republic of China are the judicial organs of the state." The Constitution continues:

(1) The People's Republic of China establishes the Supreme People's Court and the local people's courts at different levels, military courts and other special people's courts.

(2) The term of office of the President of the Supreme People's Court is the same as that of the National People's Congress; he shall serve no more than two consecutive terms.

(3) The organization of people's courts is prescribed by law.

Xian Fa art. 124 (1982) (P.R.C.).

B. GERMANY

Similarly, the Basic Law of the Federal Republic of Germany says: "The judicial power shall be vested in the judges; it shall be exercised by the Federal Constitutional Court [the Bundesverfassungsgericht], by the federal courts provided for in this the Basic Law, and by the courts of the Länder [somewhat like our states]." Grundgesetz fuer die Bundesrepublik Deutschland [GG] [Basic Law], art. 92 (F.R.G.) (hereinafter Basic Law).

In Germany the members of the Constitutional Court are chosen by the two houses of the parliament, half by the Bundestag [lower house] and Bundesrat [upper house], while judges of the other federal courts are "chosen jointly by the competent Federal Minister and a committee for the selection of judges consisting of the competent Land ministers and an equal number of members elected by the Bundestag." Basic Law, arts. 94 and 95 (F.R.G.). The Court's website explains:

The Court is made up of two Senates (panels) with eight members each. The First Senate is chaired by the President, the Second Senate by the Vice–President. The competence for constitutional complaints and review of statutes is shared between the two Senates. In all other procedures, the Second Senate decides exclusively.

Bundesverfassungsgericht, Organization, http://www.bundes-verfassungsgericht.de/en/organization/organization.html (last visited Feb. 7, 2007).

Notes

2–1. The language of the Chinese Constitution follows a form ["the people's courts ... **are** the judicial organs...."] that was common to many, but not all, civil law countries. By contrast, the German and U.S. constitutions use the word "shall be." What might explain the difference? Does the difference in form have any practical results?

2–2. What might be the reason for Germany's decision to have different selection processes for Constitutional Court judges and all other federal judges? Why have eight member Senates? Why divide the Court into two Senates?

II. JUDICIAL INDEPENDENCE

Although the U.S. Constitution does not use the phrase, constitutions of other countries commonly speak of judicial independence, but do not define it. Some courts have offered definitions.

A. SOUTH AFRICA

The South African Supreme Court has stated:

The constitutional protection of the core values of judicial independence accorded to all courts by the South African Constitution means that all courts are entitled to and have the basic protection that is required. Section 165(2) of the Constitution pointedly states that "[t]he courts *are* independent". Implicit in this is recognition of the fact that the courts and their structure, with the hierarchical differences between higher courts and lower courts which then existed, are considered by the Constitution to be independent. This does not mean that particular provisions of legislation governing the structure and functioning of the courts are immune from constitutional scrutiny. Nor does it mean that lower courts have, or are entitled to have their independence protected in the same way as higher courts. The Constitution and the existing legislation kept in force by the Constitution treat higher courts differently to lower courts. Whilst particular provisions of existing legislation dealing with magistrates' courts can be examined for consistency with the Constitution, the mere fact that they are different to the provisions of the Constitution that protect the independence of judges is not in itself a reason for holding them to be unconstitutional.

In deciding whether a particular court lacks the institutional protection that it requires to function independently and impartially, it is relevant to have regard to the core protection given to all courts by our Constitution, to the particular functions that such court performs and to its place in the court hierarchy. Lower courts are, for instance, entitled to protection by the higher courts should any threat be made to their independence. The greater the protection given to the higher courts, the greater is the protection that all courts have.

Van Rooyen v. State, 2002 (5) SA 246 (CC) (S. Afr.).

In the same case, the South African Supreme Court also quoted approvingly from the Canadian Supreme Court:

Both independence and impartiality are fundamental not only to the capacity to do justice in a particular case but also to individual and public confidence in the administration of justice. Without that confidence the system cannot command the respect and acceptance that are essential to its effective operation. It is, therefore, important that a tribunal should be perceived as independent, as well as impartial, and that the test for independence should include that perception.

Id. Protective language in a constitution does not necessarily result in true judicial independence. For example, while both the Chinese Constitution and the German Basic Law contain provisions that guarantee judicial independence, the German courts in practice enjoy greater independence.

B. CHINA

In China, "[t]he people's courts shall, in accordance with the law, exercise judicial power independently and are not subject to interference by administrative organs, public organizations or individuals." Xian Fa art. 126 (1982) (P.R.C.). However, the Constitution goes on to say: "The Supreme People's Court is responsible to the National People's Congress and its Standing Committee. Local people's courts at different levels are responsible to the organs of state power which created them." Xian Fa art. 128 (1982) (P.R.C.).

C. GERMANY

In Germany, "Judges shall be independent and subject only to the law." Basic Law, art. 97, § 1 (F.R.G.). Article 97 also protects the tenure of judges:

Judges appointed permanently to full-time positions may be involuntarily dismissed, permanently or temporarily suspended, transferred, or retired before the expiration of their term of office only by virtue of judicial decision and only for the reasons and in the manner specified by the laws. The legislature may set age limits for the retirement of judges appointed for life. In the event of changes in the structure of courts or in their districts, judges may be transferred to another court or removed from office, provided they retain their full salary.

However, the Basic Law also provides:

If a federal judge infringes the principles of the Basic Law or the constitutional order of a Land in his official capacity or unofficially, the Federal Constitutional Court, upon application of the Bundestag, may by a two-thirds majority order that the judge be transferred or retired. In the case of an intentional infringement it may order him dismissed.

Basic Law, art. 98, § 2 (F.R.G.).

D. OTHER COUNTRIES

France goes even further, providing in the Civil Code: "A judge who refuses to give judgment on the pretext of legislation being silent, obscure or insufficient, may be prosecuted for being guilty of a denial of justice." C. Civ. art. 4 (Fr.) Even if the constitution protects judicial independence by guaranteeing lifetime or lengthy tenure to judges, easy constitutional amendment may thwart that independence. Several times in Mexican history, presidents have effectively "fired" judges whose tenure was theoretically protected. In 1928, President Calles ignored the lifetime tenure of members of the Supreme Court, and fired all of them, in the course of increasing the size of the court from eleven to sixteen. President Cardenas fired the Calles appointees in 1934. Finally, in 1994, President Zedillo dissolved the existing Supreme Court and created a new one. *See* Michael C. Taylor, *Why Do Rule of Law in Mexico? Explaining the Weakness of Mexico's Judicial Branch*, 27 N.M. L.Rev. 141 (1997). Similarly, in Africa:

The Ghanaian authorities under Nkrumah ... leaned on Roosevelt's unsuccessful 'court-packing' plan as precedent when they decided to amend the constitution in 1964 to allow the president to remove judges at his pleasure:

'In the United States of America, the President has the power to 'pack' the Federal Supreme Court, that is, to appoint new Judges of his liking. He also has the power to retire Judges before the stipulated retiring age. These were powers which President Franklin Delano Roosevelt used very effectively in the mid-nineteen-thirties when he was fighting for his New Deal Programme. This is what the proposed amendment seeks to do.'

H. Kwasi Prempeh, *Marbury in Africa: Judicial Review and the Challenge of Constitutionalism in Contemporary Africa*, 80 Tul.

L.Rev. 1239, 1271 (2006) (quoting from Henry L. Bretton, *The Rise and Fall of Kwame Nkrumah: A Study of Personal Rule in Africa,* 271–72 (1966)).

Notes

2–3. What is meant by "judicial independence?" Do all courts within a judicial system share it equally? What is the difference, if any, between judicial independence and judicial impartiality? What structural protections are necessary to ensure judicial independence? Professor Prempeh observes:

> Africa's judiciaries, long considered marginal to the course of national events and politics, have emerged from current democratic and constitutional reforms with far greater prestige, authority, and confidence than they have ever enjoyed in the past. In Africa's democratizing common law countries, new and revised constitutions grant to one or more courts within the national judicial hierarchy express and unambiguous power to interpret and enforce constitutional commands, including, notably, bills of rights. Provisions designed to secure the independence of Africa's judges accompany this grant of judicial power. Generally, Africa's judges no longer hold their offices at the sufferance of the President, judicial salaries and other benefits may not be varied to the judges' detriment, and the jurisdiction of the courts may not be ousted or diminished. In Ghana, the new constitution goes even further to grant the judiciary autonomy in the preparation, administration, and control of its own budget.
>
> Even more significant is the new political context within which the African judiciary must operate. Africa's judges must work alongside multiparty parliaments, elected and term-limited presidents, opposition parties, a vibrant civil society, and an open media environment. Democracy and constitutionalism, once discredited by Africa's political elites, are now the primary sources of legitimacy for national politicians in a growing number of states. All of these make for a very favorable environment for Africa's judiciaries.
>
> At the same time, contemporary constitutions, by failing to design credible checks and balances within the political half of the state, place a disproportionate weight of the burden of promoting and sustaining constitutionalism on the African judiciary. What is yet to be seen is whether the African judiciary, in its present state, can deliver on this expectation.

Id. at 1295–96.

III. SYSTEMS OF CONSTITUTIONAL REVIEW

The systems of constitutional review seem at first glance to vary considerably. *See* Francisco Ramo Romeu, *The Establishment of Constitutional Courts: A Study of 128 Democratic Constitutions*, 2 Rev. L. & Econ. 103 (2006). England, with no written constitution, has been said not to engage in judicial review. Some countries, such as Germany and South Africa, have specialized constitutional courts. Others, such as France and China create non-judicial bodies to review constitutionality of statutes. Consider, as you read the descriptions below, how much they differ from one another or from the judicial review in the United States. Consider, also, the extent to which constitutional review is performed by the judicial system and the extent to which other institutions perform constitutional review. Finally, note that the authority to conduct constitutional review may vary depending on whether the matter being reviewed is a statute, an administrative regulation, or executive or judicial action.

A. NO TRADITIONAL JUDICIAL REVIEW

1. *England*

Until late in the twentieth century, courts and scholars followed the view that A.C. Dicey, a nineteenth century expert on English constitutional law, had advanced in his classic *Introduction to the Study of the Constitution*. Dicey argued that the English Constitution relied on two principles: "the sovereignty of Parliament," and "the 'rule of law.'" He wrote:

> This rule of law, which means at bottom the right of the courts to punish any illegal act by whomsoever committed, is of the very essence of English institutions. If the sovereignty of Parliament gives the form, the supremacy of the law of the land determines the substance of our constitution. The English constitution in short, which appears when looked at from one point of view to be a mere collection of practices or customs, turns out, when examined in its legal aspect, to be more truly than any other polity in the world, except the Constitution of the United States, based on the law of the land.

A.V. Dicey, *Introduction to the Study of the Law of the Constitution* 470–471 (10th ed. 1959). *See also British Railways Boards v Picken*, [1974] A.C. 765 (H.L.) (quoted in Allan R. Brewer–Carias, *Judicial Review in Comparative Law* 2 (1989): "The remedy for a Parliamentary wrong, if one has been committed, must be sought from Parliament, and cannot be gained from courts." One scholar suggests that "the English notion of convention is that some things are 'not done' even though the legal constitution permits them." Ernest A. Young, *English Constitutionalism Circa 2005, or, Some Funny Things Happened After the Revolution*, 21 Const. Comment. 771, 788 (2004) (reviewing Adam Tomkins, *Public Law* (2003)). By contrast, in the United States, "government actors are pushing their constitutional options as far as they can go, rather than feeling constrained by politics to do something short of what they *might* do, legally speaking" (emphasis added). *Id.*, at 789.

England has, however, begun changing the way it considers constitutional review, for at least three reasons. "The first is Europe." This cause is discussed *infra*, Part III.C. The second

> is that the political constitution has come to be widely seen as having broken down.... Were it not for the courts coming to the rescue, the government would have spun out of control, and the first task of the constitution—to hold the politically powerful to account—would be performed by nobody: constitutional government would have ended.

Adam Tomkins, *Public Law* 24 (2003). Third, "the judges changed. ... [B]y the 1970's lawyers were being appointed to the bench who had been educated in law schools which no longer incanted Dicey's views uncritically." *Id.* at 23–24.

2. *Canada*

Canada traditionally followed the English system, but the 1982 Constitution Act allowed for judicial review of deprivations of rights protected by the Charter of Rights and Freedoms. However, the Charter provides: "Parliament or the legislature of a province may expressly declare in an Act of Parliament or of the legislature ... that the Act or a provision thereof shall operate notwithstanding a provision included in section 2 or sections 7 to 15 of this Charter." Constitution Act, 1982, § 33(1) (Can.). A law passed by Parliament or a provincial legislature to override a protected right expires within five years of enactment, but may be renewed. Although the federal government has never used the override, three provinces have. Patrick Monahan, *Constitutional Law* 422–23 (2d ed. 2002). The courts will review whether a particular override of Charter rights was validly enacted. For example, *Ford c. Québec (Procureur général)*, [1988] 2 S.C.R. 712 (Can.) considered whether a Quebec law requiring commercial signs to be only in French contained a valid override of the Canadian Charter's freedom of speech. A lawyer for the Canadian government had this to say, in his book about the Canadian Constitution:

> It is submitted, however, that like parliamentary sovereignty, the right of judicial review is not in all respects absolute, and that there are occasionally conflicting principles which may support some limitation on the jurisdiction of the courts to test constitutional validity. The constitution in no place specifically provides for judicial review nor does it specifically guarantee

the jurisdiction of the courts in this regard. There is an implication in favor of judicial review, but that implication can be taken no farther than the protection of the constitution may demand, and it is subject to other limitations both express and implied in the constitution. For example, express limitations arise out of the grants of power to Parliament and the Legislatures in ss. 101 and 92(14) of the B.N.A. Act respectively, to regulate the 'Constitution, Maintenance, and Organization' of the courts. Implied limitations may be found in the fact that the B.N.A. Act created quasi-sovereign legislative bodies and executives which were to exercise the Crown prerogatives. Limitations are also suggested by the fact that our constitution does not dictate a separation of powers among co-equal branches of Government. It is therefore even more appropriate in our system that courts defer where possible to the judgment of legislative bodies which in most respects are supreme.

Barry L. Strayer, *The Canadian Constitution and the Courts: The Function and Scope of Judicial Review* 50 (2d ed. 1983).

There seem to be two bases for constitutional review in the Canadian Constitution. First, section 52(1) of the Constitution Act, 1982, provides "The Constitution of Canada is the supreme law of Canada, and any law that is inconsistent with the provisions of the Constitution is, to the extent of the inconsistency, of no force or effect." Second, the Constitution contains a special judicial review section for claims under the Charter of Rights and Freedoms: "Anyone whose rights or freedoms, as guaranteed by this Charter, have been infringed or denied may apply to a court of competent jurisdiction to obtain such remedy as the court considers appropriate and just in the circumstances." Constitution Act, 1982, § 24(1) (Can.).

In *Amax Potash Ltd. v. Saskatchewan*, [1977] 2 S.C.R. 576 (Can.),

[t]he Supreme Court struck down a Saskatchewan statute that attempted to bar recovery of taxes that had been levied pursuant to a statute that had been found to be unconstitutional. The Court held that, in a federal state, the 'bounds of sovereignty are defined and supremacy circumscribed.' While courts could not question the wisdom of enactments, they did have a responsibility to ensure that the limits imposed by the constitution were observed: '[I]t is the high duty of this Court to insure that the Legislatures do not transgress the limits of their constitutional mandate and engage in the illegal exercise of power.' The Court held that any attempt by the legislature to prevent access to the courts for purposes of determining the constitutional validity of a statute would be invalid as an

infringement of this judicial role. The attempt by Saskatchewan to limit recovery of illegally levied taxes was an attempt to do indirectly what could not be done directly, and was also invalid.

Monahan, *supra* page 34 at 139–140.

The Court's reasoning appears in this key paragraph:

The principle governing this appeal can be shortly and simply expressed in these terms: if a statute is found to be ultra vires the legislature which enacted it, legislation which would have the effect of attaching legal consequences to acts done pursuant to that invalid law must equally be ultra vires because it relates to the same subject matter as that which was involved in the prior legislation. If a state cannot take by unconstitutional means, it cannot retain by unconstitutional means. The same thought found expression in the headnote to [an Australian case] in these words:

... the immunity accorded by that Act [the State Transport Co-ordination (Barring of Claims and Remedies) Act, No. 45, of 1954] to the unlawful exactions was as offensive to the Constitution as the unlawful exactions themselves ...

Amax Potash Ltd., supra page 35, at 592.

Notes

2–4. What kind of judicial review would you expect to find in England, based on the above? Should constitutional disputes be decided by political, rather than judicial, mechanisms? Do the differing political/legal cultures affect the answer? Or does the mechanism determine the political/legal culture? Young, *supra* page 33, at 788–89. Was the Diceyan constitutional order ever realistic? To what extent did it stem from the "unwritten" nature of England's constitution?

2–5. Why is the jurisdiction-stripping statute in the *Amax Potash* case unconstitutional? Are all laws that have the effect of stripping jurisdiction from the courts to review the constitutionality of a statute unconstitutional in Canada? Do sections 52(1) and 24(1) set up one or two methods of judicial review? Is the result of § 33 that the legislative branch may overrule, at least for five years, a decision by the Supreme Court? Does § 33 solve the problem that some have with judicial review, that it is inconsistent with democratic rule? Does § 33 pose any dangers to the rule of law?

B. SPECIALIZED CONSTITUTIONAL COURTS

In the early twentieth century many European countries developed a system of constitutional review by a special constitutional court. It was thought that the existing courts lacked the needed independence. A new court, with greater independence, it was thought, could provide meaningful constitutional review of legislation. *See* Norman Dorsen, et al., *Comparative Constitutionalism: Cases and Materials* 111–112 (2003). One author suggests that Austria, Germany, Italy, France, Cyprus, Turkey, Portugal, Spain, Belgium, and Poland follow what he calls "the European model" of constitutional review: a court specially established to conduct constitutional review, and having a monopoly over constitutional litigation. Louis Favoreau, *Constitutional Review in Europe, in* Constitutionalism and Rights: The Influence of the United States Constitution Abroad 38 (Louis Henkin & Albert J. Rosenthal eds., 1990). France may not belong in this list, as we see *infra*, Part III.C.

1. Germany

Germany has a Federal Constitutional Court. The Basic Law, Arts. 93 and 100, describe the court's jurisdiction in great detail. It is worth reading these articles in their entirety.

Federal Constitutional Court; jurisdiction
Basic Law, art. 93 (F.R.G.)

(1) The Federal Constitutional Court shall rule:

1. on the interpretation of this Basic Law in the event of disputes concerning the extent of the rights and duties of a supreme federal body or of other parties vested with rights of their own by this Basic Law or by the rules of procedure of a supreme federal body;

2. in the event of disagreements or doubts respecting the formal or substantive compatibility of federal law or Land law with this Basic Law, or the compatibility of Land law with other federal law, on application of the Federal Government, of a Land government, or of one third of the Members of Bundestag;

2a. in the event of disagreements whether a law meets the requirements of paragraph (2) of Article 72, on application of the Bundesrat or of the government or legislature of a Land;

3. in the event of disagreements respecting the rights and duties of the Federation and the Länder, especially in the execution of federal law by the Länder and in the exercise of federal oversight;

4. on other disputes involving public land between the Federation and the Länder, between different Länder, or within a Land, unless there is recourse to another court;

4a. on constitutional complaints, which my be filed by any person alleging that one of his basic rights or one of his rights under paragraph (4) of Article 20 or under Article 33, 38, 101, 103, or 104 has been infringed by public authority;

4b. on constitutional complaints filed by municipalities or associations of municipalities on the ground that their right to self-government under Article 28 has been infringed by a law; in the case of infringement by a Land law, however, only if the law cannot be challenged in the constitutional court of the Land;

5. in the other instances provided for in the Basic Law.

(2) The Federal Constitutional Court shall also rule on such other matters as may be assigned to it by a federal law.

Compatibility With the Basic Law
Basic Law, art. 100 (F.R.G.)

(1) If a court concludes that a law on whose validity its decision depends is unconstitutional, the proceedings shall be stayed, and a decision shall be obtained from the Land court with jurisdiction over constitutional disputes where the constitution of a Land is held to be violated, or from the Federal Constitutional Court where this Basic Law is held to be violated. This provision shall also apply where the Basic Law is held to be violated by Land law and where a Land law is held to be incompatible with a federal law.

(2) If, in the course of litigation, doubt exists whether a rule of international law is an integral part of federal law and whether it directly creates rights and duties for the individual (Article 25), the court shall obtain a decision from the Federal Constitutional Court.

(3) If the constitutional court of a Land, in interpreting this Basic Law, proposes to deviate from a decision of the Federal Constitutional Court or of the constitutional court of another Land, it shall obtain a decision from the Federal Constitutional Court.

Notes

2–6. Does the German Federal Constitutional Court have jurisdiction over all questions arising under the Basic Law? Is the detailed description of jurisdiction preferable to a general description such as "arising under?" May the Federal Constitutional Court render advisory opinions? May the Court decline to hear constitutional issues presented to it? May the legislative branch strip jurisdiction over some matters from the court? Justice Hans G. Rupp of the Federal Constitutional Court explained the Court's approach to challenges to federal and land legislation:

the court is the supreme and only guardian against unconstitutional behavior of the political departments of government. It has the power to strike down unconstitutional laws and also to declare executive acts unconstitutional. But the political departments are the principal actors on the governmental stage and the court has only a referee-like function. For these reasons it should not unnecessarily interfere with the conduct of government.

Hans G. Rupp, *Some Remarks on Judicial Self–Restraint*, 21 Ohio St. L.J. 503, 505 (1960).

What does it mean for a court to have "only a referee-like function?" When might it be unnecessary to interfere with unconstitutional government action? Justice Wiltraut Rupp–v.Brünneck has described several cases in which the German Federal Constitutional Court has chosen to declare a statute "for the time being—still constitutional, but to announce at the same time that the statute would become unconstitutional in near future, unless the legislature should repeal or amend it." Wiltraut Rupp-v.Brünneck, *Admonitory Functions of Constitutional Courts*, 20 Am.J.Comp. L. 387, 387 (1972) For example, the Court held that a law discriminating against non-marital children was constitutional but would become unconstitutional if not promptly changed. Justice Rupp–v.Brünneck notes that such "admonitory" decisions have normally resulted in the legislative body repealing or amending the provision or replacing "it with a new one conforming to the Constitution." *Id.* When, if ever, might a court be in a position to hold that a law is constitutional only for the time being, and to warn that it will become unconstitutional in the near future? Note that the Constitutional Court sits in Karlsruhe, a small city near the French border, and far from the capital city, Berlin. Are there policy reasons for this geographic split between the judicial branch and the other branches of government?

2. *South Africa*

The South Africa Constitutional Court, in its very fine website, says the democratic constitution created a new court to provide more representative review than had existed under the apartheid constitution. Accordingly, South Africa made "a commitment to a Constitutional Court in a hybrid continental form, such as that of Germany." Constitutional Court of South Africa, About the Court, http://www.constitutionalcourt.org.za/site/thecourt/history. htm#cases (last visited on Feb. 7, 2007). According to Article 167 of the South African Constitution the Constitutional Court is the highest court in all constitutional matters. It may decide only constitutional matters and issues connected with decisions on constitutional matters. It has exclusive jurisdiction over certain cases, such as disputes between organs of state in the national or provincial sphere concerning the constitutional status, powers or functions of any of those organs of state and cases involving the constitutionality of parliamentary or provincial Bills (with some exceptions). S. Afr. Const. 1996, art. 167. The Constitution also creates a High Court, which may hear constitutional cases, except those over which the Constitutional Court has exclusive jurisdiction. S. Afr. Const. 1996, art. 169. And the Constitution creates a Supreme Court, which hears appeals from the High Court. S. Afr. Const. 1996, art. 168. Finally, it is explicitly written into the South African Constitution in Article 170 that courts lower than the High Court may not decide constitutional issues. How did South Africa depart from the German model? Why did it do so? The drafters of the constitution published explanations of how it works, including the following graphic:

Excerpted from *The Post-Apartheid Constitutions: Perspectives on South Africa's Basic Law*, p. 110, Penelope Andrews and Stephen Ellman eds., (2001)

What sort of constitutional issue does the cartoon portray?

C. REVIEW BY NON-JUDICIAL ENTITY

1. *France*

A variant on the so-called European approach is to provide for constitutional review, but not judicial review. The most well-known example is France, where the Constitution creates a nine-member Constitutional Council, with staggered nine year terms. 1958 Const. art. 56 (Fr.). The President of the Republic appoints three members, the head of the National Assembly appoints three, and the head of the Senate appoints three. The Constitutional Council reviews certain acts automatically before they enter into force and reviews other acts upon referral by the President, the Prime Minister, the heads of the National Assembly or Senate, or sixty deputies or senators. Under Article 62, if the Council declares a provision unconstitutional it "shall be neither promulgated nor implemented." The declaration is not appealable and is binding.

Note, however, that

[c]riminal courts have jurisdiction to interpret administrative decisions of a regulatory or individual nature, and to appreciate their legality where the solution to the criminal case they are handling depends upon such examination.

C. Pen., art. 111–5 (Fr.) France distinguishes between constitutional law and administrative law, even though administrative rulings may raise constitutional issues. Constitutional law refers to review of the constitutionality of proposed laws. The Constitutional Council, as originally conceived, "was not to be some form of supreme court in constitutional matters, along the lines of the German Constitutional Court, a specialist body to which references can be made from all courts during litigation." However,

[t]he scope and procedure of the constitutional review now operated by the Conseil constitutionnel is very much like that of a constitutional court, but with substantial differences from the kinds of court that exist in the United States and Germany. The Conseil constitutionnel is a court in all but name, though its procedure for reviewing legislation lacks significant attributes of a judicial process, even when compared just to ordinary French courts. Its jurisdiction is limited to reviewing *lois* before they are promulgated; once promulgated, a *loi* becomes immune from challenge in the ordinary courts.

John Bell, *French Constitutional Law* 55 (1992).

AMNESTY LAW OF 1989, LE MONDE

CC decision no. 89–258 DC, July 8, 1989

Translated in John Bell, *French Constitutional Law* 278–79 (1992).

Background: The Renault Ten had been dismissed for 'gross fault' following incidents of violence during an industrial dispute. In order to meet the aspirations of unions and the Communists, the Government sought to grant amnesty to the Ten after the labour courts and the Cour d'appel had upheld the dismissals in April 1989 (Versailles, 26 Apr. 1989, D. 1989, 386), and new industrial unrest was imminent. The amnesty law for the bicentenary of the Revolution of 1789 was drafted in such a way as to escape the restrictions imposed by decision [88–244, discussed in paragraph 1, below. The employers petitioned the Constitutional Council, claiming the amnesty law violated the constitution.]

DECISION:

1. Considering that in its decision no. 88–244 DC of 20 July 1988 and the Conseil constitutionnel declared that, within article 15–II of the amnesty law relating to the right to reinstatement, the words, 'having consisted of assaults punished by a condemnation not referred to in article 7 of the present *loi*', were contrary to the Constitution; that it is clear from the reasons given for this decision that the right of reintegration could not be extended to employees' representatives or shop stewards dismissed for reasons of grave fault; that, indeed, the decision of 20 July 1988 points out that this situation would represent 'a clear abuse of protected offices or mandates' and, furthermore, that 'the restriction that such a reinstatement would impose on the employer, who has been the victim of this abuse, or who is at least not responsible for it, would manifestly exceed the personal or property sacrifices that can be required of individuals in the public interest; that, in particular, reinstatement has to be excluded in those situations where the gross fault justifying the dismissal had harmed employees of the business, who could, moreover, themselves be employees' representatives or union officials';

2. Considering that article 3 of the amnesty law currently under scrutiny intends to complement the first paragraph of article 15–II of *loi* no. 88–828 of 20 July 1988 by the following sentence: 'These provisions apply in the case of gross fault, except where the reinstatement would impose on the employer an excessive personal or property sacrifice'; that this recognizes a right to reinstatement in the business, distinct from the amnesty already granted, to employees' representatives or shop stewards dismissed for gross fault;

3. Considering that article 3 creates an exception in those cases where reinstatement would 'impose on the employer an excessive personal or property sacrifice';

4. Considering that the tempering thus effected leaves in place the general rule laid down by this article, which recognizes a right to reinstatement in the case of serious fault; that, in particular, it does not take into consideration the case where the victims of gross fault are employees of the business, who could themselves be employees' representatives or union officials;

5. Considering that such a provision violates the authority that attaches, by virtue of article 62 of the Constitution, to the decision of the Conseil constitutionnel of 20 July 1988; that it therefore follows that article 3 of the *loi* has to be declared incompatible with the Constitution ...

2. *China*

The Chinese Constitution also grants the power of constitutional review to a non-judicial body. Article 5 provides for the supremacy of the Constitution:

> The state upholds the uniformity and dignity of the socialist legal system. No law or administrative or local rules and regulations shall contravene the constitution. All state organs, the armed forces, all political parties and public organizations and all enterprises and undertakings must abide by the Constitution and the law. All acts in violation of the Constitution and the law must be investigated. No organization or individual may enjoy the privilege of being above the Constitution and the law.

Xian Fa art. 5 (1982) (P.R.C.). According to Article 62(1–2), "The National People's Congress exercises the following functions and powers: (1) To amend the Constitution; (2) To supervise the enforcement of the Constitution;...." and Article 67(1) explains "The Standing Committee of the National People's Congress exercises the following functions and powers: To interpret the Constitution and supervise its enforcement;...." However, *Qi Yuling v. Chen Xiaoqui et al.*, CNLCAS 124 Chinalawinfo LEXIS (2001), is an example of a case in which a court engaged in constitutional review. The plaintiff had successfully passed an examination which qualified her for admission to a business school. Another person entered the school, using the plaintiff's name, apparently with the aid of the public school that had her examination certificate. She sued the person who stole her identity, the business school, and the public school. In ruling for the plaintiff, the High People's Court of

Shandong Province relied on Article 46 of the Constitution, which guarantees a right to education.

An American government commission found:

- The Chinese government has affirmed the right of citizens to petition the National People's Congress Standing Committee for review of regulations that violate the Constitution or national law. The effect of this right remains limited, however, since Chinese citizens have no right to compel such review or to challenge the constitutionality of government actions.

- Constitutional enforcement remains a politically sensitive topic in China, and the near-term prospects for the establishment of a more robust constitutional enforcement mechanism are remote. The Chinese government has ruled out establishing a constitutional court or giving people's courts the power to review the constitutionality of laws and regulations.

- The Chinese government has enacted laws to curb administrative abuses, but Chinese officials retain significant administrative discretion. Existing legal mechanisms provide only limited checks on arbitrary or unlawful government actions.

Congressional-Executive Commission on China Ann. Rep. 83–84 (2005), *available at* http://www.cecc.gov/pages/annualRpt/ annualRpt05/CECCannRpt2005.pdf.

Notes

2–7. Is all constitutional review in France and China non-judicial? What policies support non-judicial constitutional review? Why have most nations opted for judicial review? Now that you have seen the variety of constitutional arrangements, consider the argument of Professor Alec Stone Sweet, that European countries have adopted constitutional review, but not judicial review: Under the European model,

> [F]irst, constitutional judges alone exercise review powers; the 'ordinary' (that is, the nonconstitutional) judiciary may not invalidate norms or acts on grounds of unconstitutionality. Second, terms of jurisdiction restrict constitutional courts to resolving constitutional disputes. Formally, constitutional judges do not preside over litigation or appeals, per se, which remain the purview of the judiciary. Instead, constitutional judges answer the *constitutional questions* that are referred to them by, among others, elected politicians and ordinary judges. Third, constitutional courts have links with, but are detached from, the judiciary and legisla-

ture. They occupy their own 'constitutional' space, one that is neither 'judicial' nor 'political,' as those terms are commonly understood in Europe. Fourth, most constitutional courts are empowered to determine the constitutionality of statutes without respect (or even prior) to their application. (Emphasis added)

Alec Stone Sweet, *Why Europe Rejected American Judicial Review and Why It May Not Matter*, 101 Mich. L.Rev. 2744, 2769–70 (2003). What is the difference between constitutional review and judicial review? Which of the constitutions referred to above fit Sweet's description? How does this description differ from the American model of judicial review? What might be the reasons for the "European" model? Is there a difference between the way courts in these countries review claims of unconstitutional executive action and their review of legislative action? What might be the reason? Professor Jeremy Waldron describes the various types of judicial review of legislation (as distinguished from review of executive action or administrative decisionmaking):

There are a variety of practices all over the world that could be grouped under the general heading of judicial review of legislation. They may be distinguished along several dimensions. The most important difference is between what I shall call strong judicial review and weak judicial review. My target is strong judicial review.

In a system of strong judicial review, courts have the authority to decline to apply a statute in a particular case (even though the statute on its own terms plainly applies in that case) or to modify the effect of a statute to make its application conform with individual rights (in ways that the statute itself does not envisage). Moreover, courts in this system have the authority to establish as a matter of law that a given statute or legislative provision will not be applied, so that as a result of stare decisis and issue preclusion a law that they have refused to apply becomes in effect a dead letter. A form of even stronger judicial review would empower the courts to actually strike a piece of legislation out of the statute-book altogether. Some European courts have this authority. It appears that American courts do not, but the real effect of their authority is not much short of it.

In a system of weak judicial review, by contrast, courts may scrutinize legislation for its conformity to individual rights but they may not decline to apply it (or moderate its application) simply because rights would otherwise be violated. Nevertheless, the scrutiny may have some effect. In the United Kingdom, the courts may review a statute with a view to issuing a "declaration of incompatibility" in the event that "the court is satisfied that the provision is incompatible with a Convention right"—i.e., with one of the rights set out in the European Convention of Human Rights as incorporated into British law through the Human Rights Act. The Act provides that such declaration "does not affect the validity, continuing operation or enforcement of the provision in respect of which it is given; and ... is not binding on the parties to the proceedings in which it is made." But still it has an effect: A minister may use such a declaration as authorization to initiate a fast-track legislative procedure to remedy the incompatibility. (This is a power the minister would not have but for the process of judicial review that led to the declaration in the first place.)

A form of even weaker judicial review would give judges not even that much authority. Like their British counterparts, the New Zealand courts may not decline to apply legislation when it violates human rights (in New Zealand, the rights set out in the Bill of Rights Act of 1990; but they may strain to find interpretations that avoid the violation. Although courts there have indicated that they may be prepared on occasion to issue declarations of incompatibility on their own initiative, such declarations in New Zealand do not have any legal effect on the legislative process....

Jeremy Waldron, *The Core of the Case Against Judicial Review*, 115 Yale L.J. 1346, 1354–56 (2006).

IV. JUSTICIABILITY

Systems of judicial review of constitutional issues include rules regarding who may raise the issues and under what circumstances. Those rules vary widely, with many countries allowing judicial review in circumstances where the U.S. Supreme Court would find there is no justiciable case or controversy.

A. GERMANY

The question whether a federal or state statute is constitutional can arise by way of reference from a civil, criminal or administrative court, by way of a request from the federal government, a state government or one third of the Bundestag, or by way of a constitutional complaint filed by a private individual. In the first case there is an actual controversy pending before the court below which refers the constitutional question to the Constitutional Court. In the second case the constitution requires that 'differences of opinion or doubts exist on the formal and material compatibility of the statute with the Constitution.' This excludes moot questions. In the third case, petitioner must establish that his constitutional rights are impaired directly by the operation of the statute.

Rupp, *supra* page 39 at 508. The second category has been called "abstract norm control."

[T]his provision allows a losing parliamentary minority—if sufficiently strong and sufficiently enraged—to proceed directly to the Constitutional Court after the a statute is enacted....

In 1974, ... when the Social Democratic coalition relaxed criminal penalties on abortion, the losing minority of conservative members of Parliament ... successfully petitioned the Constitutional Court to have the statute declared unconstitutional—as falling short of the state's constitutional obligation to protect the life of the fetus.

Peter E. Quint, *"The Most Extraordinarily Powerful Court of Law the World has Ever Known?"—Judicial Review in the United States and Germany*, 65 Md. L. Rev. 152, 155–56 (2006). If the members had not had standing to challenge the law, could anyone else have challenged it? Professor Quint argues that Germany created an extremely strong constitutional court in reaction to the abuses of the democratic process by the Nazi regime, and that "the political and moral foundation of the German Constitutional Court as a bulwark against the catastrophes of the past still works strongly to ensure its special authority and power today." *Id.* at 169. Is judicial review a sufficient safeguard?

B. AFRICA

Although judicial review has existed in theory in most African nations, frequent rewrites of constitutions, coupled with weak judiciaries, meant that judicial review was relatively toothless until recently. More recently, however, some African courts have taken a more active stance, including adopting broad definitions of justiciability.

In Ghana, for example, where a new constitution restored democratic politics and civil liberties in 1993, the country's supreme court rejected political question objections, and enjoined the publicly funded celebration of the anniversary of the coup d'état that abolished the country's last republican constitution, holding that to allow the celebration would be inconsistent with the democratic ethos of the new constitution.

Prempeh, *supra* page 31, at 1241–1242. In *Mtikila v. the Attorney General*, the High Court of Tanzania, granted standing in a broad attack on a variety of laws and rejected narrow common law notions of standing:

The notion of personal interest, personal injury or sufficient interest over and above the interest of the general public has more to do with private law as distinct from public law. In matters of public interest litigation this Court will not deny standing to a genuine and bona fide litigant even where he has no personal interest in the matter. This position also accords with the decision in Benazir Bhutto v. Federation of Pakistan, PLD 1988 SC 46, where it was held by the Supreme Court that the traditional rule of locus standi can be dispensed with and procedure available in public interest litigation can be made use of if the petition is brought to the court by a person acting bona fide.

The relevance of public interest litigation in Tanzania cannot be over-emphasized. Having regard to our socio-economic conditions, this development promises more hope to our people than any other strategy currently in place.

Mtikila v. the Attorney General, Civil Case No. 5 of 1993 (unreported) (Tanz. H. Ct.), http://www.elaw.org/resources/printable. asp?id=167 (last visited Feb. 7, 2007). Compare the German Constitution with the South African Constitution:

Enforcement of rights.

Anyone listed in this section has the right to approach a competent court, alleging that a right in the Bill of Rights has been infringed or threatened, and the court may grant appropriate relief, including a declaration of rights. The person who may approach a court are:

a. anyone acting in their own interest;

b. anyone acting on behalf of another person who cannot act in their own name;

c. anyone acting as a member of, or in the interest of, a group or class of persons;

d. anyone acting in the public interest; and

e. an association acting in the interest of its members.

S. Afr. Const. 1996, art. 38.

C. JAPAN

THE SUZUKI DECISION

Hanreish, VI, No. 9, 783 (Sup. Ct., Oct. 8, 1952)
Translated in John M. Maki, *Court and Constitution in Japan: Selected Supreme Court Decisions, 1948–60* 362–365 (1964)

[The secretary-general of the Social Democratic party sued in the Supreme Court for a declaration that the police reserve was unconstitutional. The plaintiff argued that the existence of the police reserve violated Article 9, which forbids the maintenance of forces with war potential. The Court dismissed the case.]

If, as the plaintiff argues, the Supreme Court has the power to issue abstract declarations nullifying laws, orders, and the like, then, since anyone could bring before the Court suits claiming unconstitutionality, the validity of laws, orders, and the like, would be frequently assailed and there would be danger of the Court's assuming the appearance of an organ superior to all other powers in the land, thereby running counter to the basic principle of democratic government: that the three powers are independent, equal, and immune from each other's interference.

In short, under the system prevailing in our country, a judgment may be sought in the courts only when there exists a concrete legal dispute between specific parties. The argument that the courts have power to determine in the abstract the constitutionality of laws, orders, and the like, in the absence of a concrete case, has no foundation in the Constitution itself or in any statute. It is clear from the arguments of the plaintiff that the present case does not involve such concrete legal dispute. Therefore, the present suit does not conform with law. Neither the Supreme Court nor any lower court has the power to hear such a suit. Therefore, the suit cannot be transferred to a lower court.

D. INDIA

By contrast, P.N. Bhagwati, a former Chief Justice of India, described the expansion of standing law in India:

> where a legal wrong is done or a legal injury is caused to a person or to class of persons by violation of their constitutional or legal rights and such person or class of persons is, by reason of poverty or disability or socially or economically disadvantaged position, unable to approach the court for relief, any member of the public or social action group acting bona fide can maintain an application in the High Court or the Supreme Court seeking judicial redress for the legal wrong or injury caused to such person or class of person[s].

Prempeh, *supra* page 31, at 1300 (quoting P.N. Bhagwati, Keynote Address at the 16th Annual Session of the Organisation of Professional Associations (Oct. 4, 2003)).

Notes

Would South Africa allow standing in a case like that addressed by the Japanese Supreme Court? What is the justification for distinguishing public and private law cases for standing, as in Tanzania?

V. JUDICIAL REVIEW UNDER INTERNATIONAL LAW

All nations are subject to international law. International law defines the obligations of nations. It may be the subject of international enforcement, through the World Court, the Security Council of the United Nations, or other international bodies. However, international law may also have effect in domestic courts. For example, one kind of international law is the treaty, and the U.S. Constitution lists treaties as part of the supreme law of the land.

A. THE UNITED STATES

A recent example of United States judicial review under international law is found in *Hamdan v. Rumsfeld*, ___ U.S. ___, 126 S.Ct. 2749, 165 L.Ed.2d 723 (2006). To place the international aspect of the case into perspective, here are two relevant portions of U.S. law. President Eisenhower issued a proclamation that noted the contents of the Geneva Convention of 1949, including Article 129: "The High Contracting Parties undertake to enact any legislation necessary to provide effective penal sanctions for persons committing, or ordering to be committed, any of the grave breaches of the present Convention defined in the following Article...." Geneva Convention Relative to the Treatment of Prisoners of War art. 129, Aug. 12, 1949, 6. U.S.T. 3316, 75 U.N.T.S. 135. He noted that the Senate had ratified the treaty, as had many other listed nations, and concluded the Proclamation with:

> NOW, THEREFORE, be it known that I, Dwight D. Eisenhower, President of the United States of America, do hereby proclaim and make public the said Geneva Convention relative to the Treatment of Prisoners of War to the end that the same and every article and clause thereof, subject to the statement herein-before recited, shall be observed and fulfilled with good faith, on and after February 2, 1956, by the United States of America and by the citizens of the United States of America and all other persons subject to the jurisdiction thereof.

6 U.S.T. 3316, 3515.

Congress enacted a law enforcing the Convention:

> (a) Offense.—Whoever, whether inside or outside the United States, commits a war crime, in any of the circumstances described in subsection (b), shall be fined under this title or imprisoned for life or any term of years, or both, and if death results to the victim, shall also be subject to the penalty of death.

> (b) Circumstances.—The circumstances referred to in subsection (a) are that the person committing such war crime or the victim of such war crime is a member of the Armed Forces of the United States or a national of the United States (as defined in section 101 of the Immigration and Nationality Act).

> (c) Definition.—As used in this section the term 'war crime' means any conduct—

>> (1) defined as a grave breach in any of the international conventions signed at Geneva 12 August 1949, or any protocol to such convention to which the United States is a party;

(2) prohibited by Article 23, 25, 27, or 28 of the Annex to the Hague Convention IV, Respecting the Laws and Customs of War on Land, signed 18 October 1907;

(3) which constitutes a violation of common Article 3 of the international conventions signed at Geneva, 12 August 1949, or any protocol to such convention to which the United States is a party and which deals with non-international armed conflict; or

(4) of a person who, in relation to an armed conflict and contrary to the provisions of the Protocol on Prohibitions or Restrictions on the Use of Mines, Booby–Traps and Other Devices as amended at Geneva on 3 May 1996 (Protocol II as amended on 3 May 1996), when the United States is a party to such Protocol, willfully kills or causes serious injury to civilians.

18 U.S.C. § 2441 (2000).

Notes

2–9. Would the Geneva Convention have applied in *Hamdan* in the absence of 18 U.S.C. § 2441? The American Law Institute has explained the circumstances under which international law becomes domestic law of the United States:

§ 111 International Law and Agreements as Law of the United States

(1) International law and international agreements of the United States are law of the United States and supreme over the law of the several States.

(2) Cases arising under international law or international agreements of the United States are within the Judicial Power of the United States and, subject to Constitutional and statutory limitations and requirements of justiciability, are within the jurisdiction of the federal courts.

(3) Courts in the United States are bound to give effect to international law and to international agreements of the United States, except that a 'non-self-executing" agreement will not be given effect as law in the absence of necessary implementation.

(4) An international agreement of the United States is "non-self-executing"

(a). if the agreement manifests an intention that it shall not become effective as domestic law without the enactment of implementing legislation,

(b). if the Senate in giving consent to a treaty, or Congress, by resolution, requires implementing legislation, or (c). if implementing legislation is constitutionally required.

§ 112. Determination and Interpretation of International Law: Law of the United States

(1) [Sources and proof of international law]

(2) The determination and interpretation of international law present federal questions and their disposition by the United States Supreme Court is conclusive for other courts in the United States.

§ 115. Inconsistency Between International Law or Agreement and Domestic Law: Law of the United States

(1)(a) An act of Congress supercedes an earlier rule of international law or a provision of an international agreement as law of the United States if the purpose of the act to supersede the earlier rule or provision is clear or if the act and the earlier rule or provision cannot be fairly reconciled.

(b). That a rule of international law or a provision of an international agreement is superseded as domestic law does not relieve the United States of its international obligation or of the consequences of a violation of that obligation.

(2) A provision of a treaty of the United States that becomes effective as law of the United States supersedes as domestic law any inconsistent preexisting provisions of a law or treaty of the United States.

(3) A rule of international law or a provision of an international agreement of the United States will not be given effect as law in the United States if it is inconsistent with the United States Constitution.

Restatement (Third) of Foreign Relations Law of the United States, §§ 111–12, 115 (1987). Could Congress constitutionally adopt a law that overrules the Supreme Court's ruling that common Article 3 of the Geneva Conventions applies to the Guantanamo Bay detainees? Suppose that the Geneva Conventions provided that they were to be construed and applied only by the chief executives of each party to the Convention; could such a provision bar Congress and the courts from reviewing executive action? Note that when the Senate ratifies a treaty, it may do so with reservations and declarations. For example, the United States has ratified the International Covenant of Civil and Political Rights, but with provisions such as the following:

Reservations:

(1) That article 20 does not authorize or require legislation or other action by the United States that would restrict the right of free speech and association protected by the Constitution and laws of the United States.

Declarations:

(1) That the United States declares that the provisions of articles 1 through 27 of the Covenant are not self-executing.

B. SPAIN

Under Article 96(1) of the Spanish Constitution, "the international treaties validly ratified, once officially published in Spain, will form part of the internal order. Their guarantees should be interpreted in conformity with similar international treaties approved by Spain." C.E. art. 96(1) (Spain). In a case against Catalan separatists accused of kidnaping and blowing up a person, the Spanish courts first upheld the conviction, but then the European Court of Human Rights held that the defendants' rights under the ECHR had been violated. That decision was only declarative and left to Spain the question of what to do. The Spanish Constitutional Court read the Constitution as "effectively incorporating into Spanish constitutional law the judgments and jurisprudence of the ECHR." Dennis P. Riordan, *The Rights to a Fair Trial and to Examine Witnesses Under the Spanish Constitution and the European Convention on Human Rights*, 26 Hastings Const. L.Q. 373, 411 (1999). It therefore nullified the final judgment of conviction.

C. ENGLAND

England has enacted legislation regarding supranational judicial review. Under one law, judgments of the European Court of Justice are to "be of the same force and effect, and proceedings may be taken on the judgment, and any sum payable under the judgment shall carry interest, as if the judgment had been a judgment or order given or made by the High Court on the date of registration." The European Communities (Enforcement of Community Judgments) Order 1972, S.I. 331/72, art. 5 (EC). A later law, the Human Rights Act, 1998, c. 42 (U.K.), however, treats judgments of the European Court of Human Rights somewhat differently. Section 2 requires courts considering questions in connection with the Convention on Human Rights "to take into account any—(a) judgment, decision, declaration or advisory opinion of the European Court of Human Rights. . . ." In addition, under section 3, "So far as it is possible to do so, primary legislation and subordinate legislation must be read and given effect in a way which is compatible with the Convention rights." While the court may declare that the provision is incompatible with a Convention right, "A declaration under this section ("a declaration of incompatibility")—(a) does not affect the validity, continuing operation or enforcement of the provision in respect of which it is given; and (b) is not binding on the parties to the proceedings in which it is made."

Notes

2–10.   Has England effectively adopted judicial review, by enacting these statutes? Why would it do so? How do the review provisions of these laws differ from one another?

VI. EFFECT OF DECISIONS ON CONSTITUTIONALITY

A. EFFECT ON PARTIES

Judicial decisions on constitutionality may result in reversal of a conviction, as in the Spanish case above, in a non-binding declaratory judgment, as with England's Human Rights Act, or a binding declaratory judgment. In Germany,

> The *Gesetz über das Bundesverfassungsgericht* which lays down the rules of procedure for the court, restrains it to a ruling in a mere declaratory form. In case of a dispute between the political departments or between the federal government and a state, the court's ruling will only state that the specific course of action or measure (*Massnahme*) taken by the defendant does not violate article Y of the GG. While the court may not order the defendant to reverse its action, the defendant is under a legal obligation to comply with the *ruling* which is binding on all agencies of the Federation and the states. The same rule applies in a case concerning the validity of a statute.

Rupp, *supra* page 39, at 507.

B. EFFECT ON COURTS

Common law countries follow the doctrine of *stare decisis*, but it is often said that civil law systems do not. For example,

> Like the United States Supreme Court, the Constitutional Court [of Germany] employs a variety of interpretive modes, including arguments based on history, structure, teleology, text, interest balancing, and natural law. The one technique that is not formally followed in German constitutional analysis is that of *stare decisis*—which is unknown in the judiciaries of code-law countries—although as a matter of practice the court's opinions brim with citations to previous cases.

Donald P. Kommers, *The Constitutional Jurisprudence of the Federal Republic of Germany* 42 (2d Ed. 1997). However,

> Decisions of the [German] Federal Constitutional Court are binding on all other courts and government instrumentalities. Moreover, every decision reviewing the constitutionality of a

statute has itself the force of statute and is published in the Official Gazette....

Rupp-v.Brünneck, *supra* page 39, at 390. A variant is the Mexican writ of *amparo*, which is used to challenge the constitutionality of laws and of executive action. An *amparo* decision lacks precedential value; it applies only in the case in which it was rendered. However, the concept of *jurisprudencia* allows for the issuance of a decision with *stare decisis* effect "by holding the same point of law in five consecutive judgments...." Hector Fix Zamudio, *A Brief Introduction to the Mexican Writ of Amparo*, 9 Cal. W. Int'l. L.J. 306, 347 (1979).

Notes

2–11. Should a court be able to render more than declaratory relief where a statute is unconstitutional? Does the rule of law require that judicial rulings of unconstitutionality be given *stare decisis* effect? Are there advantages to requiring the issuance of five consecutive judgments before a decision is given *stare decisis* effect? Does the answer depend on the level of judicial independence?

Chapter Three

SEPARATION OF POWERS

Constitutions literally "constitute" the government. They create government entities—courts, legislatures, executives, heads of government—and they tell something about the functions of each. In this sense, they are political documents. However, the political constitution has legal consequences, and constitutional law depends in part on the relationship between the political arrangements and the law.

I. PRESIDENTIAL AND PARLIAMENTARY SYSTEMS

A. ATTRIBUTES

The two basic models of constitutional government are described below.

Herman Schwartz
Building Blocks for a Constitution
Issues of Democracy, 12, 14–15 (March 2004)
http://usinfo.state.gov/journals/itdhr/0304/rjde/rjde0304.pdf

The presidential system, of which the American version is the best known, usually involves the election of a chief executive by the people either directly or, as in the United States indirectly for a set period of years. In the American model, the president, who is both head of state and head of the government, sets both domestic and foreign policy and picks ministers to implement these policies. Ministers are often subject to confirmation by the legislature, but ultimately subject to direction and control by the president.

The legislature is independently elected, also for a set period of years. Neither the president nor the legislature is normally subject to dismissal by the other. This produces a system of dual legitimacy and clearly separated powers.

The presidential system offers stability and, in the hands of a strong president, can provide vigorous leadership. The stability can, however, turn into rigidity, for an unpopular or ineffective president cannot be easily removed until his or her term expires. Moreover, legislative stalemate and gridlock may result if the legislature is controlled by a different political party. If this division continues, the government may not be able to function efficiently for many years.

In a parliamentary system, the parliament is the only source of electoral legitimacy. There is no separation of powers between the legislature and the executive—the judiciary of course is independent but it stands outside the legislative sphere—for the executive branch, usually called the government and headed by a prime minister, is chosen by the party that has a majority in the parliament or from a coalition reflecting a majority of the legislators. The head of state is a president with little power, and is usually chosen by the parliament. The prime minister and the government are accountable to the parliament and can be dismissed by it. Elections can be called at any time, providing flexibility. Since there is no formal separation of powers between legislative and executive, there is little chance of an impasse since a government or prime minister who loses the confidence of the parliament can be dismissed by it.

The parliamentary system can, however, produce a frequent turnover of governments and great instability. It can also produce sudden drastic changes of policy when an opposition gains a majority, which can create a different kind of instability.

B. PARLIAMENTARY SYSTEM

Although parliamentary systems share the attribute of legislative supremacy—at least over the executive branch—systems vary in how they distribute powers between the prime minister [or premier], who is a member of parliament and its leader, and the other executive official, called a president or head of state [or monarch].

1. Strong Head of State

A strong head of state has more than symbolic authority, with powers that are different from and independent of, those wielded by the prime minister.

The French Constitution provides for a president, who is elected for seven-year terms, by a majority vote of the entire nation. 1958 Const. arts. 6–7 (Fr.). His role is spelled out in Article 5:

The President of the Republic shall supervise respect for the Constitution. By his arbitrament [*arbitrage*], he shall ensure the proper functioning of public authorities, as well as the continuity of the State. He is the guarantor of the nation's independence, of the integrity of its territory, and of respect for Community agreements and for treaties.

The President appoints the Prime Minister and, on the latter's recommendation, the members of the Government [Article 8]. The President has power to dissolve and call new elections for the National Assembly [Article 12]. He "is the head of the army," and:

When the institutions of the Republic, the nation's independence, the integrity of its territory, or the implementation of international agreements are threatened seriously and immediately, and the proper functioning of constitutional public authorities is interrupted, the President of the Republic shall take such measures as these circumstances require, having consulted officially the Prime Minister, the Presidents of the chambers, and also the Conseil constitutionnel.

1958 Const. arts. 15–16 (Fr.). However, "a declaration of war shall be authorized by Parliament [Article 35]," and although the President negotiates and ratifies treaties [Article 52], certain treaties must be ratified or approved by a *loi*, passed by the National Assembly. This limitation applies to "[P]eace treaties, commercial treaties, treaties relating to international organizations, those which commit the finances of the State, those relating to the status of persons, and those which involve the transfer, exchange, or addition of territory...." 1958 Const. arts. 53 (Fr.). The President shares some power with the Prime Minister, because the Constitution provides: "Acts of the President of the Republic, other than those provided for under [certain specified] articles, shall be countersigned by the Prime Minister and, where required, by the appropriate ministers." 1958 Const. art. 19 (Fr.).

The duties of the Prime Minister are set forth in Title 3: The Government. That title begins by declaring: "The Government shall determine and conduct national policy. It shall have the administration and the army at its disposal. It shall answer to Parliament under the terms of, and following the procedures set out in, articles 49 and 50 [regarding censure of the government and requiring the Prime Minister to offer the resignation of the Government to the President]." 1958 Const. art. 20 (Fr.). The Prime Minister "directs the operation of the Government. He is responsible for national defence. He ensures the implementation of laws." He makes appointments to the civil and military service [Article 21], but that power is held jointly with the President [Article 13].

The main power of Parliament is to pass *lois* (statutes). The French Constitution sets out the subjects on which Parliament may legislate,

1958 Const. art. 34 (Fr.)

(2) Statutes shall determine the rules concerning:

—civic rights and the fundamental guarantees granted to citizens for the exercise of their public liberties; the obligations imposed for the purposes of national defence upon citizens in respect of their persons and their property;

—nationality, the status and legal capacity of persons, matrimonial regimes, inheritance and gifts;

—the determination of serious crimes and other major offences and the penalties applicable to them; criminal procedure; amnesty; the establishment of new classes of courts and tribunals and the regulations governing the members of the judiciary;

—the base, rates and methods of collection of taxes of all types; the issue of currency.

(3) Statutes shall likewise determine the rules concerning:

—the electoral systems of parliamentary assemblies and local assemblies;

—the creation of categories of public establishments;

—the fundamental guarantees granted to civil and military personnel employed by the State;—the nationalization of enterprises and transfers of ownership in enterprises from the public to the private sector.

(4) Statutes shall determine the fundamental principles of:

—the general organization of national defence;

—the self-government of territorial units, their powers and their resources;

—the preservation of the environment;

—education;

—the regime governing ownership, rights *in rem* and civil and commercial obligations;

—labour law, trade-union law and social security.

(5) Finance Acts shall determine the resources and obligations of the State in the manner and with the reservations specified in an institutional Act.

(6) Programme Acts shall determine the objectives of the economic and social action of the State.

(7) The provisions of this article may be enlarged upon and complemented by an institutional Act.

Article 37(1) provides that "matters other than those within the province of *loi* (legislation) have a regulatory character."

Notes

3–1.   The first President under the 1958 Constitution, Charles de Gaulle, "said that the entirety of the state's authority is devolved to him." Denis Baranger, *Executive Power in France, in* The Executive and Public Law 217, 226 (Paul Craig and Adam Tomkins, eds. 2006). Is that a fair reading of the 1958 Constitution's allocation of powers? Does the 1958 Constitution follow the separation of powers? What principle determines allocation of power? Could the President of France have taken actions akin to those in *The Steel Seizure Cases*, 343 U.S. 579, 72 S.Ct. 863, 96 L.Ed. 1153 (1952) or *Dames & Moore v. Regan*, 453 U.S. 654, 101 S.Ct. 2972, 69 L.Ed.2d 918 (1981)? Could the Prime Minister? What is the impact of Article 37 of the French Constitution on the separation of powers?

2. Weak Head of State

In many countries a monarch or president acts as the head of state, but the executive power belongs to a prime minister, appointed by the head of state based on support of a parliament. For example, in Japan, "[t]he Emperor shall be the symbol of the State...." Kenpo, art. 1 (Japan). "The Emperor shall appoint the Prime Minister as designated by the Diet [legislature]." Kenpo, art. 6, para. 1 (Japan). The Prime Minister is the chief executive and appoints the Cabinet, submits bills, and "exercises control and supervision over various administrative branches." Kenpo, arts. 68 & 72 (Japan). The critical question in such countries is the relationship between the legislative power and the executive power.

II. DELEGATION OF LEGISLATIVE POWER

Delegation of legislative power to the executive blurs the separation between the two branches. Constitutions differ as to the extent to which they've been interpreted to allow this.

The Constitutional Court of South Africa summarized the law in commonwealth countries in which the Western Cape Legislature challenged the validity of proclamations issued by the President of South Africa amending a law relating to provincial elections.

THE EXECUTIVE COUNCIL OF THE WESTERN CAPE LEGISLATURE AND OTHERS v. THE PRESIDENT OF THE REPUBLIC OF SOUTH AFRICA

1995 (10) BCLR 1289 (CC) (S. Afr.)
available at http://www.concourt.gov.za/
text/court/cases/wpcape.pdf, at 29–39

JUSTICE CHASKALSON:

[52] In the past our courts have given effect to Acts of parliament which vested wide plenary power in the executive. *Binga v Cabinet for South West Africa and Others* 1988 (3) SA 155(A) and *R v Maharaj* 1950 (3) SA 187(A) are examples of such decisions. They are in conformity with English law under which it is accepted that parliament can delegate power to the executive to amend or repeal acts of parliament. S. Wade and C. Forsyth, *Administrative Law* 863–864 (Clarendon Press, Oxford, 7th ed. 1994). These decisions were, however, given at a time when the Constitution was not entrenched and the doctrine of parliamentary sovereignty prevailed. What has to be decided in the present case is whether such legislation is competent under the new constitutional order in which the Constitution is both entrenched and supreme. This requires us to consider the implications of the separation of powers under the Constitution, the "manner and form" provisions of sections 59, 60 and 61, the implications of the supremacy clause (section 4) and the requirement that parliament shall make laws in accordance with the Constitution (section 37).

[53] In the United States of America, delegation of legislative power to the executive is dealt under the doctrine of separation of powers. Congress as the body in which all federal lawmaking power has been vested must take legislative decisions in accordance with the "single, finely wrought and exhaustively considered, procedure" laid down by the US Constitution, which requires laws to be passed bicamerally and then presented to the President for consideration for a possible veto. *INS v Chada* 462 US 919 (1983) per Burger CJ at 951. Delegation of legislative power within prescribed limits is permissible because, as the Supreme Court has said, "[w]ithout capacity to give authorizations of that sort we should have the anomaly of legislative power which in many circumstances calling for its exertion would be but a futility." Per Hughes CJ in *Panama Refining Co. v Ryan* 293 US 388, 421 (1935). The delegation must not, however, be so broad or vague that the authority to whom the power is delegated makes law rather than acting within the framework of law made by Congress. . . .

[54] In Ireland, under the influence of the United States jurisprudence, the courts have adopted a similar approach. The Supreme Court held that whilst parliament cannot delegate its power to make laws to the executive, it is competent for it to make laws under which a regulatory power is delegated to the executive. The test as to whether lawmaking or regulatory powers have been delegated is "whether what is challenged as an unauthorised delegation of parliamentary power is more than the mere giving effect to principles and policies which are contained in the statute itself. If it be, then it is not authorised; for such would constitute a purported exercise of legislative power by an authority which is not permitted to do so under the Constitution."

[55] The courts of some Commonwealth countries seem to take a broader view of the power to delegate legislative authority than the courts of the United States, and to permit parliament to delegate plenary law-making powers to the executive, including the power to amend Acts of parliament. In part this is due to the influence of English law and decisions of the Privy Council, and in part to the form of government in such countries. In the United States there is a clear separation of powers between the legislature and the executive. In Commonwealth countries there is usually a clear separation as far as the judiciary is concerned, but not always as clear a separation between the legislature and the executive. Many of the Commonwealth countries have followed the English system of executive government under which the head of the government is the Prime Minister, who sits in parliament and requires its support to govern. Although there is a separation of functions, the Prime Minister and the members of his or her cabinet sit in parliament and are answerable to parliament for their actions.

[56] The influence of English law is referred to in [an Australian High Court case] in which the Court declined to follow the United States cases. In the same case, Evatt J ... drew attention to the differences in the form of government of Commonwealth countries and that of the United States, saying:

> In dealing with the doctrine of "separation" of legislative and executive powers, it must be remembered that, underlying the Commonwealth frame of government, there is the notion of the British system of an Executive which is responsible to Parliament. That system is not in operation under the United States Constitution.

> . . .

> This close relationship between the legislative and executive agencies of the Commonwealth must be kept in mind in examining the contention that it is the Legislature of the Common-

wealth, and it alone, which may lawfully exercise legislative power.

In Australia, it seems to have been accepted that the Commonwealth parliament can delegate a legislative power to the executive and vest in the executive the power to make regulations which will take precedence over Acts of Parliament. In *Cobb & Co Ltd and Others v. Kropp and Others* 1967 (1) AC 141 the Privy Council upheld a decision of the Supreme Court of Queensland finding that it was competent for the state legislature to vest in its Commissioner for Transport the power to impose taxes in the form of license fees on transport operators, as well as the power to determine the amount of the fees, which could be made to vary between operator and operator. Queensland had a bi-cameral legislature and the Order in Council under which it was established provided that "all bills for appropriating any part of the public revenue for imposing any new rate tax or impost" should originate in the Legislative Assembly. It was held that the plenary powers vested in the Queensland legislature entitled it to vest this authority in the Commissioner for Transport....

[57] Seervai in his work on the Indian Constitution deals at length with the Indian jurisprudence on the power of parliament to delegate legislative power to the executive. He refers to various judgments and decisions of judges in the Supreme Court of India which in his view contradict each other and vacillate between on the one hand sanctioning a broad delegation of law-making power by parliament to the executive, and on the other, requiring such delegation of legislative power to be carried out within a policy framework prescribed by parliament. Seervai himself takes the view that under the Indian Constitution a legislature has the power to pass a law under which the executive is given the power to implement an Act and to modify its provisions to enable it to work smoothly. He states ... that:

> [L]egislative power is not "property" to be jealously guarded by the legislature, but is a means to an end, and if the end is desired by the legislature and the difficulties in achieving that end cannot be foreseen, it is not only desirable but imperative that the power to remove difficulties should be entrusted to the executive Government which would be in charge of the day-to-day working of the law. (Citation omitted).

. . .

[58] In Canada, under the influence of the Privy Council decision in *Hodge v. The Queen* (1883) 9 AC 117 and *Shannon v. Lower Mainland Dairy Products Board* [1938] AC 708, it seems to be accepted that parliament has wide powers of delegation. Hogg,

Constitutional Law of Canada (3d ed. 1992) at paragraph 14.2, notes:

> The difference between the Canadian and the American systems resides not only in the different language of the two constitutional instruments, but in Canada's retention of the British system of responsible government. The close link between the executive and the legislative branches which is entailed by the British system is utterly inconsistent with any separation of executive and legislative functions.

According to Hogg, although delegation of legislative power between parliament and provincial legislatures is not permitted, delegation of such power by parliament to the executive, "short of a complete abdication of its power", is permissible. . . .

[60] Whilst it seems to be accepted in most of the Commonwealth that parliament can delegate wide powers to the executive, the separation of powers as far as the judiciary is concerned has been strictly enforced, and the Privy Council has held to be invalid legislation which encroaches upon the judicial power. *Attorney General for Australia v. The Queen* (supra) and *Liyanage v. The Queen* 1967 (1) AC 259 at 286C (an appeal from the Supreme Court of Ceylon). In *Liyanage*'s case it was said that the power to make laws derived from the Constitution and had to be exercised in accordance with its provisions.

Those provisions prevented parliament from issuing bills of attainder to the judiciary.

[61] This brief and somewhat limited survey of the law as it has developed in other countries is sufficient to show that where Parliament is established under a written constitution, the nature and extent of its power to delegate legislative powers to the executive depends ultimately on the language of the Constitution, construed in the light of the country's own history. Our history, like the history of Commonwealth countries such as Australia, India and Canada was a history of parliamentary supremacy. But our Constitution of 1993 shows a clear intention to break away from that history. The preamble to the Constitution begins by stating the "need to create a new order." That order is established in section 4 of the Constitution which lays down that:

> (1) This Constitution shall be the supreme law of the Republic and any law or Act inconsistent with its provisions shall, unless otherwise provided expressly or by necessary implication in this Constitution, be of no force and effect to the extent of the inconsistency.

> (2) This Constitution shall bind all legislative executive and judicial organs of the State at all levels of government.

Sub-section (2) is of particular importance in the present case.

[62] The new Constitution establishes a fundamentally different order to that which previously existed. Parliament can no longer claim supreme power subject to limitations imposed by the Constitution; it is subject in all respects to the provisions of the Constitution and has only the powers vested in it by the Constitution expressly or by necessary implication. Section 37 of the Constitution spells out what those powers are. It provides that:

> The legislative authority of the Republic shall, subject to this Constitution, vest in Parliament, which shall have the power to make laws for the Republic in accordance with this Constitution.

The supremacy of the Constitution is reaffirmed in section 37 in two respects. First, the legislative power is declared to be "subject to" the Constitution, which emphasises the dominance of the provisions of the Constitution over Parliament's legislative power, *S v. Marwane* 1982(3) SA 717(A) at 747 H—748 A, and secondly laws have to be made "in accordance with this Constitution." In paragraph [51] of this judgment we pointed out why it is a necessary implication of the Constitution that Parliament should have the power to delegate subordinate legislative powers to the executive. To do so is not inconsistent with the Constitution; on the contrary it is necessary to give efficacy to the primary legislative power that Parliament enjoys. But to delegate to the executive the power to amend or repeal Acts of Parliament is quite different. To hold that such power exists by necessary implication from the terms of the Constitution could be subversive of the "manner and form" provisions of sections 59, 60 and 61. Those provisions are not merely directory. They prescribe how laws are to be made and changed and are part of a scheme which guarantees the participation of both houses in the exercise of the legislative authority vested in Parliament under the Constitution, and also establish machinery for breaking deadlocks. There may be exceptional circumstances such as war and emergencies in which there will be a necessary implication that laws can be made without following the forms and procedures prescribed by sections 59, 60 and 61. Section 34 of the Constitution makes provision for the declaration of states of emergency in which provisions of the Constitution can be suspended. It is possible that circumstances short of war or states of emergency will exist from which a necessary implication can arise that Parliament may authorise urgent action to be taken out of necessity. A national disaster as a result of floods or other forces of nature may call for urgent action to be taken inconsistent with existing laws such as environmental laws. And there may well be other situations of urgency in which this type of action will be necessary. But even if this is so (and there is no need to decide this issue in the present case) the conditions in which section 16A were enacted fall short of such an emergency. There was, of course, urgency associated with the implementation of the Transition Act, but the Minister has regulatory powers under the Act, and legislation could have been passed to authorise the President to issue proclamations not inconsistent with the Act. Whether this could have included a power to amend other Acts of Parliament need not now be decided. An unrestricted power to amend the Transition Act itself cannot be justified on the grounds of necessity, nor can it be said to be a power which by necessary implication is granted by the Constitution to the President. Sections 59, 60 and 61 of the Constitution are part of an entrenched and supreme Constitution. They can only be departed from where the Constitution permits this expressly [section 235 (8) is such a case] or by necessary implication. In the present case neither of these requirements is present.

[63] Insistence upon compliance with the manner and form provisions of the Constitution in these circumstances is not elevating form above substance. The authorisation of legislation such as section 16A allows control over legislation to pass from Parliament to the executive. Later this power could be used to introduce contentious provisions into what was previously uncontentious legislation. Assuming this is done at a time party A has a majority in the Assembly, but not in the Senate, it would be difficult for other parties to secure a resolution of Parliament which would be needed to invalidate the delegation. It would also render ineffective the special procedures prescribed by sections 60 and 61. A contention that this would be a consequence of the Assembly and the Senate having passed the legislation in the first place, would be of little solace to parties in the Senate in a situation in which the authorisation is given at a time when Party A has a majority in the Assembly and the Senate, but later loses its majority in the Senate. In such circumstances, it could block a resolution objecting to legislation enacted under the delegation which could never have been passed without such delegation.

Notes

3–2. Does the South African Parliament have as much power to delegate legislative power to the executive as the English Parliament? As the U. S. Congress? What accounts for the variations in power among the Parliaments of the various commonwealth nations? Note that the separation of powers can be approached from another perspective: whether the legislature is encroaching on executive power. In the *Stendhal South Railway Line Bypass Case*, the German Federal Constitutional Court considered a claim that a federal law providing for the construction of a railway line was incompatible with the separation of powers because it included detailed maps, construction details, land acquisition lists, and the like. The plaintiff claimed that planning the details of a railway route was an executive function and that the parliament could only set general norms. The court rejected the claim. It held that "[u]nless it is a matter of the government's 'central spheres of independent executive responsibility' ..., the legislature may also decide fundamental questions itself." *Stendhal South Railway Line Bypass Case*, 1 BverfGE 95 (1996) (F.R.G. Fed. Const. Ct.), translated in 3 *Decisions of the Bundesverfassungsgericht* 706, 709 (F.R.G. Fed. Const. Ct. ed., 2005). Therefore, "in the planning of an individual project, the legislature therefore does not necessarily encroach on the function which the constitution has reserved to the executive power or to the judiciary...." *Id.* How would the case be decided under the U.S. Constitution? What values are encompassed within the general antipathy against legislative encroachment on the other two branches? Are they put at risk by the *Stendhal* decision?

III. WAR POWER

Article Two of the United Nations Charter provides, in part:

3. All Members shall settle their international disputes by peaceful means in such a manner that international peace and security, and justice, are not endangered.

4. All Members shall refrain in their international relations from the threat or use of force against the territorial integrity or political independence of any state, or in any other manner inconsistent with the Purposes of the United Nations.

U.N. Charter art. 2, paras. 3–4. The constitutions of member states differ both with respect to how they address this ideal and with respect to the procedures for waging war. In the wake of World War II, the allied victors required that the aggressive nations build a prohibition against aggressive war into their constitutions.

The Japanese Constitution provides:

(1) Aspiring sincerely to an international peace based on justice and order, the Japanese people forever renounce war as a sovereign right of the nation and the threat or use of force as a means of settling international disputes.

(2) In order to accomplish the aim of the preceding paragraph, land, sea, and air forces, as well as other war potential, will never be maintained. The right of belligerency of the state will not be recognized.

Kenpo, art. 9 (Japan).

Germany's Basic Law provides:

(1) Acts tending to and undertaken with intent to disturb the peaceful relations between nations, especially to prepare for a war of aggression, shall be unconstitutional. They shall be made a criminal offense.

(2) Weapons designed for warfare may be manufactured, transported, or marketed only with the permission of the Federal Government. Details shall be regulated by a federal law.

Basic Law, art. 26 (F.R.G.).

Other constitutions limit the purposes for war in other ways. In South Africa, the Constitution refers to "the defence force," whose "primary object ... is to defend and protect the Republic, its territorial integrity and its people in accordance with the Constitution and the principles of international law regulating the use of force." S. Afr. Const. 1996, art. 200. The President has sole authority to authorise the employment of the defence force, and the purposes for which he may do so are "(a) in cooperation with the police service; (b) in defence of the Republic; or (c) in fulfillment of an international obligation." S. Afr. Const. 1996, art. 201(2). The President must promptly report to Parliament on any such use of the defence force. *See* Stephen Ellmann, *War Powers Under the South African Constitution, in* Comparative Constitutionalism and Rights: Global Perspectives (P. Andrews ed., forthcoming 2007), *available at* http://ssrn.com/abstract=938103. Other constitutions define the respective roles of the executive and legislative branches with respect to war differently. Article 35 of the French Constitution provides for the Parliament to declare war, and under Article 15 the President is the head of the army. In China, the Constitution authorizes the President to proclaim war and martial law and mobilize the military. Xian Fa art. 80 (1982) (P.R.C.).

Notes

3–3. Are there differences in the types of military force that these other nations and the United States may maintain, under their constitutions? In the roles of the branches of government in authorizing or reviewing the use of military force? Would the War Powers Resolution comport with the constitution in these countries? Note that Japan, after World War II, did not maintain armed forces. It then created a Self Defense Force (SDF). In the primary case challenging the existence of the SDF as violating Article 9 of the Constitution, the lower court agreed that the SDF violated Article 9, an intermediate court disagreed, and the Supreme Court found a lack of standing and so did not directly address the issue. The intermediate court argued that Article 9 forbids aggressive war but does not forbid defense. It said that

the question is whether or not, objectively speaking, our country's ability to carry on war is clearly sufficient for aggression as compared with other countries.... Because such an evaluation cannot be settled upon objectively and unequivocally in the present situation, we cannot say that the SDF is at first sight and most clearly aggressive.

Minister of Agriculture, Forestry and Fisheries v. Ito., 27 Gy_sai Reish_ 1175 (Sapporo H. Ct., Aug. 5, 1976), translated in Lawrence W. Beer and Hiroshi Itoh, *The Constitutional Case Law of Japan, 1970 through 1990* 112, 121–22 (1996). Therefore, the question is one of state governance, committed to the Diet (legislature) and Cabinet. Would the question be phrased similarly in other countries? What is the impact of the United Nations Charter on the war power?

Chapter Four

VERTICAL DISTRIBUTION
OF POWERS

In study of the U.S. Constitution, "federalism" refers to the vertical distribution of powers between the nation and states and localities. Other constitutions, too, divide powers between the national government and subunits, but in different ways. Additionally, many European nations have, by treaty, agreed to so-called supranational governance to enforce treaty provisions, which means norms interpreted or established by government bodies outside the nation may modify national law, including constitutional law.

I. GEOGRAPHICAL DISTRIBUTION OF POWERS WITHIN A NATION

Constitutions not only "constitute" a central government, they also establish the division of authority between the central government and smaller government units. Constitutions vary in how they address this division—from strong federalism, as in the United States, to highly centralized states.

A. OTHER FEDERALIST NATIONS

1. *Germany*

Soon after Hitler took power in 1933, he instituted a series of measures that by 1936 had substantially liquidated the Länder [states] and had transferred all power to the central government. Roger H. Wells, *The Liquidation of the German Länder*, 30 Am Pol. Sci. Rev. 350 (1936). When the German government was reconstituted after World War II, the Basic Law instituted a federal system, with a national government and [after reunification] sixteen Länder. Article 28 requires that "the constitutional order of the Länder must conform to the principles of a republican, democratic, and social state governed by the rule of law...." Basic Law, art. 28 (F.R.G.). The Basic Law spells out in great detail the powers of the national government and powers that the two hold concurrently. Under Article 30, "[e]xcept as otherwise provided or permitted by this Basic Law, the exercise of state powers and the discharge of state functions is a matter for the Länder." On the other hand, Article 31 states: "Federal law shall take precedence over Land [state] law." The national government's exclusive legislative powers include foreign affairs and defense, citizenship, currency, foreign commerce, and intellectual property, among others. Basic Law, art. 73 (F.R.G.). Article 74 lists twenty six subjects of concurrent legislation, including civil and criminal law, court organization, public welfare, labor law, education, and property law, among others. Where there is concurrent power, "the Länder shall have power to legislate so long as and to the extent that the Federation has not exercised its legislative power by enacting a law," and "The Federation shall have the right to legislate on these matters if and to the extent that the establishment of equal living conditions throughout the federal territory or the maintenance of legal or economic unity renders federal regulation necessary in the national interest." Basic Law, art. 72 (F.R.G.). Moreover, the national government may adopt "framework legislation" on some subjects, and "When the Federation adopts framework legislation, the Länder shall be obliged to adopt the necessary Land laws within a reasonable period prescribed by the law." Basic Law, art. 75 (F.R.G.). The Länder may execute national laws [except where the Basic Law says otherwise], subject to federal supervision. The national government may also delegate execution of national laws to the Länder. Basic Law, arts. 83–85 (F.R.G.). The Basic Law also specifies how tax revenues are to be apportioned between the national government and Länder. Länder are autonomous in managing their budgets. Basic Law, arts. 106 & 109 (F.R.G.).

2. Canada

When the predecessor to the modern Canadian Constitution was being considered, the drafters looked to the experience of the United States. Thus, Sir John A. Macdonald explained:

We have given the General Legislature all the great subjects of legislation. We have conferred on them, not only specifically and in detail, all the powers which are incident to sovereignty, but we have expressly declared that all subjects of general interest not distinctly and exclusively conferred upon the local governments and local legislatures shall be conferred upon the

General Government and Legislature. We have thus avoided that great source of weakness which has been the cause of the disruption of the United States. *We have avoided all conflict of jurisdiction and authority.*

Parliamentary Debates on the Subject of Confederation, 8th Parl., 3rd sess. at 33 (1865) (emphasis added), quoted in Barry L. Strayer, *The Canadian Constitution and the Courts: The Function and Scope of Judicial Review* 16 (2d ed. 1983). The modern Constitution carries forward that provision and modified versions of two lists from the 1867 Constitution: exclusive legislative authority of the national government and exclusive legislative authority of the provinces. Constitution Act, 1867, 30 & 31 Vict., c. 3, §§ 91–92 (U.K.) A Canadian constitutional scholar writes that the case law interpreting these articles "contributed to a fiscal and constitutional crisis that emerged in the 1930's, a crisis that forced governments at both the federal and provincial levels to begin to search for new solutions." Patrick J. Monahan, *Constitutional Law* 235 (2d ed. 2002). He continues: "In Canada in the 1990s, the watertight compartments that were idealized by the Privy Council have been supplanted by a norm of shared and divided jurisdiction." *Id.* at 249.

B. UNITARY STATES

1. *South Africa?*

Is South Africa a federal state or a unitary state? The Constitution recognizes nine provinces, each with its own legislature and executive. One observer writes:

> If the South African constitutional schema were to be analysed against a formal federal checklist it could, with justification, be classified as federal. . . . Yet a closer examination would also reveal that the treatment of provincial or regional powers in the final Constitution promotes or sanctions an integrated system of government in which national and sub-national governments are deeply implicated in each others' functioning.

Nicholas Haysom, *Federal Features of the Final Constitution, in* The Post–Apartheid Constitutions: Perspectives on South Africa's Basic Law 504, 504 (Penelope Andrews and Stephen Ellman eds., 2001). Chapter Three of the Constitution provides that "government is constituted as national, provincial and local spheres of government, which are distinctive, interdependent and interrelated." S. Afr. Const. 1996, art. 40. It requires the levels of government to "co-operate with one another in mutual trust and good faith by—. . . (iv) co-ordinating their actions and legislation with one another . . .", and "An Act of Parliament must—(a) establish or provide for structures and institutions to promote and facilitate intergovernmental relations; and (b) provide for appropriate mechanisms and procedures to facilitate settlement of intergovernmental disputes." S. Afr. Const. 1996, arts. 40–41. Provincial legislative powers are found in two schedules, one listing concurrent powers and the other listing exclusive powers. The latter are minimal in scope.

2.   *France and China*

Although France divides its territory into communes, departments, and the overseas territories, the French constitution notes that they are "created by *loi*." 1958 Const. art. 72 (Fr.). The powers of the local governments are thus determined by the national government. Similarly, China divides its territory into administrative divisions, with some legislative power. However, the national government retains ultimate legislative authority on all matters.

C.   HYBRIDS

Italy is an example of a country that combines the federalist and unitary structures.

Italy was formed in the Nineteenth Century by the merger of several kingdoms and other entities. Today the government is divided between the State [national] and the Regions. The Regions do not correspond to the historical entities that united to form Italy.

> Although Italy is a Regional state and member of a supranational community to which it has ceded significant sovereignty, it retains elements of national control typical of a unitary state. Its courts are national, as are its legal professions and training. Its civil, commercial, corporate, criminal and family laws remain uniform national bodies of law. Its Parliament retains the power to establish essential principles to bound Regional discretion.... Italy's Constitutional Court, a national institution, continues at the forefront of defining the relationships between Italy's Regions and its central State authorities.

Louis F. Del Duca and Patrick Del Duca, *An Italian Federalism?— the State, its Institutions and National Culture as Rule of Law Guarantor*, 55 Am J. Comp. L.—(forthcoming 2007), *available at* http://ssrn.com/abstract=942868, at 25–26. After the collapse of fascism and the end of World War II, "rule of law under the Constitution and regional autonomy emerge as key themes in modern Italy.... The provision for Regionalization ... was also a reaction to the fascist dictatorship's association with a high degree of centralization." *Id.* at 30–31. Regionalization came through a 2001 amendment to the Constitution, which:

(1) reserves to the State exclusive legislative power in limited matters, (2) enumerates matters of concurrent State and Regional legislative power, subject to State legislative determination of "fundamental principles," and (3) grants Regions legislative power in every other matter. Regions may not restrict free circulation of persons and goods, nor may they limit the right to work.

Id. at 15. The Del Ducas conclude

The continuing invention of an Italian federalism under the 1948 Constitution is not fundamentally the accommodation of territorial cleavages, *i.e.* a self-aware minority's concentration in a specific territorial area, but rather redefinition of the State to accommodate national political impasse through invention of governmental levels other than the State itself, accompanied by devolution and delegation of responsibilities.... The ongoing evolution of Regionalization and Supranationalism within the constraint of State assurance of the constitutional rule of law affirms and deepens the State's role of assuring the Constitutional rule of law and the application of its fundamental principles.

Id. at 46–48.

Notes

4–1. Does the system for allocating powers between the central government and regions have any legal significance? Do you think that Canada's system is clearer than the U.S. system? Is a centralized system more harmonious?

II. IMPACT OF TRANSNATIONAL LAW ON DOMESTIC GOVERNANCE

Transnational law is law that has binding force across nations. European countries, in different combinations, have united to form two different sources of transnational law with different enforcement mechanisms. The European Convention on Human Rights is a treaty, which establishes certain human rights. Individuals from signatory nations who believe that their Convention rights have been violated may file petitions with the European Court of Human Rights, which issues decisions that then bind signatory nations. The European Union (EU) is a grouping of nations initially formed to promote economic unity, but which has since adopted human rights norms as well. A European Council, with representatives from each member nation, makes rules for the EU within the scope of the subject matters the member nations have delegated to it. European Council rules and directives bind member nations.

A. EUROPEAN CONVENTION ON HUMAN RIGHTS

In the following, the German Constitutional Court describes the impact of a ruling of the European Court of Human Rights on domestic law.

ORDER OF THE SECOND SENATE
OF 14 OCTOBER 2004

2 BvR 1481/04 (2004) (F.R.G. Const. Ct.)
http://www.bundesver fassungsgericht. de/en/decisions/rs
20041014_2bvr148104en.html

[I]n the proceedings on the constitutional complaint of the Turkish citizen G., . . . against

(a) the order of the Naumburg Higher Regional Court (Oberlandesgericht) of 30 June 2004—14 WF 64/04—,

(b) the order of the Naumburg Higher Regional Court of 30 March 2004–14 WF 64/04—

[In this case the European Court of Human Rights had held that the German court had violated rights of the plaintiff under the European Convention on Human Rights; on remand, the Naumberg Higher Regional Court continued to deny an injunction against the adoption of the plaintiff's child, and this appeal resulted].

I.

In the German legal system, the European Convention on Human Rights has the status of a federal statute, and it must be taken into account in the interpretation of domestic law, including fundamental rights and constitutional guarantees (1.). The binding effect of a decision of the ECHR extends to all state bodies and in principle imposes on these an obligation, within their jurisdiction and without violating the binding effect of statute and law (Article 20.3 of the Basic Law), to end a continuing violation of the Convention and to create a situation that complies with the Convention (2.). The nature of the binding effect depends on the sphere of responsibility of the state bodies and on the latitude given by prior-ranking law. Courts are at all events under a duty to take into account a judgment that relates to a case already decided by them if they preside over a retrial of the matter in a procedurally admissible manner and are able to take the judgment into account without a violation of substantive law (3.). A complainant may challenge the disregard of this duty of consideration as a violation of the fundamental right whose area of protection is affected in conjunction with the principle of the rule of law (4.).

1. a) The European Convention on Human Rights and its protocols are agreements under public international law. The Con-

vention leaves it to the States parties to decide in what way they comply with their duty to observe the provisions of the Convention. The federal legislature consented to the above treaty in each case by a formal statute under Article 59.2 of the Basic Law.

This classification [as statute] means that German courts must observe and apply the Convention within the limits of methodically justifiable interpretation like other statute law of the Federal Government. But the guarantees of the European Convention on Human Rights and its protocols, by reason of this status in the hierarchy of norms, are not a direct constitutional standard of review in the German legal system (see Article 93.1 no. 4.a of the Basic Law, § 90.1 of the Federal Constitutional Court Act). A complainant can therefore not directly challenge the violation of a human right contained in the European Convention on Human Rights by a constitutional complaint before the Federal Constitutional Court. However, the guarantees of the Convention influence the interpretation of the fundamental rights and constitutional principles of the Basic Law. The text of the Convention and the case-law of the European Court of Human Rights serve, on the level of constitutional law, as guides to interpretation in determining the content and scope of fundamental rights and constitutional principles of the Basic Law, provided that this does not lead to a restriction or reduction of protection of the individual's fundamental rights under the Basic Law—and this the Convention itself does not desire.

b) This constitutional significance of an agreement under international law, aiming at the regional protection of human rights, is the expression of the Basic Law's openness towards international law (Völkerrechtsfreundlichkeit); the Basic Law encourages both the exercise of state sovereignty through the law of international agreements and international cooperation, and the incorporation of the general rules of public international law, and therefore is, if possible, to be interpreted in such a way that no conflict arises with duties of the Federal Republic of Germany under public international law. The Basic Law has laid down in its programme that German public authority is committed to international cooperation (Article 24 of the Basic Law) and to European integration (Article 23 of the Basic Law). The Basic Law has granted the general rules of public international law priority over ordinary statute law (Article 25 sentence 2 of the Basic Law) and has integrated the law of international agreements, by Article 59.2 of the Basic Law, into the system of the separation of powers. In addition, it has opened the possibility of joining systems of mutual collective security (Article 24.2 of the Basic Law), created the duty to ensure the peaceful settlement of international disputes by way of arbitration (Article 24.3 of the Basic Law) and declared that the disturbance of the peace, and in particular preparing a war of aggression, is unconstitutional (Article 26 of the Basic Law). In this complex of norms, the German constitution, as is also shown by its preamble, aims to incorporate the Federal Republic of Germany into the community of states as a peaceful member having equal rights in a system of public international law serving peace (see also BVerfGE 63, 343 (370)).

However, the Basic Law did not take the greatest possible steps in opening itself to international-law connections. On the domestic level, the law of international agreements is not to be treated directly as applicable law, that is, without an Act subject to the consent of the German parliament under Article 59.2 of the Basic Law, and—like customary international law (see Article 25 of the Basic Law)—not endowed with the status of constitutional law.

. . .

d) The legal effect of a decision of the ECHR, under the principles of public international law, is directed in the first instance to the State party as such. In principle, the Convention takes a neutral attitude towards the domestic legal system, and, unlike the law of a supranational organisation, it is not intended to intervene directly in the domestic legal system. On the domestic level, appropriate Convention provisions in conjunction with the consent Act and constitutional requirements bind all organisations responsible for German public authority in principle to the decisions of the ECHR.

This legal position corresponds to the conception of the European Convention on Human Rights as an instrument for protection and for the enforcement of particular human rights. The obligation of the States parties, integrated into federal law by the consent Act, to create a domestic instance at which the person affected can have an "effective remedy" against particular conduct by the state (Article 13 of the Convention) already extends into the domestic structure of the state system and is not restricted to the executive branch, which is competent to act externally. In addition, the States parties must guarantee the "effective implementation of any of the provisions" of the European Convention on Human Rights in their domestic law (see Article 52 of the Convention), which is possible in a state under the rule of law governed by the principle of the separation of powers only if all the organisations responsible for sovereign power are bound by the guarantees of the Convention. In this view, the German courts too are under a duty to take the decisions of the ECHR into account.

3. The binding effect of decisions of the ECHR depends on the area of competence of the state bodies and the relevant law. Administrative bodies and courts may not free themselves from the

constitutional system of competencies and the binding effect of statute and law (Article 20.3 of the Basic Law) by relying on a decision of the ECHR. But the binding effect of statute and law also includes a duty to take into account the guarantees of the Convention and the decisions of the ECHR as part of a methodologically justifiable interpretation of the law. Both a failure to consider a decision of the ECHR and the "enforcement" of such a decision in a schematic way, in violation of prior-ranking law, may therefore violate fundamental rights in conjunction with the principle of the rule of law.

a) The obligation created by the consent Act to take into account the guarantees of the European Convention on Human Rights and the decisions of the ECHR at least demands that notice is taken of the relevant texts and case-law and that they are part of the process of developing an informed opinion of the court appointed to make a decision, of the competent authority or of the legislature. Domestic law must if possible be interpreted in harmony with public international law, regardless of the date when it comes into force (see BVerfGE 74, 358 (370)).

. . .

b) aa) If the ECHR has declared a domestic provision to be contrary to the Convention, either this provision may be interpreted in conformity with public international law when applied in practice, or the legislature has the possibility of altering this domestic provision that is incompatible with the Convention. If the violation of the Convention consists in effecting a specific administrative act, the authority responsible has the possibility of cancelling this act under the provisions of the law of administrative procedure. Administrative practice that is in violation of the Convention can be amended, and courts may establish the duty to do this.

. . .

Under Article 20.3 of the Basic Law, judicial decisions are bound by statute and law. The constitutionally guaranteed independence of the judge, who is subject to the law, is not affected by this commitment, which is derived from the principle of the rule of law.... Both the commitment to law and the commitment to statute put into concrete terms the judicial power that is entrusted to the judges (Article 92 of the Basic Law). Since the European Convention on Human Rights—as interpreted by the ECHR—has the status of a formal federal statute, it shares the primacy of statute law and must therefore be complied with by the judiciary.

. . .

Admittedly, as part of its competence the Federal Constitutional Court is also competent to prevent and remove, if possible, violations of public international law that consist in the incorrect application or non-observance by German courts of international-law obligations and may given rise to an international-law responsibility on the part of Germany (see BVerfGE 58, 1 (34); 59, 63 (89); 109, 13 (23)). In this, the Federal Constitutional Court is indirectly in the service of enforcing international law and in this way reduces the risk of failing to comply with international law. For this reason it may be necessary, deviating from the customary standard, to review the application and interpretation of international-law treaties by the ordinary courts.

This applies in a particularly high degree to the duties under public international law arising from the Convention, which contributes to promoting a joint European development of fundamental rights.... In Article 1.2 of the Basic Law, the Basic Law accords particular protection to the central stock of international human rights. This protection, in conjunction with Article 59.2 of the Basic Law, is the basis for the constitutional duty to use the European Convention on Human Rights in its specific manifestation when applying German fundamental rights too (see BVerfGE 74, 358 (370)). As long as applicable methodological standards leave scope for interpretation and weighing of interests, German courts must give precedence to interpretation in accordance with the Convention. The situation is different only if observing the decision of the ECHR, for example because the facts on which it is based have changed, clearly violates statute law to the contrary or German constitutional provisions, in particular also the fundamental rights of third parties. "Take into account" means taking notice of the Convention provision as interpreted by the ECHR and applying it to the case, provided the application does not violate prior-ranking law, in particular constitutional law.

. . .

II.

The challenged decision of the Naumburg Higher Regional Court of 30 June 2004 violates Article 6 of the Basic Law in conjunction with the principle of the rule of law. The Higher Regional Court did not take sufficient account of the judgment of the ECHR of 26 February 2004 when making its decision, although it was under an obligation to do so.

1. The challenged decision does not reveal whether and to what extent the Higher Regional Court considered the fact that the right of access asserted by the complainant is in principle protected by Article 6 of the Basic Law ["(1) Marriage and the family shall

enjoy the special protection of the state. (2) The care and upbringing of children is the natural right of parents and a duty primarily incumbent upon them. The state shall watch over them in the performance of this duty. (3) Children may be separated from their families against the will of their parents or guardians only pursuant to a law, and only if the parents or guardians fail in their duties or the children are otherwise in danger of serious neglect. (4) Every mother shall be entitled to the protection and care of the community. (5) Children born outside of marriage shall be provided by legislation with the same opportunities for physical and mental development and for their position in society as are enjoyed by those born within marriage."]. This constitutional protection is to be seen against the background of the court's remarks on the complementary guarantee in Article 8 of the Convention. The Higher Regional Court should have considered in an understandable way how Article 6 of the Basic Law could have been interpreted in a manner that complied with the obligations under international law of the Federal Republic of Germany.

Here it is of central importance that the Federal Republic of Germany's violation of Article 8 of the Convention established by the ECHR is a continuing violation from the perspective of Convention law, for the complainant still has no access to his son. In its judgment, the ECHR held that the Federal Republic of Germany, in the choice of the means with which the judgment has to be enforced on the domestic level, is free, insofar as these means are compatible with the conclusions from the judgment. In the view of the ECHR, this means that it must at least be possible for the complainant to have access to his child (ECHR, Judgment of 26 February 2004, no. 64). This opinion of the ECHR should have caused the Higher Regional Court to consider the question as to whether and how far personal access of the complainant to his child might precisely be in the best interest of the child and what obstacles that could be documented—if necessary by way of a new expert witness's report—are presented by the consideration of the best interest of the child to the access which the ECHR regards as appropriate and which are protected by Article 6.2 of the Basic Law.

2. The Higher Regional Court in particular assumes in a manner that is not acceptable under constitutional law that a judgment of the European Court of Human Rights binds only the Federal Republic of Germany as a subject of public international law, but does not bind German courts. All the state bodies of the Federal Republic of Germany are—to the extent set out here under C. I. above—bound by operation of law within their jurisdiction by the Convention and the protocols that have entered into force in Germany. They must take into account the guarantees of the

Convention and the case-law of the ECHR when interpreting fundamental rights and constitutional guarantees.

In the present case, the Higher Regional Court, by reason of the judgment of the ECHR of 26 February 2004, had particular cause to consider the grounds of that judgment, because the judgment, which established a violation of the Convention by the Federal Republic of Germany, dealt with the matter with which the Higher Regional Court was again concerned. The duty to take the decision into account neither adversely affects the Higher Regional Court's constitutionally guaranteed independence, nor does it force the court to enforce the ECHR decision without reflection. However, the Higher Regional Court is bound by statute and law, which includes not only civil law and the relevant procedural law, but also the European Convention on Human Rights, which has the status of an ordinary federal statute.

In the legal analysis in particular of new facts, in weighing conflicting fundamental rights such as those of the foster family and in integrating the individual case in the overall context of family-law cases relating to the right of access, the Higher Regional Court is not bound in its particular conclusion. The order challenged, however, lacks a discussion of the connections set out above.

B. THE EUROPEAN UNION

The European Union (EU) has a separate, but overlapping membership, to that of the nations that have agreed to be bound by decisions of the European Court of Human Rights.

As of January 2007, the European Union (EU) consisted of twenty-seven countries, bound together by treaties that create the EU's structure. The treaties provide for the EU to regulate such areas as trade and movement barriers, antitrust, employment discrimination, and some social policies. They establish legislative, executive, and judicial bodies to create rules, administer them, and enforce them.

Members of the European Union have agreed by treaty to be bound by directives of the European Parliament (a rule-making body comprised of one representative from each member nation). The following excerpt describes the effect the EU Race Equality Directive, Council Directive 2000/43/EC, 2000 O.J. (L180) 22 (EC), would have on domestic law:

> Even the most optimistic Euro–MPs have been surprised at how fast the European Union turned aspiration into reality: a new race equality directive has been approved by the European parliament and passed unanimously by the council of ministers that will compel member states to rewrite their laws by the end of 2002. For

the United Kingdom, which already has a race relations statutes, the directive will still provoke major reforms.

In an EU where most countries have no comprehensive race legislation, the new directive enforces the principle of equal treatment irrespective of ethnic origin. European involvement in this area is based on article 13 of the Amsterdam Treaty of June 1997, allowing "appropriate action to combat discrimination based on sex, racial or ethnic origin, religion or belief, disability, age or sexual orientation".

The directive outlaws both direct and indirect discrimination. Practices that are apparently neutral but disadvantage those of a particular ethnic origin will be banned. Incitement to discriminate is to be treated as equivalent to actual discrimination.

EU members will be obliged to ensure that their domestic law complies. Statutes must be put in place that ensure equal treatment in both public and private sectors, including social security and health, as well as in the supply of goods and services, such as housing.

. . .

The effect of the equal treatment directive will vary from country to country. The Race Relations Act here [UK] already includes many of the required provisions. But [not all.] . . .

Even more dramatic will be the directive's impact on other countries. In Germany the constitution can be invoked by individuals in court cases alleging discrimination, but there is no specific race legislation. The French constitution and civil and labour codes mention race. Politicians have been discussing new anti-discrimination proposals; the directive now gives them a comprehensive framework.

Austria ... has no general anti-discrimination law and its constitution has no reference to "race". It is a measure of the importance of the directive that the government, Freedom party included [which had opposed such a measure], will have to implement a race relations act.

The EU's southern members are interesting, too. The Portuguese, who during their presidency of the EU have been leading the debate, have no constitutional provision on race, though Portuguese labour law prohibits dismissal on grounds of race or ethnic origin. Portugal's institutional architecture includes the office of high commissioner for immigration and ethnic minorities.

The constitution of Greece states that all Greeks are equal before the law, but civil and labour law entirely omit any protection against discrimination on the grounds of race. Netherlands law offers a comprehensive framework around equal opportunities and race and probably comes closest among EU members to the UK. The Dutch 1994 Equal Treatment Act explicitly mentions race, nationality and race discrimination—yet even the Netherlands will not be immune from the directive's effects.

There is no doubt that buried in the various European constitutions there are commitments to equal treatment, but they are vague and inexplicit. The new directive will bring consistency to the way all EU citizens are treated, whatever their race or origin.

Claude Moraes, *Race Against Time: The European Union's New Directive will Enforce the Principle of Equal Treatment Regardless of Ethnic Origin*, Guardian, June 30, 2000, available at http://www. guardian. co.uk/analysis/ story/0,,338078,00.html.

The European Court of Justice [ECJ] hears cases arising out of the European Union. Professor Michel Rosenfeld describes the ECJ:

In contrast to the USSCt, the ECJ is the creature of a treaty rather than a constitution and its mission is to interpret EU treaties and the laws issued from, or pursuant to, them. In the broadest term, treaties are typically concluded to regulate external relations between two or more sovereigns whereas constitutions typically regulate internal matters within a unified whole, most commonly a nation-state. Thus, for example, a free trade treaty between two nation-states usually creates legal obligations that may well require judicial interpretation and adjudication, but the latter is clearly distinguishable from constitutional review. From a formal standpoint, therefore, the ECJ appears to have no legitimate constitutional review function and does not engage in constitutional interpretation.

From a practical and functional standpoint, however, matters seem quite different. Many contemporary treaties, such as the European Convention on Human Rights("ECHR") deal with subjects that are much more "internal" than "external" and have a far more extensive impact on the relationship between a citizen and her own state than on relationships among states. Consistent with this, moreover, the European Court of Human Rights ("ECHR"), while a transnational court interpreting and applying ECHR treaty based rights, engages *substantively* in what is very much akin to adjudication of constitutional rights. In the context of the EU, the relevant treaties also deal with "internal" as well as "external" matters in relation to the member-states, though arguably their "internal" impact is less comprehensive than that of the ECHR. Nevertheless, early in its tenure the ECJ itself played a key role in widening and deepening the "internal" reach of the relevant treaty-based supra-national European order. Indeed, in its landmark 1963 decision in *Van Gend en Loos,* the ECJ held that Community law has direct effect conferring rights on citizens against their own state for the latter's violations of certain of its treaty-based obligations.

Michel Rosenfeld, *Comparing Constitutional Review by the European Court of Justice and the U.S. Supreme Court,* Cardozo Legal Stud. Res. Paper No. 157, at 4–5, http://ssrn.com/abstract=917890.

The U.S. Supreme Court has interpreted the Constitution's system of federalism to prohibit "commandeering", meaning direct orders by Congress requiring states to implement congressional policy. By contrast, Professor Neil S. Siegel has pointed out that

> the general view of member states of the European Union on commandeering is the opposite of the U.S. Supreme Court's position: member states tend to prefer directives, which 'command a Member State to regulate in a particular area and thus require further Member State legislative action to become fully effective within that state,' to regulations, which 'have immediate legal force for individuals within a Member State.'

Neil S. Siegel, *Some Modest Uses of Transnational Legal Perspectives in First–Year Constitutional Law,* 56 J. Legal Educ. 201, 204–5 (2006) (quoting Daniel Halberstam, *Comparative Federalism and the Issue of Commandeering, in* The Federal Vision: Legitimacy and Levels of Governance in the United States and the European Union (Kalypso Nicolaïdis and Robert Howse eds., 2001)). Siegel notes that Justice Breyer referred to "this perceived virtue of commandeering on the other side of the Atlantic" in his dissent in *Printz v. United States,* 521 U.S. 898, 976–77, 117 S.Ct. 2365, 2404, 138 L.Ed.2d 914 (1997).

Notes

4–2. Why does the decision of the European Court of Human Rights bind the German courts? Does the ECHR create a supranational form of government similar to a federal system? What is the same? What is different? What is the difference between the direct application of European Union law and the indirect application of the European Convention on Human Rights? What is the impact of the transnational arrangements such as the ECHR and the European Union on federalism within member states? Note that international agreements affect the power of states in the United States. For example, *see Asante Technologies v. PMC–Sierra, Inc.,* 164 F.Supp.2d 1142 (N.D. Cal. 2001), a suit between two Delaware corporations for breach of contract. One party's principal place of business was in California and the other's in British Columbia. The federal district court held that the case could be removed from state court, because the United Nations Convention on Contracts for International Sale of Goods applied. The Convention applied even though different from California law, because "California is bound by the Supremacy Clause to the treaties of the United States." *Asante Technologies,* 164 F.Supp.2d at 1150.

4–3. How does the European Council's authority over the race discrimination policies of the EU member states compare to Congress's authority over state law? How does it compare to the U.S. Supreme Court's authority over state action through interpretation of the equal protection clause? How might the European Council's authority change if the EU members were to ratify the proposed "constitution"?

4–4. The United States does not belong to an organization like the EU, which has a Council with the authority to issue binding human rights directives. It is, however, a signatory to numerous international treaties that contain equality guarantees. How do these guarantees affect the U.S. Supreme Court's interpretation of the Constitution's equal protection guarantee? *See infra*, Fundamental Rights, Ch. 6, Part III.

4–5. Would the EU position, noted above, necessarily lead to a different result than that in *Printz*, if the case had arisen in Europe? What might explain the differing approaches in the U.S. and EU? Professor Mark Tushnet points out that "the political safeguards of federalism are stronger in Germany than in the United States" because "the German lander have a higher degree of direct representation in the German policy-making process than U.S. states do." Mark Tushnet, *How (and How Not) to Use Comparative Constitutional Law in Basic Constitutional Law Courses*, 49 St. Louis Univ. L.J. 671, 677 (2005).

Chapter Five

EQUALITY

Problems of equality both persist around the world, and differ in specifics according to national histories. These samenesses and differences are reflected in the different constitutional equality guarantees.

I. RACE DISCRIMINATION

A. *BROWN'S* LEGACY

The following lecture, delivered to celebrate the fiftieth anniversary of *Brown v. Board of Education*, 347 U.S. 483, 74 S.Ct. 686, 98 L.Ed. 873 (1954), which interpreted the U.S. Constitution's equal protection guarantee, describes its impact on other nations with different constitutions and different histories, and particularly on one country, Brazil, which shares the American history of race-based slavery.

Robert J. Cottrol
**Brown and the Contemporary Brazilian
Struggle Against Racial Inequality: Some
Preliminary Comparative Thoughts**

66 U. Pitt. L. Rev. 113, 116–129 (2004)

Brown has a significance that is even broader than its pivotal role in the struggle against a legally-sanctioned caste system in American culture. *Brown* must be seen as part of a larger movement in the postwar World: the struggles against traditional systems of inequality, hierarchy and disadvantage. The struggle against the Nazis and the revulsion toward Nazi racism helped generate new ways of thinking about race in many societies. It certainly helped play a role, if perhaps a hard-to-define role, in the

Brown decision itself. If *Brown* helped to fuel the postwar civil rights movement in the United States, that civil rights movement was also fueled by the knowledge that similar struggles were occurring in other societies. The relationship was symbiotic-the struggles for human dignity in other societies in turn were fed and continue to be fed by the example of the Civil Rights movement in the United States. The movement against apartheid in South Africa drew inspiration from the fight against Jim Crow in the United States. The movement for equal rights for Catholics in Northern Ireland saw parallels with the Afro–American fight against American segregation. India, home of the religiously-based caste system that helped inspire segregation and exclusion in the United States, today is attempting to institute affirmative action programs designed to bring into that society's mainstream people from castes traditionally excluded from positions of power and respect. This process continues world-wide.... [O]ne of the heroes of the *Brown* litigation effort ... ha[s] ... returned from Eastern Europe where he was helping governments in that region dismantle the systems of separate and decidedly unequal schools for Roma children.

... Among the nations currently struggling with issues of a legacy of discrimination and inequality and how to remedy the exclusions of the past and present is Brazil....

Brazil's path ... has some interesting parallels and differences with the American odyssey with race and rights. Brazil had a history of African slavery and the enslavement of the descendants of Africans that was longer and more profound than the history of slavery in the United States. Brazilian slavery began before Portuguese settlement of the Americas. African slaves toiled in the cities of Portugal and in the sugar plantations of the Azores even before the Columbian voyages to the Americas. Unlike the English, who had to develop systems of slavery in the Americas, the Portuguese were able to import an already-existing system of slavery to Brazil. More than three million African captives went to the sugar and coffee plantations and mines of Brazil, dwarfing the 500,000 to 600,000 Africans that are estimated to have been brought, enslaved, to what is now the United States. Slavery was finally abolished in Brazil in 1888, more than a generation after Appomattox and the Thirteenth Amendment. Today, Brazil has an African-descended population of over fifty million, the second-largest population of African descent in the world after Nigeria.

... It would be accurate to say that for many decades, the literature on race in Brazil celebrated the notion of Brazil as a "racial democracy." There were many reasons for this, but one reason was, perhaps, more important than the others, particularly for our purposes. Brazil lacked the kind of state-sponsored, legally-mandated system of racial discrimination that prevailed for many years in the United States. The two American Republics have had similarities in their racial histories-African and Afro–American slavery, the virtual continuation or attempt at continuation of the master-slave relation in some regions after formal emancipation, industrial competition between Afro–American populations and later immigrants from Europe and Asia, often-significant regional differences in race relations, and negative stereotyping of people of African descent. But still, there were significant differences. The United States had a much longer history of erecting formal caste-like barriers between black and white. This had been true even during the long slave era in both societies. If Brazilian slavery was physically harsher than slavery in the United States, Brazil as a slave society was nonetheless more comfortable with its free Negro population and more willing to recognize free Afro–Brazilians as citizens entitled to the rights of other citizens. The southern states of the United States were largely uncomfortable with their free black population. This discomfort was reflected in the law of the southern states which, particularly in the nineteenth century, increasingly curbed the limited set of rights enjoyed by free African–Americans.

. . .

By and large, Brazil lacked this history of legal [Jim Crow-era] discrimination that characterized American race relations for much of the post-emancipation era. With the principal exception of its immigration laws that favored European immigration, and to varying degrees prohibited the immigration of others, Brazilian law in the twentieth century has lacked the caste-like character of its American counterpart. This contrast with the patent, legally-mandated system of racial discrimination in the United States contributed to the notion of Brazil as a racial democracy-a harmonious society where blacks, whites, and particularly mulattoes, all interacted and blended together with ease and without discrimination. . . .

And yet, the image was very much belied by stubborn facts. Brazil has been a nation of often-startling inequalities-inequalities not coincidentally correlated with race. Although Brazilian law has not had a history of mandating discrimination, strong discrimination has nonetheless existed against Afro–Brazilians. For example, the passage of Brazil's first civil rights statute, Lei Afonso Arinos, in 1951, was occasioned by Brazil's international embarrassment over an incident involving discrimination against a visiting black celebrity from the United States. . . .

I think it is fair to say that despite the very real persistence of both inequality and discrimination in Brazilian life, an Afro–Brazilian effort to combat these evils remained quite underdeveloped until relatively recently. I think this is certainly so when contrasted with the Civil Rights movement in the United States. Several explanations might be advanced to explain this fact. First, the lack of the kind of clear and formal, indeed legally-required, barriers that existed in the United States gave potential Afro–Brazilian activists less of a clear target. How do you attack a barrier that few are willing to acknowledge even exists? Second, flexible definitions of racial categories and a tendency to "promote" successful Brazilians with African ancestry out of the black category and sometimes out of the mulatto category, have led to a lesser sense of racial cohesion among those who might be categorized as "Afro–Brazilians" than has been the case among those currently categorized as "African–Americans" in the United States. This is what historian Carl Degler once termed "the mulatto escape hatch." Third, an authoritarian government in Brazil, including a better than twenty-year reign of military government between 1964 and 1985, discouraged protest movements. This curtailed the possibilities of racial protest, including potential Afro–Brazilian protests or civil rights movements.

Here is where *Brown,* and the movements for civil rights and racial remedy that were partly inspired by that decision, become important to this discussion. The successes of the U.S. civil rights movement helped spur a reassessment of the role of race in Brazilian life. . . .

Persisting inequality in the land of "racial democracy" forced a reconsideration of anti-discrimination law in Brazil. Brazil was a pioneer in the passage of anti-discrimination law. If Brazilian law, enshrined in the 1988 Constitution, criminalized racial discrimination and represented a national normative consensus concerning the evils of racism, why did so much in the way of inequality and discrimination still persist? A number of Brazilian legal scholars were beginning to wonder if they might fruitfully study the North American experience, and if civil rights law in the United States might provide some answers.

Inequality in education, particularly higher education, has been one such point of comparison. Brazil has a first-class system of public universities, both state and federal. Students admitted to these universities are entitled to tuition-free educations. Admission to public universities is governed by a stringent admission exam entitled "the vestibular." Although the exams are vigorously defended by their champions as fair and meritocratic, success on the exams is highly correlated with family income. In brief, well-to-do families, whose children have had strong secondary educations in private schools, tend to score higher on vestibular exams and thus receive the benefit of free public universities. Children of poor families, who have had weak public school secondary educations, tend to score lower and are denied the benefit of free public universities. As a disproportionate percentage of the nation's poor, Afro–Brazilians have historically been significantly under-represented in the nation's public universities.

Throughout the 1990s, Brazilian scholars in law and the social-sciences began looking toward affirmative action as one way of ameliorating the effects of both outright discrimination and the kind of structural inequality represented in university admissions, employment, and other facets of Brazilian life. Although advocacy of affirmative action was gaining momentum in the 1990s, Brazilian law, particularly the Constitution of 1988, was seen as posing formidable barriers to race-conscious measures as a means of redressing deeply rooted inequalities.

Undoubtedly, one of the more important of the Brazilian legal scholars arguing that affirmative action could be reconciled with the anti-discrimination provisions of the Brazilian Constitution was Joaquim B. Barbosa Gomes. [Gomes cited from the Warren opinion in *Brown* to argue that affirmative action to remedy the racial stratification in higher education would be consistent with the Brazilian constitution.] . . .

. . . By 2001, tentative steps were being made toward affirmative action programs in governmental ministries and higher education. In that year, with the support of Bernadette da Silva, Rio de Janeiro's first Afro–Brazilian governor, the state legislature passed three statutes instituting a system of quotas for the state's two public universities, the State University of Rio de Janeiro and the University of North Fluminense. The legislation called for a quota of 50 percent for graduates of public schools, 40 percent for Afro–Brazilians and 10 percent for the physically disabled. Some other states also followed with affirmative action programs of their own.

The program quickly came under intense criticism. . . .

The newly instituted affirmative action measures are being challenged in the Brazilian courts and face a potentially uncertain future. Arguments that are certainly familiar to students of the affirmative action debate in the United States are being advanced in Brazilian courts. These arguments, concerning stark inequalities of results, meritocracy in university admissions, the possibility of color-blind alternatives, and the possibilities of taking race into account in the face of anti-discrimination constitutional provisions, have become part of the Brazilian debate, as indeed they are clearly part of the debate in the United States.

The American experience with the modern civil rights move-ment-an experience *Brown* did much to precipitate and help shape-contributed to the growth of the Brazilian struggle against racial inequality in several important ways. First, by taking the civil rights struggle beyond the mere breaking of caste or caste-like barriers, the American civil rights movement helped to demonstrate the limitations of formal egalitarianism.... By the 1970s, having largely won the battle to dismantle formal discrimination in law, civil rights advocates in the United States increasingly turned their attention to the law's actual impact. American law was becoming increasingly concerned with the question of whether or not the law, as a substantive matter, treated people of different races equally. For example, that concern came in the form of the Supreme Court's finding that some level of affirmative action in university admissions is constitutional, or the Court's creation of a body of law in the field of employment discrimination that allowed discrimination to be inferred from statistical, rather than direct, evidence.

This concern led to a second American contribution to Brazilian civil rights discourse. Critics of Brazilian jurisprudence have stressed the formalistic nature of Brazilian judicial reasoning. Brazilian supporters of affirmative action have contrasted this formalism with the flexibility of the U.S. common law system and how that flexibility has allowed both the executive branch and the courts to accommodate a system of affirmative action that takes into account social and economic disparities in American life. Some Brazilian scholars have also noted how American courts have managed to find the constitutional space to permit affirmative action, while also ruling that quotas violate the equal protection principle. This latter point may become particularly important as the quotas adopted at the state universities of Rio de Janeiro and other institutions come under constitutional challenge. In my view, Brazilian legal scholars, ... may be trying to carve out a constitutional space that would allow public institutions in Brazil to take race into account, even if they do not employ the kind of rigid quotas that have developed in some public institutions in Brazil. In short, Brazilian advocates of affirmative action were arguing for the importation of the kind of legal realism that has long been influential in American jurisprudence, was critical in the development of American civil rights law, and played a critical part in the *Brown* decision.

Notes

5–1. The Supreme Court of Brazil dismissed the initial constitutional challenge to the university affirmative action plan on technical grounds. Other challenges in state courts, however, remain pending, as states continue to implement various affirmative action measures. *See* Marion Lloyd, *In Brazil, A Different Approach to Affirmative Action: Latin America's First University for Black Students Open Amid a Countrywide Debate About Quotas*, Chronicle Higher Ed., Oct. 29, 2004, at A49. Both a draft law establishing similar quotas for enrollment at public universities and a Racial Equality Statute, which mandates affirmative action and provides incentives for inclusion and advancement of Afro–Brazilians in public and private employment are pending in the national Congress. The Senate's approval of the Racial Equality Statute in 2005 provoked a wave of protests and the exchange of "manifestos" signed by prominent figures on both sides of the debate. *See* Mario Osava, *Brazil: Race Quotas—Accused of Racism*, Inter Press Service, July 26, 2006, available at http://ipsnews.net/news.asp?idnew= 34111.

5–2. In arguing from the similarities of the current Brazilian situation and the one confronted by the U.S. Supreme Court in *Brown*, advocates challenge "the traditional view, stated in "We Are Not Racists," a new best-selling book that criticizes quotas, that in contrast to "a segregated society like America," Brazil's institutions are "completely open to people of all colors, our judicial and institutional framework is completely colorblind." Larry Rohter, *Soccer Skirmish Turns Spotlight on Brazil's Racial Divide*, N.Y. Times, Sept. 19, 2006, at A4 (reporting on a case that has "reverberated throughout Brazil," in which, at a police league soccer game, a retired police colonel, irate at seeing a teammate penalized, called the referee, an Afro–Brazilian, a "monkey" and said his skin was the color of excrement; the referee, who is also a soccer player, brought a criminal complaint for libel, slander and "incitement to racism"). Core elements of the "traditional" view are "first. . . . the widely disseminated belief that Brazil is a racial 'paradise' or, more recently, 'democracy.' The second . . . . . is that Brazilian society is 'multi-racial,' in contrast to the 'bi-racial' society of the United States." Gail D. Timor, *Race, With or Without Color? Reconciling Brazilian Historiography*, 10 Estudios interdisciplinarios de America Latina y El Caribe (1999), http://www.tau.ac.il/eial/X_1/triner.html. The "racial democracy" ideal stems from a scholarly work published in the 1940's, which argued that, for a number reasons, including the mutually advantageous miscegenation among owners and slaves, race relations both during and after slavery in Brazil were more harmonious than in the United States. *Id.* Additionally, racial classifications differ in Brazil from those employed in the United States. Along the black/white divide, the Brazilian population census categorizes people according to whether they are *branco* (white), *pardo* (gray-brown) or *preto* (black), while popular definitions include a range of intermediate shades. Edward E. Telles, *Race in Another America: The Significance of Skin Color in Brazil* 22 (2004). Brazilian classifications add complexity, too, in that they consider a range of features, such as nose shape and hair type, along with skin color. "The Portuguese word that in the Brazilian folk taxonomy corresponds to the American 'race' is 'tipo.' Tipo, a cognate of the English word 'type,' is a descriptive term that serves as a kind of shorthand for a series of physical features. Because people's physical features vary separately from one another, there are an awful lot of tipos in Brazil." Jefferson M. Fish and Ken Schles, *Mixed Blood—The Myth of Racial Classifications*, Psychology Today, Dec. 1995, available at http://www.psychology today.com/articles/ PTO–19951101–000038.html. How would you expect these elements of the traditional view of race relations in Brazil as contrasted with the United States to impact the affirmative action debate?

5–3.   Should arguments from *Brown* and the U.S. Supreme Court equal protection clause jurisprudence be persuasive in Brazil? Consider the following:

> [A] ... fundamental difference ... must be taken into account when transferring legal knowledge: the distinct legal *traditions* of the two countries. The *common law* tradition as found in the United States creates legal conclusions built upon the legal conclusions of earlier cases, in essence incorporating social and legal history into its constantly growing legal framework. Brazil follows a *civil law* tradition which sees precedence as relevant but non-binding, allowing judges to make decisions based upon the independent interpretation most relevant to each situation. It could be said that, unlike the civil law tradition, the common law has a "memory" of its past decisions, both good and bad, built into its ever-growing structure. Whether it is expedient for Brazil to arrive at the same conclusions as the United States regarding affirmative action, any expectation of transplantation without Brazil constructing its own rigorous legal underpinning would be as unwise as making a decision totally based upon a stranger's memories.
>
> . . .
>
> One of the most touted distinctions between the common law and civil law traditions is the different weight given to past judicial decisions. Under a civil law system such as Brazil's, the judge's role is to determine the decision mandated by written legislation. Although other sources—notably past cases and writings by experts—play a role in the decision-making process, the judge is not expected to create new law. Legislating is reserved for the legislature.
>
> A common law system, by contrast, builds its entire corpus of law on the notion of *stare decisis*, under which past judicial decisions are controlling. The outcomes of past cases will dictate, as a matter of legality, the correct decision in a present case. Law students in common law countries learn the art of distinguishing past cases on their facts as one means to get around this limitation.
>
> Constitutional Equal Protection jurisprudence in the United States especially exemplifies the common/civil tradition divide. The respective textual constitutional bases for equal protection vary little between the United States and Brazil. The Fourteenth Amendment of the United States Constitution declares, "No state shall ... deny to any person within its jurisdiction the equal

protection of the laws." Brazil's Constitution includes the assurance that, "all are equal before the law, without distinction of any kind ..." coupled with an objective "to promote the well-being of all, without prejudice as to origin, race, sex, color, age and any other forms of discrimination."

In the United States, however, the Supreme Court's interpretation of "equal protection" must be followed in all subsequent cases until modified or overruled by a later Supreme Court decision. For this reason the "separate but equal" doctrine "derived" from the Constitution by the Court in *Plessy v. Ferguson* remained constitutionally steadfast law for over 50 years until its reversal in *Brown v. Board of Education*. Speaking to the strength of *stare decisis*, Equal Protection jurisprudence after *Brown* continued to cast the debate in terms molded by the original *Plessy* decision: either the Constitution allows discriminatory laws aimed at persecuting minorities, as claimed the majority; or the Constitution is "color-blind" in the words of the dissent. The United States' common law context, it might be argued, has forced the issue of affirmative action to remain under the constraints of its seminal case, even after that case has been overturned.

As the history of racial discrimination in the United States makes evident, the evolution of a framework of "scrutiny" for race-related cases was built with an eye first to abolish the system of Jim Crow persecution that had taken hold across the country. No wonder, then, that the Supreme Court ruled that any government action that makes a distinction based on race requires the highest level of scrutiny. By the time affirmative action appeared, this same system of scrutiny, through the power of *stare decisis*, resulted in a ruling that quotas are categorically illegal under a "color-blind" Constitution, even if meant to assist those against whom discrimination had originally been directed. Justice Powell in *Bakke* went further, saying that individual efforts to make up for general past persecution is similarly proscribed.

This entire judge-constructed framework contrasts with the Brazilian equal protection landscape. Granted, there was historically no regime of racially discriminating laws to abolish, and therefore less impetus for constructing strict barriers against race-conscious legislation. Brazil's recently-born constitution has likewise not grown old enough to have constructed such an elaborate framework as Equal Protection in the United States. Beyond these historical factors, however, it remains that Brazil's constitutional judges will *not* be constructing any rigid set of hard-and-fast rules outlining equal protection. Following civil law tradition, any constitutionally-mandated framework for discerning solutions to equal protection dilemmas must be created by the legislature. Brazil's approach to the constitutionality of its affirmative action, including Rio's recent attempt at public university quotas, will be made on a case-by-case evaluation of the constitutionality of racially-conscious policies.

Garret Wilson, *The Effect of Legal Tradition on Affirmative Action in the U.S. and Brazil*, Feb. 25, 2005, http://www.garretwilson.com/essays/law/brazilaffirmativeaction.html.

B. AFFIRMATIVE ACTION

The U.S. Supreme Court has struggled since the mid 1970's to define the limits that the general guarantee of "equal protection" imposes on government choices to employ race-conscious measures to address the lingering effects of past discrimination. A number of constitutions explicitly provide for the possibility of affirmative action, often alongside an equality guarantee. South Africa's constitution provides: "9(1)Everyone is equal before the law and has the right to equal protection and benefit of the law; 9(2) Equality includes the full and equal enjoyment of all rights and freedoms. To promote the achievement of equality, legislative and other measures designed to protect or advance person, or categories of person, disadvantaged by unfair discrimination may be taken." S. Afr. Const. 1996, ss. 9(1) and 9(2), available at http://www.acts.co.za/constitution/index.htm. The proposed constitution for the European Union, which is consistent with an anti-discrimination directive that currently binds the member states, provides: "Equality between men and women must be assured in all areas, including employment, work and pay," but this "shall not prevent the maintenance or adoption of measures providing for specific advantages in favour of the under-represented sex". A Treaty Establishing a Constitution for Europe, art. II–83, Oct. 29, 2004, http://europa.eu/constitution/en/lstoc1_en.htm.

India's constitution, effective in 1950, not only provides for the possibility of affirmative action, but embodies the expectation that such programs will occur. Unlike the United States, its deep social and economic divisions trace not to slavery, but to a rigid and complex Hindu caste system, imposed at birth according to the family's traditional occupation, and reinforced by British colonial rule. The system arranged cases in a hierarchy from priests and the educated elite at the top to the peasants and working class at the bottom. Outcasts, or untouchables, were outside the caste system entirely. In addition to abolishing untouchability and generally guaranteeing equality on grounds including race, religion, caste, and sex, India's Constitution provides for "reservations" of government employment positions and other opportunities, such as university student slots, for members of indigenous "scheduled tribes," and of the former untouchables, labeled "scheduled castes." A 1951 amendment empowered the government to make any "special provision for the advancement of any socially and educationally backward classes of citizens or for the scheduled castes and the scheduled tribes." In response to the mandate to identify other backward classes, in additional to the former untouchables, a first Backward Classes Commission produced a report in 1955 identifying thousands of different groups as "backward" and recommending a range of reservations for government jobs and university slots. The Indian Parliament rejected the report and it was never implemented, although certain states took affirmative action measures. A 1963 Supreme Court decision held that the total reservations could not exceed 50%. A second Backward Classes Commission headed by B.P. Mandal produced another report in 1980. The government's announcement in 1990 that it would implement the recommended reservations in government employment

> provoked a torrent of criticism and an orgy of anti-reservation violence that included burning buses, trains and government buildings, blocking road and rail traffic, police firings, and as many as 100 suicides. The army was called out in several states to restore peace and order. The epicenter of the turbulence was New Delhi, the nation's capital, and spread throughout northern India. Prime Minister Singh's clarifications that the Mandal recommendations would not apply initially to educational institutions and promotions in government jobs did little to diminish the passion and anger. Virtually all accounts identified upper caste, middle class students, who saw the Mandal recommendations as denying them job and educational opportunities, as the largest protesting group; certainly it was students setting themselves on fire that attracted the most national and international press coverage. In an effort to curb the caste violence and self-immolations, the Supreme Court on October 1st issued a stay order, directing the government to suspend implementation of the ... recommendations pending the Court's decisions on the various constitutional and legal challenges. . . .

George H. Gadbois, Jr., *International Insight: Mandal And The Other Backward Classes: Affirmative Action In India In The 1990s,* 1 J.L. & Soc. Challenges 71, 74 (1997).

In 1992, the Indian Supreme Court issued a 900 + page decision *(Indra Sawhney v. Union of India,* (1992) 3 S.C.C. 212

(Ind.)) in which it in large part upheld the government's adoption of the commission's recommendations, with several modifications. It affirmed the 50% limit on total reservations(to be comprised of 22.5% for scheduled castes and scheduled tribes combined with 27% for other backward classes (OBCs) designated by the commission). It disagreed with a state government proposal to give preference to poorer sections of the OBCs, instead charging the national government with dividing the entire class of OBCs into "more backward" and "backward" categories and assigning a separate quota for each. It introduced the concept of a "creamy layer" or most advanced segment of each class designated as backward and required the government to create criteria for eliminating these segments from the set-asides. Additionally, the Court held that the reservations should apply only to hiring, and that promotions must be allocated according to merit independent of class designation.

In the following case, the Supreme Court of India addressed an effort by one of the Indian states to subdivide and treat differently sub-castes within the "scheduled castes" category identified by the President of India as entitled to reservations under the Indian Constitution.

EV CHINNAIAH v. STATE OF ANDHRA PRADESH & ORS

[2004] 4 LRI 705 (Ind.)

N Santosh Hegde J (delivering judgment of the court):

. . .

[43] Legal constitutional policy adumbrated in a statute must answer the test of art 14 of the Constitution of India. Classification whether permissible or not must be judged on the touchstone of the object sought to be achieved. If the object of reservation is to take affirmative action in favour of a class which is socially, educationally and economically backward, the state's jurisdiction while exercising its executive or legislative function is to decide as to what extent reservation should be made for them either in Public Service or for obtaining admission in educational institutions. In our opinion, such a class cannot be sub-divided so as to give more preference to a miniscule proportion of the scheduled castes in preference to other members of the same class.

. . .

[49] The appeals are allowed, impugned Act is declared as ultra vires the Constitution.

. . .

[50] SB Sinha J (delivering judgment of the court): . . .

[51] The scheduled castes and scheduled tribes occupy a special place in our Constitution. The President of India is the sole repository of the power to specify the castes, races or tribes or parts of or groups within castes, races or tribes which shall for the purpose of the Constitution be deemed to be scheduled castes.

[52] Clause (2) of art 341 of the Constitution confers power only on the Parliament to include therein or exclude therefrom castes, races or part or group within any caste etc. By reason of the provisions of the said Act, the members of the scheduled castes specified for the state of Andhra Pradesh had been divided in four different categories and reservations both in public office as also in education had been earmarked in the manner specified therein.

. . .

[62] The short question which arises for consideration is as to whether by reason of the impugned legislation the State has exceeded its legislative power.

Constitutionality of the Act: Equality Clause:

[64] By reason of the impugned legislation, the State although had not sought to alter or amend the Scheduled Castes Order made by the President of India, but, admittedly, it sub-divided the members of scheduled castes in four different categories.

. . .

[68] Equal protection clause mandates that all persons under like circumstances should be treated alike. Article 14 is in many respects similar to Fourteenth Amendment of the American Constitution. . . .

. . .

[70] Although in the United States of America, affirmative action based on race is a deeply divisive issue. . . .

[71] In a recent decision a question came up before the US Supreme Court in *Jennifer Gratz & Patrick Hamacher v Lee Bollinger* (Decided on 23 June 2003) as regard the validity of guidelines providing for selection method under which every applicant from an underrepresented racial or ethnic minority groups was to be automatically awarded 20 points out of 100 points needed to guarantee admission. The said provision was struck down as being violative of equality protection clause. . . .

[72] Delivering his [sic] minority opinion on his own behalf as also on behalf of Souter, Ginsburg, Justice however held: Our

jurisprudence ranks race a 'suspect' category, 'not because (race) is inevitably an impermissible classification, but because it is one which usually, to our national shame, has been drawn for the purpose of maintaining racial inequality' ... *Norwalk Core v Norwalk Redevelopment Agency* 395 F 2d 920, 931–932 (CA2 1968). But where race is considered 'for the purpose of achieving equality', ibid, at 932, no automatic proscription is in order.... [T]he Constitution is colour conscious to prevent discrimination being perpetuated and to undo the effects of past discrimination....

[73] The minority opinion of Ginsburg J appeals to us and is in tune with our Constitutional scheme.

[74] Can having regard to the constitutional scheme, the conglomeration of the members of scheduled castes be subjected to further classification is the question.

[75] Article 14 of the Constitution of India aims at equality. It prohibits discrimination in any form. At its worst form, it will be violative of basic and essential feature of the Constitution.

[76] Reasonableness of sub-classification of the scheduled castes must be judged on the touchstone of the equality clause.

[77] Having regard to the decision of this court in [the case reviewing the recommendations of the second Backward Classes Commission], the backward class citizens can be classified in four different categories—(i) more backward, (ii) backward, (iii) scheduled caste and (iv) scheduled tribe....

. . .

[79] There appears to be no good reason for classifying the backward classes of citizens in four categories; as noticed in the judgment of Brother Hegde J and furthermore the Scheduled Caste Order and Scheduled Tribe Order provide for conglomeration of castes and tribes and, thus, must be treated as a distinct and separate class for the purpose of the Constitution. We may notice that there is not such express provision in the Constitution in respect of 'other backward class'.

[80] The preamble to the Constitution proclaims that 'we the people of India' adopt, enact and give to ourselves the Constitution of India to secure to all its citizens justice, liberty and equality. There are a few Articles in Part IV of the Constitution of India like arts 38, 39 and 47 which aim at securing equality of opportunity and social justice. The State in terms of arts 14, 15(1) and 15(4) of the Constitution had inter alia made special provisions with regard to admissions in educational institutions for advancement of sched-

uled castes. Article 16(4) likewise enables the State from making any provision for the reservation of appointments or posts in favour of the backward classes under the State. Inevitably, its meaning is influenced by the legal context in which it must operate.

[81] Indisputably, only because the scheduled castes and scheduled tribes and other socially and economically backward class of citizens are not in a position to compete with the general category candidates, the equality principle has been adopted by way of affirmative action by the state government in making reservations in their favour both as regard admission in educational institutions and public employment. The doctrine of equality is the fibre with which constitutional scheme is woven.

[82] Our Constitution permits application of equality clause by grant of additional protection to the disadvantaged class so as to bring them on equal platform with other advantaged class of people. Such a class which requires the benefit of additional protection, thus, cannot be discriminated inter se, ie, between one member of the said class and another only on a certain pre-supposition of some advancement by one group over other although both satisfy the test of abysmal backwardness as also inadequate representation in public service.

[83] In a case of this nature, the burden of reasonable classification and its nexus with the object of the legislation is on the State. The State, in my opinion, has not been able to discharge the said burden.

. . .

[119] The power of a state legislature to decide as regard grant of benefit of reservation in jobs or in educational institutions to the backward classes is not in dispute. It is furthermore not in dispute that if such a decision is made the state can also lay down a legislative policy as regard extend of reservation to be made for different members of the backward classes including scheduled castes. But it cannot take away the said benefit on the premise that one or the other group amongst the members of the scheduled castes has advanced and, thus, is not entitled to the entire benefit of reservation. The impugned legislation, thus, must be held to be unconstitutional.

What is the Remedy?

[120] There is one practical aspect of the matter which may not also be lost sight of. The chart produced before us clearly shows

that the members belonging to Relli and Adi–Andhra are hardly educated. What was necessary in the situation was to provide to them scholarships, hostel facilities, special coaching, etc, so that they may be brought on the same platform with the member of other scheduled tribes, viz, Madiga and Mala, if not with the other backward classes. It is not in dispute that members belonging to Relli are hardly educated. Only two per cent of the members of the said community have studied in secondary school. No one has ever been admitted in any engineering discipline or other professional disciplines. The said facts clearly go to show that providing reservation for them in engineering or medical discipline or in public service would not solve their problem. Without such basic education, the members belonging to the said community would not be getting admission either in the engineering or medical colleges or other professional courses and as such the question of their joining public service may not arise at all. Now, even for the post of class IV employees, qualification of passing matriculation examination is provided. Unless children of the said community are educated, the provisions for both the education as also public service would be a myth for them and ultimately in view of the impugned legislation for all intent and purport, the benefit thereof would go to other categories. The state, in our opinion, should take positive steps in this behalf.

[121] I entirely agree with the opinion of Brother N Santosh Hegde J that the appeals be allowed.

Notes

5–4. Controversy over the Indian government's plans to implement affirmative action plans continues.

a government decision "to reserve almost 50% of seats in colleges and universities for lower-caste and other disadvantaged Indians" led to violent demonstrations, a hunger strike by medical students, the disruption of medical services, and violent police crowd control measures.

Randeep Ramesh, *Violence Feared in Indian Caste Row*, Guardian (London), May 17, 2006, at 23, available at http://www.guardian.co.uk/india/story/0,1776450,00.html.

5–5. How are the issues confronted by the Indian Supreme Court and the U.S. Supreme Court with respect to affirmative action the same? How are they different? How does India's history, and the fact that its embedded discrimination is based on caste, not race, affect the constitutional analysis? *See id.* ("'We feel very strongly that the student intake should be based on merit, not on birth,' said Sajanjiv Singh, a 20–year-old medical student on hunger strike. 'We do not even know what caste people are here, yet the politicians want to label us and use this as a factor in university admissions. It will mean fewer places for the talented.' '').

5–6. Compare the discussion of remedy by the Indian Supreme Court with those in U.S. Supreme Court affirmative action decisions. Would the U.S. Supreme Court ever propose what the Indian Supreme Court does? If not, why?

5–7. European countries generally employ affirmative action measures to benefit women, rather than racial or ethnic minorities. *See* Ivana Krstic, *Affirmative Action in the United States and the European Union: Comparison and Analysis, Facta Universitatis,* 1 Law and Politics 825 (2003), available at http://facta.junis.ni.ac.yu/facta/lap/lap 2003/lap2003–06.pdf. The concept of what constitutes affirmative action, or "positive action" as it is called there, is broader in Europe, encompassing for women "norms of preferential treatment to enable women to accomplish their dual roles in the family and at the workplace. It means that positive action must require reorganization in the workplace to make it easier for women to work in and outside the home. These measures include access for all pregnant women to adequate periods of maternity leave, insurances that the health of the mother and the child is not in danger, time off for pre-natal and post-natal care, proper care during pregnancy, and safety from exposure to hazardous working conditions." *Id* at 830. Nevertheless, such measures have generated far less social controversy than in the U.S. or India. Consider the following explanation of why:

> [A]s the term woman is pretty clear, the EU law does not pass through all controversies that are encountered in the US law.
>
> . . .
>
> Another model that all European countries implemented in the last century is based on the equal distribution of positive rights and is generally known as the welfare state model. The development of this idea began in Germany about century ago, and spread through all Western industrialized countries with the idea that the term "welfare state" includes the obligations and commitments of the state in many spheres of economic development, such as full employment, social security, and guarantees of certain minimal limits as to income, health care and education. The state obligations were seen as caring for all parts of the population, especially for groups in weak economic positions, to enable all citizens to live a life of human dignity and to take responsibility to equalize any imbalance in society.
>
> Since work has been seen as an essential means whereby individuals may preserve positive rights, the government has posi-

tive duties and has concentrated these in the social and economic spheres. The original aims of the EU were, therefore, to promote improved working conditions within the Union and to increase the standard of living of individuals living in the EU.

The idea of a welfare state, deeply, rooted in the mind of the European people is certainly an important reason why the public for the most part supports positive action, and sees it as a part of the policy to solve imbalances in a society.

. . .

The US Supreme Court almost always discussed the burden imposed on innocent whites by an affirmative action plan that it is reviewing.... The EU situation is different because positive action includes women, meaning half of the population that extends through all social categories; thus many people recognize its need and its opposition is, therefore, much weaker.

Id. at 832–42.

C. OTHER WAYS OF IMPLEMENTING EQUALITY GUARANTEES

1. *Building Legal Infrastructure and Looking to International Law*

Perhaps nothing so poignantly illustrates the chasm between a formal constitutional guarantee and its realization as the contrast between the equality guarantee of the world's most recent constitution, that of Iraq ("Article 14: Iraqis are equal before the law without discrimination based on gender, race, ethnicity, origin, color, religion, creed, belief or opinion, or economic and social status") and the rampant sectarian violence that is a day-to-day reality. In other countries as well, a threshold level of social stability and development of legal infrastructure is a prerequisite to realizing individual rights guarantees.

Open Society, Justice Initiative
Antidiscrimination in Russia
Combating Discrimination in Russia:
Strategies for Lawyers and NGOs
http://www.justiceinitiative.org/activities/ec/ec_russia (last visited Nov. 29, 2006)

Over the past few years, anecdotal evidence and the reports of non-governmental monitoring organizations have noted an increase in discriminatory practices and violence against racial/ethnic minorities on the territory of the Russian Federation. One effect of discriminatory practices has been the precarious legal status of a large number of former Soviet citizens who previously resided legally in the Russian Federation, but who have been considered illegal migrants since the entry into force in 2002 of the Federal Laws on Russian Citizenship and on the Legal Status of Foreign Citizens. Other human rights problems include racially selective inspections and identity checks by law enforcement targeting people from specific minorities, including those from the Caucasus and Central Asia and Roma minority, and numerous reports that residence registration is used as a means of discriminating against certain ethnic groups (UN Committee on the Elimination of Racial Discrimination Concluding Observations CERD/C/62/CO/7, March 2003).

Article 19 of the Russian Constitution stipulates that everyone is equal before the law and prohibits any restriction of rights on the grounds of race, ethnicity, national origin, or language–an "equal rights" provision that is reproduced in the civil code, criminal code, labor law, and administrative legislation. However, there exists no specific, binding anti-discrimination legislation that defines discrimination (not to mention the distinct meanings of "direct" or "indirect" discrimination) nor a list of legal mechanisms, judicial or otherwise, for redress of harm caused by discriminatory treatment.

In theory, the Constitution is an act of direct effect, and its equal rights provisions can be directly applied by a court. However, lawyers are not accustomed to seeking–nor are judges accustomed to sanctioning–the application of constitutional provisions in ordinary courts. Judges, defence lawyers and the Russian public are not familiar with discrimination as a concept of law. In a number of cases where discrimination occurred, complainants have failed to argue it, confining themselves to the "substantive" right at issue (i.e., denial of residence permit, employment dismissal, refusal to grant refugee status). In such cases, the courts' legal reasoning does not reach the question of whether persons were treated differently in similar situations.

Though international treaties such as the International Covenant on Civil and Political Rights (ICCPR), the International Covenant on Economic, Social, and Cultural Rights (ICESCR), and the International Convention on the Elimination of All Forms of Racial Discrimination (ICERD) can be used in domestic courts, lawyers and judges rarely cite them in practice.

Russian lawyers are, however, increasingly turning to the European Court of Human Rights. In the last two years, applications from Russia to the Court have exceeded 10,000, outnumbering those from any other country in the Council of Europe. During this period, however, only 14 cases from Russia were ruled admissible. Clearly the demand for skilled human rights litigation in Russia is matched by the need for training and strategic thinking in the use of domestic and regional human rights instruments. The Court in Strasbourg has generated case law in areas, such as police brutality, that matter to discrimination's victims. Additionally, the evolution of European Union law—particularly the adoption of prohibitions against discrimination on grounds of race and gender and in the field of employment—also offers additional tools to antidiscrimination litigators seeking to call upon European norms.

Notes

5–8. The fourteenth amendment became a part of the Constitution in 1868, the U.S. Supreme Court issued the Brown decision in 1954, and still in the United States substantial race-based differences in resources, opportunities and treatment remain. How do the impediments to implementing the U.S. equal protection guarantee compare with the Russian situation today? What lessons might the U.S. experience offer to others who seek to implement constitutional equal rights guarantees?

5–9. How might the European Court of Human Rights help Russian lawyers who are already armed with a constitutional equality guarantee? Why do you suspect so few Russian applications have been ruled admissible? An international non-governmental organization (NGO) issued the above excerpted press release. To what extent can or should organizations from outside a country intervene with respect to national discrimination issues?

2. Ensuring Legislative Representation

The U.S. Supreme Court has addressed the constitutionality of government attempts to secure minority participation in the political process through the drawing of voting district lines. Other countries address the issue of participation more directly, by providing for proportional representation of previously under-represented groups in the national or regional legislatures. See Daniela Estrada, *Chile: Parties not Keen on Push for More Women Legislators*, Inter Press Service, July 20, 2006 ("At present, 50 of the world's countries have adopted ... laws" which set gender quotas for legislative seats.). Although explicit proportional representation overcomes some of the obstacles to participation that exist in U.S. constitutional jurisprudence, other issues arise.

Integrated Regional Information
Networks (IRIN)
UN Office for the Coordination
of Humanitarian Affairs
**BOTSWANA: Minority Ethnic Groups Feel
New Bill Still Discriminates**

April 13, 2005
http://www.irinnews.org/report.asp?
ReportID=46625&SelectRegion=Southern_Africa

Member of parliament Filbert Nagafela has decided to register his own personal protest against the Botswana constitution by refusing to sing the national anthem until all references to the country's ethnic groups are removed.

Nagafela is a member of the Kgalakgadi people, one of the eight ethnic groups not recognised by the current constitution and, as such, he feels he is unable to identify with the phrase "this land is our inheritance" in the anthem.

Sections 77, 78 and 79 of the constitution guarantee automatic membership of the House of Chiefs to the eight Setswana-speaking paramount chiefs, while minority groups are represented by three members, regarded as sub-chiefs, who are elected to the assembly on a rotating basis and serve a four-year term.

The Khoisan, the first people to inhabit the country, are among those excluded from full representation in the House of Chiefs, as they are considered "minor tribes".

A bill introduced last year to address this discrimination by giving permanent seats in the House of Chiefs to the smaller ethnic groups has continued to fuel debate. The House of Chiefs plays an advisory role to the government and parliament.

The Constitution Amendment Bill, while still allowing the eight Setswana-speaking people the right to continue designating their traditional leaders to the house, provides for the election of 20 representatives from the eight so-called minor groups.

It also allows the president to appoint five additional members to the house, increasing the total from 15 to 35.

The 20 additional representatives from non-Setswana groups, including the Khalanga, the Wayeyi and the Khoisan, would be selected by district electoral colleges, to be chaired by a civil servant appointed by the Minister of Local Government.

However, there has been concern that traditional leaders might not make it to the house via an electoral process.

Nagafela questioned the need for elections. "Every tribe knows its history and traditional leadership; even bees have a king," he said.

Letshwiti Tutwane, a political analyst from the University of Botswana, said the process would confer a greater degree of authority on the eight Setswana-speaking chiefs, who would not have to undergo the rough and tumble of elections. "We will still have a situation where some chiefs will be superior than others."

The amendment bill was introduced last year after a report by a presidential commission of enquiry, established in July 2000 under former minister Patrick Balopi to look into complaints by non-Setswana speaking people that the constitution was biased.

The Chieftainship Act states that the "principal tribes" are defined as the Setswana-speaking Bamangwato, Batawana, Bakgatla, Bakwena, Bangwaketse, Bamalete, Barolong and Batlokwa. The Tribal Territories Act defines ethnic territory in terms of these eight groups, which means that all land is distributed under their jurisdiction.

Membership of the House of Chiefs is important because it confers constitutional recognition on the existence of a particular ethnic group. A lack of representation also means the lack of a voice in the development of customary law: for instance, the Wayeyi and some Basarwa and Herero groups are matrilineal, but the imposition of Setswana patriarchal customary law has nullified their own laws of inheritance, marriage and succession.

The issue of ethnic discrimination has been a sensitive one since independence; two previous attempts to reform the constitution—in 1969 and 1998—failed.

. . .

The "discrimination" against non-Setswana speakers is described by Lydia Nyathi–Ramahobo, the secretary general of Reteng, a coalition of ethnic cultural groups, as "a blemish on Botswana's deservedly good reputation for democracy and good governance".

"Non–Setswana speaking groups are not recognised or consulted on decisions affecting their lives through their chiefs, and do not have their languages used in education, on the national radio and in other social domains," she pointed out.

Nyathi-Ramahobo is unhappy with the provisions of the Constitutional Amendment Bill. "In our view, neither tribal neutrality nor tribal discrimination has been effectively addressed," she said.

According to Reteng, if the constitution is to reflect ethnic neutrality, it should accord all groups equal status.

Notes

5–10. Why do you think so many other countries perceive explicit legislative quotas as consistent with their constitutional equality guarantees? What additional "equality" issues does a system of quotas produce?

II. SEX DISCRIMINATION

A. INCLUDING WOMEN IN CONSTITUTION–DRAFTING AND CONSTITUTIONAL TEXT

Women did not participate in the drafting or ratification of the U.S. Constitution or of the fourteenth amendment, which added the equality guarantee. At the same time that the states were considering an Equal Rights Amendment, which would have explicitly prohibited discrimination based upon sex, the U.S. Supreme Court interpreted such a prohibition into the more general equal protection guarantee. In other countries with constitutions drafted more recently, women's participation in the constitution-making process has been more extensive, and the provisions more explicit and detailed with respect to sex-based equality.

Martha I. Morgan
Emancipatory Equality: Gender Jurisprudence under the Colombian Constitution

in The Gender of Constitutional Jurisprudence 75,
80 (B. Baines & R. Rubio–Marin eds., 2005)

After decades of extreme violence, many Colombians eagerly embraced the 1991 Colombian Constitution....

Despite the broadly proclaimed representativeness of the 1991 constituent assembly, women were vastly underrepresented—only four of the seventy-four members were women. But women and organizations advocating their causes were active outside the assembly as well.

. . .

As a result of the efforts of these advocates for women's rights, and of the parallel efforts of supportive men and women within the constitutional assembly, the Constitution contains several explicit guarantees related to women's rights. First, it expressly reflects CEDAW's dual strategy of prohibition of discrimination against women and approval of special positive measures as a means of assuring substantive rather than merely formal equality. Article 13 of the new Constitution incorporates these twin principles of equality in the following terms:

All persons are born free and-equal before the law, shall receive the same protection and treatment from the authorities, and shall enjoy the same rights, liberties and opportunities without any discrimination for reasons of sex, race, national or family origin, language, religion, or political or philosophical opinion.

The State shall promote conditions so that equality will be real and effective and adopt measures in favor of groups discriminated against or marginalized.

The State shall specially protect those persons who because of their economic, physical or mental condition find themselves in circumstances of manifest weakness and punish abuses and mistreatment that are committed against them.

The Constitutional Court's decisions under Article 13 have used both principles of reasonableness and proportionality developed by the European Court of Human Rights and the concept of levels of scrutiny from the United States Supreme Court's opinions. Unlike the U.S. Supreme Court, which has applied a "heightened" review but not "strict scrutiny" to gender classifications, the Colombian Court has applied "strict scrutiny" and has placed a heavy burden of proof on the defender of the challenged action when faced with discrimination based on sex (and, more recently, sexual orientation) as well as when dealing with infringements upon fundamental rights.

In addition to Article 13's general equality provisions, Article 40 provides that "the authorities will guarantee the adequate and effective participation of women in the decision-making levels of Public Administration," Article 42 recognizes equal rights and responsibilities between spouses and Article 43 prohibits discrimination against women and declares equal rights and opportunities between women and men. Finally, Article 53 includes equality of opportunity and special protection for women, maternity, and minors among the fundamental principles to be considered by Congress in enacting a labor law.

One of the most controversial features of the new Constitution was its extension of civil divorce to religious marriages. According to Article 42, "The civil effects of all marriages will be terminated by divorce according to the civil law." Article 42 also recognizes that a family can be formed by "natural or judicial bonds, by the free decision of a man and a woman to contract marriage or by the responsible will to form it," and, as mentioned above, guarantees equality of rights among couples. It further provides: "Any form of violence within the family is considered destructive of its harmony and unity, and will be punished according to the law."

Although Article 42 also recognizes the right of couples "to freely and responsibly decide the number of their children," the constitutional assembly rejected demands of women's groups that free choice about motherhood, including the right to legalized abortion, be explicitly guaranteed. By contrast, Article 43 guarantees special state assistance and protection to women during pregnancy and after childbirth, including "support benefits from it if they then become unemployed or abandoned." It further provides that the "State will provide help in a special manner to women heads of family." And, as mentioned earlier, protection for maternity is among the fundamental principles that Article 53 directs lawmakers to consider in enacting a labor law.

Notes

5–11. Another aspect of the Colombian Constitution important to the protection of individual rights is the tutela action, which allows any citizen to file "public actions in defense of the Constitution and the law." Pol. Const. Colombia 1991, as amended, art. 40(6), available at http://confinder.richmond.edu/admin/docs/colombia_const2.pdf. Courts must rule on tutelas within 10 days, and those decisions are subject to discretionary review by the Constitutional Court. Colombia Const., art. 86. The Constitutional Court held that domestic abuse was an actionable violation of numerous parts of the Constitution, including articles 42 and 43. Martha I. Morgan, *Taking Machismo to Court: The Gender Jurisprudence of the Colombian Constitutional Court*, 30 U. Miami Inter–Am. L. Rev. 253, 284–5 (1999) (noting that the Court stopped hearing such cases under the Constitution after the legislature passed a statute protecting women from spousal abuse). Why doesn't domestic violence violate the U.S. Constitution's equal protection guarantee? What other types of discrimination might form the basis for a constitutional action in Colombia but not the United States?

5–12. Although women did not participate in drafting the equal protection clause, since that time they have obtained the right to vote, as well as substantial political power. Why hasn't this change resulted in amendments to the U.S. Constitution's text, similar to the explicit and detailed Colombian constitutional guarantees?

5–13. In the wake of the war to oust the Saddam Hussein regime in Iraq, the United States provided extensive assistance in drafting the new Iraqi Constitution, including assistance to assure women's participation in the constitution-drafting process. *See* USAID, *Assistance for Iraq: Supporting Iraq's Constitution,* June 21, 2006, http://www.usaid.gov/iraq/accomplishments/constitution.html (detailing activities to assist organizations and women leaders to advocate for stronger legal rights in the Constitution and to build public awareness of women in the Constitution). The United States, of course, had a special interest in Iraq. To what extent is "assistance" from other countries in drafting foreign constitutions appropriate more generally? Consider the following commentary.

> [T]he impact of American constitutional rhetoric [on the new Ethiopian Constitution] is staggering.... What I'm observing is the impact of the rhetoric of American modern law professors which appears rather ridiculous out of context.... Talking about fashionable provisions (within the American academia) we will find that the press should not only be free but "diverse"; women are entitled to "affirmative" action in order to be able to "compete on the basis of equality with men in political, economic and social life". The problems that may arise from the competition between men and women should be resolved "in the best interests of the child." ... The rhetoric of individual rights, or individualism and of competition that is produced by the American model could not be more foreign to the African mentalite. A strong and ideological assertiveness of rights can have very destabilizing impact on the Ethiopian society.... In Africa, right assertiveness is particularly dangerous if it is understood as rights of a clan to be asserted against the others. The traditional decentralized ethnic African society endorsed and endorses a decision making style that could not be more far from the western right assertiveness. It was a culture of mediation, of unanimity, of peacekeeping not much different from the international law which governs the international community.

Ugo Mattei, *The New Ethiopian Constitution: First Thoughts on Ethnical Federalism and the Reception of Western Institutions*, 1 Cardozo Electronic L. Bull. (1995), www.jus.unitn.it/cardozo/Review/Constitutional/Mattei2.html.

B. IDENTIFYING INEQUALITY

A male plaintiff claimed unequal treatment in *Craig v. Boren*, 429 U.S. 190, 97 S.Ct. 451, 50 L.Ed.2d 397 (1976), the case in which the U.S. Supreme Court established intermediate scrutiny as the appropriate analysis for sex discrimination claims. Although the Court held the state's discrimination against males in access to 3.2% beer unconstitutional, in other cases it has found "real" sex-based differences to justify classifications that discriminate against men. As of 2005, males were the plaintiffs in two of the four cases directly asserting sex discrimination before the South African Supreme Court, and that Court has struggled to identify the kinds of "real differences" that can justify different government treatment of the sexes as well.

PRESIDENT OF THE REPUBLIC OF SOUTH AFRICA AND ANOTHER v. HUGO

1997 (6) BCLR 708 (CC) (S. Afr.)

JUDGMENT: BY Goldstone J

[2] On 27 June 1994, acting pursuant to his powers under section 82(1)(k) of the interim Constitution, the President (first appellant) and the two Executive Deputy Presidents signed a document styled Presidential Act No. 17 (the "Presidential Act"), in terms of which special remission of sentences was granted to certain categories of prisoners. The category of direct relevance to these proceedings was "all mothers in prison on 10 May 1994, with minor children under the age of twelve (12) years". It is common cause that the respondent would have qualified for remission, but for the fact that he was the father (and not the mother) of his son who was under the age of twelve years at the relevant date.

. . .

[32] The respondent argued that the Presidential Act was in conflict with section 8 of the interim Constitution in that by releasing all mothers whose children were under the age of twelve, it discriminated against fathers of children of a similar age. Section 8 of the interim Constitution provides as follows:

(1) Every person shall have the right to equality before the law and to equal protection of the law.

(2) No person shall be unfairly discriminated against, directly or indirectly, and, without derogating from the generality of this provision, on one or more of the following grounds in particular: race, gender, sex, ethnic or social origin, colour, sexual orientation, age, disability, religion, conscience, belief, culture or language.

(3)(a) This section shall not preclude measures designed to achieve the adequate protection and advancement of persons or groups or categories of persons disadvantaged by unfair discrimination, in order to enable their full and equal enjoyment of all rights and freedoms.

. . .

[37] The reason given by the President for the special remission of sentence of mothers with small children is that it will serve the interests of children. To support this, he relies upon the evidence of Ms Starke that mothers are, generally speaking, primarily responsible for the care of small children in our society. Although no statistical or survey evidence was produced to establish this fact, I see no reason to doubt the assertion that mothers,

as a matter of fact, bear more responsibilities for child-rearing in our society than do fathers. This statement, of course, is a generalisation. There will, doubtless, be particular instances where fathers bear more responsibilities than mothers for the care of children. In addition, there will also be many cases where a natural mother is not the primary care giver, but some other woman fulfils that role, whether she be the grandmother, stepmother, sister, or aunt of the child concerned. However, although it may generally be true that mothers bear an unequal share of the burden of child rearing in our society as compared to the burden borne by fathers, it cannot be said that it will ordinarily be fair to discriminate between women and men on that basis.

.   .   .

[41] The prohibition on unfair discrimination in the interim Constitution seeks not only to avoid discrimination against people who are members of disadvantaged groups. It seeks more than that. At the heart of the prohibition of unfair discrimination lies a recognition that the purpose of our new constitutional and democratic order is the establishment of a society in which all human beings will be accorded equal dignity and respect regardless of their membership of particular groups. The achievement of such a society in the context of our deeply inegalitarian past will not be easy, but that that is the goal of the Constitution should not be forgotten or overlooked. . . .

It is not enough for the appellants to say that the impact of the discrimination in the case under consideration affected members of a group that were not historically disadvantaged. They must still show in the context of this particular case that the impact of the discrimination on the people who were discriminated against was not unfair. In section 8(3), the interim Constitution contains an express recognition that there is a need for measures to seek to alleviate the disadvantage which is the product of past discrimination. We need, therefore, to develop a concept of unfair discrimination which recognises that although a society which affords each human being equal treatment on the basis of equal worth and freedom is our goal, we cannot achieve that goal by insisting upon identical treatment in all circumstances before that goal is achieved. Each case, therefore, will require a careful and thorough understanding of the impact of the discriminatory action upon the particular people concerned to determine whether its overall impact is one which furthers the constitutional goal of equality or not. A classification which is unfair in one context may not necessarily be unfair in a different context.

.   .   .

[44] The power to pardon duly convicted prisoners in terms of which the President acted is conferred upon him by the interim Constitution. The power of pardon is one which is recognised in many democratic countries

[45] There are at least two situations in which the power to pardon may be important. First, it may be used to correct mistaken convictions or reduce excessive sentences.

[46] In addition, however, it will also provide an opportunity to the President to release groups of convicted prisoners where he or she considers it desirable in the public interest. This is such a case. Here the pardon was not to an individual to correct a miscarriage of justice, but to a group to confer an advantage upon them as an act of mercy at a time of great historical significance.

The considerations mentioned here would well nigh have made it impossible for the President to release all fathers who were in prison as well as mothers. Male prisoners outnumber female prisoners almost fiftyfold. A release of all fathers would have meant that a very large number of men prisoners would have gained their release. As many fathers play only a secondary role in child rearing, the release of male prisoners would not have contributed as significantly to the achievement of the President's purpose as the release of mothers. In addition, the release of a large number of male prisoners in the current circumstances where crime has reached alarming levels would almost certainly have led to considerable public outcry. In the circumstances it must be accepted that it would have been very difficult, if not impossible, for the President to have released fathers on the same basis as mothers. Were he obliged to release fathers on the same terms as mothers, the result may have been that no parents would have been released at all.

. . .

[52] In the result, however, it has been established that the President has exercised his discretion fairly and in a manner that was consistent with the interim Constitution. The court a quo therefore should have dismissed the application.

(Chaskalson P, Mahomed DP, Ackermann, Langa, Madala, and Sachs JJ concurred in the judgment of Goldstone J).

BY Kriegler J (dissenting)

[63] This is a very hard case indeed.

[64] . . . I endorse the general observations in the majority judgment regarding gender discrimination. In the result my conclusion is that the President not only transgressed the provisions of s 8(2) in distinguishing between classes of parents on the basis of their gender (on which the majority seem to agree with me) but also that the presumption of unfairness attaching to that distinc-

tion has not been rebutted. That is the point at which our paths diverge.

. . .

[77] What kinds of facts are likely to discharge the burden of rebuttal imposed on the President by s 8(4)? I would make three observations here. First, the fact that discrimination is unintended or in good faith does not render it fair. Once the subject action or legislation is found to create adverse effects on a discriminatory basis, there is no further requirement, eg of bad faith or malice. My second observation is that the "rebutting" factors can seldom, if ever, in themselves be discriminatory or otherwise objectionable. True as it may be that our society currently exhibits deeply entrenched patterns of inequality, these cannot justify a perpetuation of inequality. A statute or conduct that presupposes these patterns is unlikely to be vindicated by relying on them. One that not only presupposes them but is likely to promote their continuation, is even less likely to pass muster. Third, factors that would or could justify interference with the right to equality in a section 33(1) analysis, are to be distinguished from those relevant to the enquiry under section 8(4). The one is concerned with justification, possibly notwithstanding unfairness; the other is concerned with fairness and with nothing else. I turn from these general comments to the case at hand.

[78] In my respectful view, the majority errs on all three counts.

. . .

[80] One can accept for the sake of argument that the President's belief is empirically confirmed. The question then is whether the fact that in South Africa mothers are the primary care givers can establish fairness under s 8(4). In this regard I agree with the majority judgment that the fact that women generally "bear an unequal share of the burden of child rearing" cannot render it ordinarily "fair to discriminate between women and men on that basis". What I cannot endorse, is the majority's conclusion that although the discrimination inherent in the Act was based on that very stereotyping, it is nevertheless vindicated. In my view the notion relied upon by the President, namely that women are to be regarded as the primary care givers of young children, is a root cause of women's inequality in our society. It is both a result and a cause of prejudice; a societal attitude which relegates women to a subservient, occupationally inferior yet unceasingly onerous role. It is a relic and a feature of the patriarchy which the Constitution so vehemently condemns. Section 8 and the other provisions mentioned above outlawing gender or sex discrimination were designed to undermine and not to perpetuate patterns of discrimination of

this kind. Indeed I find it startling that the appellants could have placed this fact before the Court in order to establish that their conduct does not constitute unfair discrimination. I would have thought that this is precisely the kind of motive that the respondent might have attempted to divine in the appellant's conduct in order to condemn it. It hardly has justificatory power. One of the ways in which one accords equal dignity and respect to persons is by seeking to protect the basic choices they make about their own identities. Reliance on the generalisation that women are the primary care givers is harmful in its tendency to cramp and stunt the efforts of both men and women to form their identities freely.

[81] Is it relevant that an inherently objectionable generalisation has been used in this case for the benefit of a particular group of women prisoners? The majority judgment regards this as an important—if not a decisive—factor in its reasoning. My first response is a narrow one. It is merely to say that the President has nowhere mentioned that it was his purpose to benefit women generally or the released mothers in particular .There is no suggestion of compensation for wrongs of the past or an attempt to make good for past discrimination against women. On the contrary, the whole thrust of the President's affidavit, and the raison d'être for the main supporting affidavit, is the interest of children. The third category of prisoners released under the Act was not women in their own right but solely in their capacity as perceived child minders.

. . .

[85] I must emphasise that I am not suggesting that gender or sex discrimination of any kind must always and inevitably be found to be irrevocably unfair. There is no question that gender or sex discrimination can be shown to be fair. All I am contending is that the evidence must be persuasive. In cases such as these the United States Supreme Court requires "exceedingly persuasive justification"—a rigorous test in the context of their equality provision, which makes no express mention of discrimination and contains no deemed unfairness. We should do no less. Mothers are no longer the "natural" or "primary" minders of young children in the eyes of the law, whatever tradition, prejudice, male chauvinism or privilege may maintain. Constitutionally the starting point is that parents are parents.

. . .

[88] In the result I would order as follows:

   1.   The appeal is upheld.

Notes

5–14.   How would the U.S. Supreme Court have ruled in the face of an identical government action? Compare the result and reasoning of the opinions in the above case with the opinions of the U.S. Supreme Court Justices in *Nguyen v. Immigration and Naturalization Service*, 533 U.S. 53, 121 S.Ct. 2053, 150 L.Ed.2d 115 (2001) (upholding a statutory requirement that fathers, but not mothers, of children born abroad engage in certain affirmative acts to confer U.S. citizenship on the child). Are the cases the same, or different, in important ways?

5–15.   Compare the text of the equality guarantees of the South African Constitution with the text of the U.S. Constitution's equal protection clause. Are the differences between them important to the result? In what kind of case might the differences in text influence the result?

5–16.   The dissenting justice refers to the U.S. Supreme Court's "exceedingly persuasive" standard. The South African Constitution states that "[w]hen interpreting the Bill of Rights, a court ... (b) must consider international law; and (c) may consider foreign law.". S. Afr. Const. 1996, s. 39(1). Should the U.S. Supreme Court refer to South African jurisprudence, such as the case above, in deciding future constitutional cases?

C.   THE INFLUENCE OF CUSTOMARY AND RELIGIOUS LAW ON CONSTITUTIONAL SEX EQUALITY RIGHTS

Constitutional equality guarantees require interpretation and implementation. Conflicts arise when different sources of law, such as customary or religious law, which incorporates gender inequality, coexist with constitutional equality guarantees. In the following excerpt, the Tanzanian High Court interprets the interaction of a new constitutional gender equality guarantee with traditional tribal law.

EPHRAHIM v. PASTORY AND KAIZILEGE

1990 (87) Int. L. Rep. 106 (Tanz. H. Ct.)

Mwalusanya, J:

This appeal is about women's rights under our Bill of Rights. Women's liberation is high on the agenda in this appeal. [Respondent] inherited some clan land from her father by a valid will [and sold it. Appellant] prayed for a declaration that the sale of the clan land by his aunt ... was void as females under Haya customary law have no power to sell clan land. . . .

Indeed the Haya customary law is clear on this point. It ... provides:

Women can inherit, except for clan land, which they may receive in usufruct but may not sell. However, if there is not [sic] male of that clan, women may inherit such land in full ownership.

  . . .

[S]ince the Bill of Rights was incorporated in our 1977 Constitution vide Act No 15/1984 by Article 13(4) discrimination against women has been prohibited. . . . It is clear . . . that the customary law under discussion flies in the face of our Bill of Rights as well as the international conventions to which we are signatories.

  . . .

Courts are not impotent to invalidate laws which are discriminatory and unconstitutional.

  . . .

I have found as a fact that [the law restricting sale of clan land by women] is discriminatory of females in that unlike their male counterparts, they are barred from selling clan land. That is consistent with Article 13(4) of the Bill of Rights of our Constitution which bars discrimination on account of sex. Therefore . . . I take Section 20 of the Rules of Inheritance GN No 436/1963 to be no modified and qualified such that males and females have now equal rights to inherit and sell clan land. . . . Females just like males can now and onwards inherit clan land or self-acquired land of their fathers and dispose of the same when and as they like. The disposal of the clan land to strangers without the consent of the clansmen is subject to the fiat that any other clan member can redeem that clan land on payment of the purchase price to the purchaser. That now applies to both males and females. . . .

From now on, females all over Tanzania can at least hold their heads high and claim to be equal to men as far as inheritance of clan land and self-acquired land of their father's is concerned. It is part of the long road to women's liberation. But there is no cause for euphoria as there is much more to do in other spheres. One thing which surprises me is that it has taken a simple, old rural woman to champion the cause of women in this field but not the elite women in town who chant jejune slogans years on end on women's lib but without delivering the goods. . . .

Like the District Court I hold that the sale was valid. . . . The appeal is dismissed with costs. Order accordingly.

Notes

5–17. Another court in Africa several years after the decision of the Tanzanian High Court in Ephrahim reached a "diametrically opposed" result, as explained below.

In 1999, a similar issue arose in Zimbabwe in the Magaya case [1999 (1) ZLR 100 (S)]. Venia Magaya, the daughter of her deceased father's first wife, claimed ownership of the estate; this was opposed by a son of the father's second wife. The Supreme Court-relying on an exemption for customary law under the Constitution and rejecting the binding effect of the international human rights instruments to which Zimbabwe was party-refused to invalidate a customary law rule that gave preference to males in inheritance. Judge Muchechetere held that this customary law rule was part of the fabric of the African socio-political order, at the heart of which lies the family. He said: "At the head of the family there was a patriarch, or a senior man, who exercised control of the property and lives of women and juniors. It is from this that the status of women is derived. The woman's status is therefore basically the same as that of any junior male in the family." He added: "While I am in total agreement with the submission that there is a need to advance gender equality in all spheres of society, I am of the view that great care must be taken when African customary law is under consideration ... I consider it prudent to pursue a pragmatic and gradual change which would win long term acceptance rather than legal revolution initiated by the courts.".

Frances Raday, *Culture, Religion, and Gender*, 1 Int'l J. Const. L. 663, 683–84 (2003).

According to Professor Raday

Many of the practices, defended in the name of culture, that impinge on human rights are gender specific; they preserve patriarchy at the expense of women's rights. Such practices include: a preference for sons, leading to female infanticide; female genital mutilation (FGM); sale of daughters in marriage, including giving them in forced marriage as child brides; paying to acquire husbands for daughters through the dowry system; patriarchal marriage arrangements, allowing the husband control over land, finances, freedom of movement; husband's right to obedience and power to discipline or commit acts of violence against his wife, including marital rape; family honour killings by the shamed father or brothers of a girl who has been sexually violated, whether with consent or by rape; witch-hunting; compulsory restrictive dress codes; customary division of food, which produces female malnutrition; and restriction of women to the roles of housewives or mothers, without a balanced view of women as autonomous and productive members of civil society.

Id. at 670.

5–19. Religion and custom are often closely related. Judicial deference to either can impact constitutionally guaranteed equality rights.

We can sum up the current clash between monotheistic religious norms [Christian, Islamic and Jewish] and women's right to equality in both the private (family) and the public (political and economic) spheres of their lives, as follows. Under most of the monotheistic religious norms, women are not entitled to equality in inheritance, guardianship, custody of children, or division of matrimonial property. In most of the branches of the monotheistic religions, women are not eligible for religious office and, in some, they are limited in their freedom to participate in public life, whether political or economic.

Id. at 675.

5–19. As with customary law, difficult issues of constitutional meaning arise when religious law is recognized in a nation's constitution as authoritative generally or in certain realms of activity. Consider the following description of a recent dispute in Israel:

The Bavli case, in 1994, involved the division of matrimonial property. Jurisdiction for determining the division of matrimonial property is sometimes under the rabbinical courts and sometimes the civil courts. Different regimes regarding the division of matrimonial property are applied in the two jurisdictions; in the rabbinical courts, the Jewish law regime of property separation is applied, and, in the civil courts, there is both a judicial and statutory presumption of community property, which is to be divided equally between the spouses on dissolution of the marriage. In the case in hand, the rabbinical courts had jurisdiction and refused to divide the matrimonial property equally. The divorced wife's petition to the High Court of Justice was accepted and the case returned to the rabbinical courts. Justice Barak, the president of the High Court, rejected the claim that the Jewish law regime of separate matrimonial property could not be considered discriminatory as it applied to men and women equally, holding that the social facts showed women are disadvantaged where a separate property regime is applied. Following this decision, there were vociferous protests from Orthodox Jewish groups, and it is common knowledge that the rabbinical courts do not apply the ruling by the High Court of Justice.

In Rephaeli, a woman petitioned to overturn the refusal of the Grand Rabbinical Court to oblige her husband, separated from her for more than six years, to give her a divorce. The High Court of Justice ruled unanimously to dismiss, holding that it could not intervene in the Grand Rabbinical Court's decision. Justice Cheshin, although concurring in the ruling, remarked that, under Jewish law, the situation of a slave was preferable to that of a wife since even a slave would have been released after seven years of bondage.

In Hoffman I, in 1994, Israel's High Court of Justice rejected the petition of the Women of the Wall (WOW) to pray at the Kotel (the Western Wall of the second Temple and a central national, cultural, and religious site for Jews) in a group, wearing prayer shawls and reading aloud from the Torah Scroll, a manner of prayer customary for men but not for women and a subject of much controversy among Orthodox Jewish authorities. The women's prayer in this manner had been greeted with violent opposition from other Orthodox worshippers and prohibited by the secular authorities. Although rejecting the petition, the Court recognised, in principle, the WOW's right of access and freedom of worship, and Justice Shamgar recommended that the government make arrangements to enforce this right with minimum injury to the sensitivities of other worshippers. In 1998, after a series of governmental committees had failed to find a solution, WOW petitioned the High Court of Justice again. The Court, in Hoffman II, composed of two women justices and one man, directed the government to implement the WOW's prayer rights at the Kotel within six months. Orthodox Jewish political parties immediately presented a bill to convert the area in front of the Kotel into a religious shrine exclusively for Orthodox religious practice with a penalty of seven years' imprisonment for any person violating the current Orthodox custom of prayer. The attorney general requested a further hearing and the president of the Supreme Court appointed an expanded panel of nine justices to reconsider the issue. The Court held by a majority of nine to two that the members of WOW were entitled to pray at the Kotel; however, it also decided, by a majority of five to four, that, in order to prevent injury to the sensitivities of other worshippers, the government should make arrangements for a suitable prayer area for WOW at an adjacent site (Robinson's Arch) and only if the government failed to do so within a year would the WOW have the right to pray at the Kotel.

Id. at 688–89.

Has the U.S. Supreme Court addressed a similar conflict as between the Orthodox Jewish practitioners and the women who wanted to pray at the Western Wall?

5–20.   The clash between religious norms and sex equality arises in both the drafting and implementation of new constitutions. The following describes the drafting of the new Afghanistan Constitution.

Given the decades-old struggle within Afghan society between secularists and fundamentalists, the role of religion in the new constitution was bound to be contentious....

Afghan activists ... demanded strong protection for women's rights. Afghanistan's Deputy Minister for Women's Affairs argued for an express ban on all forms of discrimination against women and a clear requirement of universal education of Afghan women. A conference convened in Kandahar of women leaders from across Afghanistan went further, demanding an "Afghan Women's Bill of Rights" that included equal representation in parliament and the Constitutional Loya Jirga, compulsory education through high school with opportunities for higher education, full property and inheritance rights and participation in economic life, access to modern health services and reproductive care, freedom to decide whom to be married to, enforcement of criminal laws against violence and sexual abuse, and an end to the exchange of women as compensation for crimes by one family against another (known as Bad).

. . .

On January 4, 2004, the 1,500 Afghan delegates to the Constitutional Loya Jirga (CLJ) ratified the new constitution. . . .

The Afghans who participated in the constitutional drafting process, and the international community, crafted a charter for their country that stands as an unqualified improvement over the Taliban's unwritten code of theocratic oppression. Among other improvements, the constitution remedied the draft's failure to enshrine women's rights. It now provides that: "Any kind of discrimination and privilege between the citizens of Afghanistan are prohibited. [P] The citizens of Afghanistan—whether man or woman—have equal rights and duties before the law." This clause revives precedents in the 1977 and 1987 constitutions that specifically guaranteed that Afghan women would enjoy equal rights before the law and protection against discrimination. Moreover, the new constitution envisions a level of participation by Afghan women in their country's parliament that surpasses any historical precedent in that country, or indeed in most other countries. On paper, women are guaranteed over 25% of the seats in the lower house of parliament, and almost 17% of the upper house.

But a close examination of the tight relationship the constitution establishes between religious doctrine and the judiciary reveals that the claim that the new constitution is the most "enlightened" in the region, even in the entire Islamic world, is implausible. Although women are equal "before the law," the intention of the Afghan courts and many of the constitution's drafters is that the laws will treat them very differently in many respects, and deny them many liberties available to men. And while they may be ensured a say in parliament, their ability to pass laws improving women's plight in their country will be strictly limited by a veto power the constitution grants to radical fundamentalists in the Afghan judiciary. The constitution also omits elementary protections available to women in other countries where they have not been subjected to the kind of treatment suffered in Afghanistan for many years, such as a ban on slavery and slave-like practices, or a requirement that both parties consent to a marriage.

Many Afghans and international human rights groups have accordingly tempered their praise of the constitution. They have expressed fears that several provisions could be used to enforce medieval interpretations of Islamic Sharia law, suppress religious expression and political speech, and perpetuate Afghan laws and customs that ruthlessly oppress Afghan women. An agenda to accommodate a fundamentalist future for Afghanistan permeated the CLJ, and prevented the new constitution from realizing the promises of the U.S. and U.N. that Afghanistan would henceforth abide by international human rights standards. The warlords and fundamentalist leaders, who issued death threats against more moderate Afghan men and women to deter them from participating in or even attending the CLJ, prevailed on several critical issues that the assembly addressed. Their death threats and vote buying ensured that the "majority" of CLJ delegates were tied to the "warlord controlling the province they came from." Nor did the intimidation end at the doors of the CLJ. The chairman of the CLJ, a former *mujahideen* leader, announced that female delegates should not "try to put yourself on a level with men. Even God has not given you equal rights, ... because under his decision two women are counted as equal to one man." The chairman called for delegates who circulated a petition proposing the removal of the word "Islamic" from the name of the country to be "identified and punished" as infidels, an offense worthy of the death penalty during Afghanistan's recent history.

At the CLJ, the warlords that have ruled most of Afghanistan since the fall of the Taliban succeeded in transforming a clause providing that no law could be contrary to the religion of Islam "and the values of this Constitution" into one that says that "no law can be contrary to the beliefs and provisions of the sacred religion of Islam." Afghan experts and human rights activists regard the new clause as much more subject to abuse by fundamentalists who seek to impose Taliban-like theocratic rule, because the "provisions" of Islam were precisely what the Taliban claimed to be enforcing. Female CLJ delegates and human rights activists therefore view this provision as introducing a strict version of Sharia law by the "back door." The "beliefs and provisions" clause means "that Islamic law is the supreme law of the land," and its content will inevitably be left for a Supreme Court staffed by "hard line Shariah jurists" to interpret. Under the new constitution, the Supreme Court, whose Chief Justice has consistently pushed for a theocratic state in which his interpretation of Islam would hold sway, "can review compliance with the Constitution of laws, legislative decrees, international treaties, and international conventions, and interpret them, in accordance with the law." The constitution grants the Supreme Court, which the Chief Justice has packed with many sympathetic judges who lack training in Afghanistan's civil and secular laws, the "power to reject virtually any law or treaty as un-Islamic."

Hannibal Travis, *Freedom or Theocracy?: Constitutionalism in Afghanistan and Iraq*, 3 Nw. U.J. Int'l Hum. Rts. (2005) at 17–20, http://www.law.northwestern.edu/journals/jihr/v3/4/Travis.pdf.

The U.S. Constitution does not grant religious courts the same control over family law matters as in Israel and many Muslim countries. It does, however, within a certain range, permit lawmakers to accommodate the autonomy of religious institutions. So, for example, Title VII of the Civil Rights Act of 1964 permits religious discrimination by religious organizations. 42 U.S.C. § 2000e–1 (2000). Additionally, relying on the first amendment's free exercise guarantee, circuit courts have crafted a "ministerial exception," which allows religious organizations to discriminate on the basis of sex with respect to positions integral to the entity's religious or spiritual activities or necessary to maintain its internal operations. Do these types of permissive accommodations raise the same issues and/or concerns with respect to sex equality as in countries that more explicitly incorporate religion into their constitutional law?

Chapter Six

FUNDAMENTAL RIGHTS

All constitutions guarantee some fundamental rights. They differ, however, in the degree to which the government is required to affirmatively guarantee the rights, the rights guaranteed and the specific contents of those rights. The following presents some selected topics in comparative fundamental rights.

I. POSITIVE RIGHTS

The explicit guarantees of the U.S. Constitution protect so-called "negative rights," meaning rights against government interference as opposed to rights to affirmative government assistance to obtain things like minimal subsistence income, housing, health care or protection from private violence. Although the U.S. Constitution set the standard for rights when it was written, it is now the anomaly.

Cass R. Sunstein

Why Does the American Constitution Lack Social and Economic Guarantees?

56 Syracuse L. Rev. 1, 2–4 (2005)

The Universal Declaration of Human Rights protects a wide range of social and economic rights. It proclaims, for example, that "everyone has the right to work, to free choice of employment, to just and favourable conditions of work and to protection against unemployment." It also provides a "right to equal pay for equal work," a "right to form and to join trade unions for the protection of his interests," and a "right to just and favourable remuneration ensuring for himself and his family an existence worthy of human dignity, and supplemented, if necessary, by other means of social protection." More broadly still, the Declaration proclaims that

125

everyone has the right to a standard of living adequate for the health and well-being of himself and of his family, including food, clothing, housing and medical care and necessary social services, and the right to security in the event of unemployment, sickness, disability, widowhood, old age or other lack of livelihood in circumstances beyond his control.

The Declaration also provides a "right to education" and a "right to social security."

The International Covenant on Social, Economic, and Cultural Rights follows the Declaration in creating social and economic rights, as do many constitutions, which guarantee citizens a wide range of social entitlements. Of course, this was true for the Soviet Constitution. But many non-communist and post-communist constitutions contain these rights as well. The Constitution of Norway imposes on the state the responsibility "to create conditions enabling every person capable of work to earn a living by his work." The Romanian Constitution includes the right to work, the right to equal pay for equal work, and measures for the protection and safety of workers. The Constitution of Peru announces, "The worker has the right to an equitable and sufficient remuneration, that procures, for him and his family material and spiritual welfare." The Syrian Constitution proclaims that "the state undertakes to provide work for all citizens." The Bulgarian Constitution offers the right to work, the right to labor safety, the right to social security, and the right to free medical care. The Hungarian Constitution proclaims, "People living within the territory of the Republic of Hungary have the right to the highest possible level of physical and mental health." It also provides that "everyone who works has the right to emolument that corresponds to the amount and quality of the work performed."

Not every modern constitution creates rights of this sort; such rights are entirely absent from a number of contemporary constitutions. Indeed, some nations recognize such rights, but in a way that seems to make them goals and not rights at all. The Constitution of Switzerland, for example, says that "the Confederation and the Cantons shall strive to ensure" certain rights, including social security, necessary health care, and more. The Constitution of India offers a range of civil and political rights, and also offers "Directive Principles of State Policy," saying that "the State shall ... direct its policy towards securing" certain rights, including "an adequate means of livelihood," "equal pay for equal work for both men and women," and more. This strategy is taken as well in the constitutions of Ireland, Nigeria, and Papua New Guinea. The South African Constitution recognizes a wide range of social and economic rights, but also acknowledges resource constraints, typically obliging the state to "take reasonable legislative and other measures, within its available resources, to achieve the progressive realisation of" the relevant right. Provisions of this kind are ambiguous, but they have been held to be justiciable, obliging the government not to default in its basic obligations.

... The constitutions of most nations create social and economic rights, whether or not they are enforceable, but the American Constitution does nothing of the kind. Why is this? What makes the American Constitution so distinctive in this regard?

Richard J. Goldstone[1]
A South African Perspective on Social and Economic Rights

Hum. Rts. Br. 4, 4–6 (Winter 2006)

THE DEVELOPMENT OF SOCIAL AND ECONOMIC RIGHTS IN SOUTH AFRICA

In South Africa the Constitution's drafters believed that the overwhelming majority of South Africans, in particular the previously oppressed black South Africans, would not be particularly concerned with so-called "first-generation" rights, such as freedom of speech, assembly, association, and movement. All of these first generation rights were thought not to be of great concern to individuals who did not have enough food to eat, or a roof above their heads, or money to send their children to school. Rather, it was felt that for South Africa's new constitution in 1994 and its final constitution in 1996 to be relevant to the majority of South Africans, it would have to include "third-generation" rights, such as rights to housing, health care, and education.

The South African Constitution very carefully delineates social and economic rights, and provides that "everyone" is entitled to reasonable access to housing, health care, and education. The Constitutional Court has held, however, that "reasonable access" does not mean that an individual is entitled to these provisions. Rather, these provisions should be progressively provided, taking into account the financial ability of the state. Indeed, the Constitution is carefully worded to give appropriate deference to the legislature, and it can be very difficult for courts and judges in the context of that careful wording to determine at what point the legislature or executive can be faulted and told that it is acting unconstitutionally.

1. From July 1994 to October 2003, Richard Goldstone served as a Justice on the Constitutional Court of South Afri- ca, which was charged with interpreting South Africa's post-Apartheid constitu- tional individual rights guarantees.

SOUTH AFRICA'S RIGHT TO HEALTH CARE

The first case the South African Constitutional Court heard on social and economic rights was the worst possible beginning. In *Soobramoney v. Minister of Health,* an Indian South African living in the city of Durban had an ischemic heart, a failed liver, and a life expectation of approximately 18 months. Soobramoney's condition required that he receive treatment at least once a week. He went to a public government hospital for dialysis, but was denied treatment because the hospital only had provisions for 78 patients in any given week. Therefore, the hospital gave priority to patients who were in line to receive transplants, who needed only short-term treatment, and who would make a full recovery. In other words, to give Soobramoney dialysis would have prevented a different patient from receiving the long-term benefits of treatment. When hospital authorities reluctantly explained to him that the treatment was not available, Soobramoney brought an urgent application to the High Court at Durban, which ordered the government to provide him with the dialysis. The government urgently appealed, and the Constitutional Court heard the appeal. . . .

The Constitutional Court held that it could not order the dialysis treatment. First, the Court rejected Soobramoney's argument that this was emergency treatment, which is an absolute right under the South African Constitution and not, like other forms of health care, something to which the government must only provide reasonable access. The Court said emergency treatment is the sort of treatment that an individual receives in trauma and emergency wards following a serious accident. Soobramoney's situation, as grave as it was, did not require such a level of care. Second, the Court unanimously held that it could not order the hospital to purchase more dialysis machines. The budget had been carefully drafted in the state hospitals, and more machines would have meant less money for medicines, which would have altered the hospital's budgetary determinations. In the judges' conference room, it was noted that ordering more dialysis machines would open the door to situations where individuals could demand non-emergency treatments that would cost hospitals significant amounts of money.

The Court held that it could not interfere and tell the government how to stock its medical supplies. Rather, the Court said that it could only interfere in situations where there was an unconstitutional violation of equality; for example, if the priority list prepared by the doctors gave preference to individuals of a particular race. Unfortunately, national television stations took their cameras to Soobramoney's home the day the opinion came down rejecting the claim for dialysis treatment. He was sitting with his wife and three children, and they asked him how he felt about the decision to deny him dialysis treatment. Before he could even begin to answer, however, he had a stroke and died within the hour. The Court was criticized by much of the media for effectively sentencing Soobramoney to death.

Perhaps the most dramatic case in the Constitutional Court's history thus far has been *Minister of Health v. Treatment Action Campaign.* This particular case involved the supply of a drug called Nevirapine to pregnant mothers. The drug has been very successful in stopping the transmission of the HIV virus from HIV-positive mothers to their newborn children. It is inexpensive and easily dispensed; the mother has to have one small dose during labor and the child a very small dose at birth. But the South African government has an ambivalent and in some ways irrational approach to HIV/AIDS. Some senior ministers, and even President Thabo Mbeki at one stage, have denied that the HIV virus is the cause of AIDS. As such, only two test stations in two medical facilities were set up within the country, effectively denying Nevirapine to 90 percent of South Africa's pregnant mothers.

Because the government could not challenge the undeniable efficacy of the drug, it argued that too many obstacles prevented it from safely and effectively administering the drug. [The Constitutional Court rejected these claims.] . . .

As a result, the government was ordered to supply the drug to every hospital in South Africa. In its decision, the Court relied not only on the right to medical treatment but also equality: Nevirapine could not be supplied to some mothers and not others. The government, to its great credit in this and other cases where the Court has ruled against it, has quickly implemented the orders of the Constitutional Court.

A CONSTITUTIONAL RIGHT TO HOUSING

In addition to the right to health care, the Constitutional Court has also pushed the South African government to ensure the rights of its citizens in cases concerning the right to housing. In *Government of the RSA v. Grootboom,* hundreds of squatter-dwellers who lived in an area on the banks of a river outside of Cape Town lost their homes during a flood. The squatter-dwellers moved onto private property and built makeshift homes with cardboard and plastic that provided minimal protection from the elements. Shamefully, the owner of this private property was encouraged by local authorities to apply for their eviction, which the lower court granted. In response, the squatter-dwellers brought an application against Cape Town's provisional government and the city government, which asserted that the South African Constitution provided a right to housing.

The government argued that its housing scheme, which provided housing for over three million families, as well as electricity and water for millions of South Africans, was evidence that it had taken the social and economic rights provisions of the Constitution seriously. In a unanimous decision, the 11 members of the Constitutional Court praised the government housing policy and its significant achievements. The Court noted, however, that the policy did not provide for the poorest of the poor or for emergency situations. It said that where reasonable access to housing had been provided as a constitutional requirement, there had to be minimal provisions for emergencies and for individuals of lower socio-economic status. The government's response was that these provisions would drain its resources.

Notably, the Court was urged in an *amicus curiae* brief to adopt the "minimum core" approach of the United Nations Committee on Social and Economic Rights that has been developed over decades, and that identifies minimum core social and economic rights. The Court refused to implement this approach, however, because there was insufficient information to determine what constitutes a minimum core for housing or, by extension, what would be a minimum core for health care. Instead it reiterated that although there must be adequate provisions for the country's neediest, such determinations were not the business of the judiciary. The Court recommended that the government address these problems and requested that the Human Rights Commission, which was established by the Constitution, monitor the government and, if necessary, come back to the Court if it was of the view that the government was not taking the decision seriously. To date, the Human Rights Commission has not returned to the Court.

Notes

6–1. How would you answer Professor Sunstein's question of why the U.S. Constitution does not contain positive rights guarantees? Professor Sunstein considers four possible answers: the Constitution's age, the incompatibility of positive rights with judicial review, the absence of a significant socialist movement in the U.S. and the identity and judicial philosophies of the individuals who have happened to serve on the U.S. Supreme Court. He settles on the last explanation, namely that "[t]he Constitution means what the Supreme Court says that it means, and with a modest shift in personnel, the Constitution would have been understood to create social and economic rights of the sort recognized in many modern constitutions, and indeed in the constitutions of some of the American states." Sunstein, *supra* page 125, at 5. Do you agree?

6–2. Is the recognition of positive rights inconsistent with U.S.-style judicial review? Consider Justice Goldstone's response:

Let me first refer to what I would suggest is the false distinction between positive and negative rights that one often reads, for example, in the decisions of some American judges. They argue that negative rights, which protect individuals from interference, can be enforced, but positive rights, such as social and economic rights, encroach on the powers of the legislative and executive branches. In the view of many American courts, because these rights involve enabling individuals through the allocation of public funds, they cannot be enforced. The question thus becomes whether courts should become involved in instructing the legislature or executive how to allocate such funds. Many individuals believe that it is not the province of the judiciary to do so.

What these proponents of positive and negative rights fail to realize, however, is that most court decisions involve spending public money. Take, for instance, judicial decisions ordering the improvement of prison conditions. Such decisions may be based on the premise of protecting the negative rights of incarcerated individuals; however, they also entail a positive obligation because they compel government action that is likely to cost hundreds of millions of dollars. In California, for example, a federal judge issued an order threatening to take over California's prisons if the state did not take bolder steps to ensure prison reform. Sufficient steps were not taken and the whole state prison system is now under federal court control. Similarly, the mandated bussing that followed *Brown v. Board of Education* is an example of judicial enforcement that has cost taxpayers huge amounts of money. Ultimately, this dichotomy between positive and negative rights breaks down at a fundamental level because many judicial decisions involve some determination of the allocation of public funds."

Goldstone, *supra* page 127, at 4. Do you agree that the dichotomy between negative and positive rights is essentially "false"? *See* Frank B. Cross, *The Error of Positive Rights*, 48 UCLA L. Rev. 857, 866 (2001) ("I propose the following simple test for distinguishing between positive and negative rights—if there was no government in existence, would the right be automatically fulfilled?").

6–3. Notice the remedy ordered by the South African Court in *Grootboom*. Does the remedy appropriately vindicate the South African Constitution's "housing" right? Would the U.S. Supreme Court order such a remedy after finding a violation of a constitutional right? *See Brown v. Board of Education of Topeka (Brown II)*, 349 U.S. 294, 75 S.Ct. 753, 99 L.Ed. 1083 (1955) (ordering that defendants make "a prompt and reasonable start toward full compliance [with the *Brown I* decision]" and that the parties to the cases be admitted to public schools on a nondiscriminatory basis "with all deliberate speed."). Does the availability of such a remedy make positive constitutional rights more compatible with judicial review?

II. SOME COMPARISONS: PRIVACY

A. CHILDBEARING

In *Griswold v. Connecticut*, 381 U.S. 479, 85 S.Ct. 1678, 14 L.Ed.2d 510 (1965), and subsequent cases, the Supreme Court interpreted the U.S. Constitution to contain a privacy right, which includes the right to obtain and use contraceptives. In 1974, the Irish Supreme Court found a similar right in its own Constitution, which invalidated a law restricting importation and sale of contraceptives. *McGee v. Attorney General*, [1974] I.R. 284 (Ir.). In the last number of years, rights to reproductive freedom have been included in a number of constitutions, and in international agreements that may impact domestic contraceptive restrictions. Article 16(1) of The Convention on the Elimination of All Forms of Discrimination Against Women provides, "States Parties shall ... ensure, on a basis of equality of men and women ... (e) The same rights to decide freely and responsibility on the number and spacing of their children and to have access to the information, education and means to enable them to exercise these rights...." Although emergency contraception is controversial, and a number of countries have prohibited it as akin to abortion, use of other types of contraceptives is legal in most countries. Access to legal products for those in need is often what is hard to obtain.

Many countries actively promote contraception to achieve the goal of reducing population size, which can raise constitutional issues as well.

JAVED & ORS v. STATE OF HARYANA & ORS

(2003) 90 A.I.R. 3057, 3063–74 (Ind.)

RC LAHOTI, J. (delivering judgment of the court):

Placed in plain words the provision [at issue] disqualifies a person having more than two living children from holding the specified offices in Panchayats [local governing units]....

Several persons ... have been disqualified or proceeded against for disqualifying either from contesting the elections for, or from continuing in, the office of panchas/sarpanchas in view of their having incurred the disqualification.... As agreed to at the Bar, the grounds of challenge can be categorized into five—(i) that the provision is arbitrary and hence violative of art 14 of the Constitution; (ii) that the disqualification does not serve the purpose sought to be achieved by the legislation; (iii) that the provision is discriminatory; (iv) that the provision adversely affects the liberty of leading personal life in all its freedom and having as many children as one chooses to have and hence is violative of art 21 of the

Constitution; and (v) that the provision interferes with freedom of religion and hence violates art 25 of the Constitution.

. . .

Submissions (i), (ii) and (iii)

The first three submissions are based on art 14 of the Constitution and, therefore, are taken up together for consideration.

Is the classification arbitrary?

It is well-settled that art 14 forbids class legislation; it does not forbid reasonable classification for the purpose of legislation. To satisfy the constitutional test of permissibility, two conditions must be satisfied, namely; (i) that the classification is founded on an intelligible differentia which distinguishes persons or things that are grouped together from others left out of the group, and (ii) that such differentia has a rational relation to the object sought to be achieved by the statute in question. The basis for classification may rest on conditions which may be geographical or according to objects or occupation or the like.... The classification is well-defined and well-perceptible. Persons having more than two living children are clearly distinguishable from persons having not more than two living children. The two constitute two different classes and the classification is founded on an intelligible differentia clearly distinguishing one from the other. One of the objects sought to be achieved by the legislation is popularizing the family welfare/family planning programme. The disqualification enacted by the provision seeks to achieve the objective by creating a dis-incentive. The classification does not suffer from any arbitrariness. The number of children, viz, two is based on legislative wisdom. It could have been more or less. The number is a matter of policy decision which is not open to judicial scrutiny.

The legislation does not serve its object?

It was submitted that the number of children which one has, whether two or three or more, does not affect the capacity, competence and quality of a person to serve on any office of a panchayat and, therefore, the impugned disqualification has no nexus with the purpose sought to be achieved by the Act. There is no merit in the submission. We have already stated that one of the objects of the enactment is to popularize family welfare/family planning programme. This is consistent with the National Population Policy....

In our opinion, the impugned disqualification does have a nexus with the purpose sought to be achieved by the Act. Hence it is valid.

The provision is discriminatory?

To make a beginning, the reforms may be introduced at the grass-root level so as to spiral up or may be introduced at the top so as to percolate down. Panchayats are grass-root level institutions of local self-governance. They have a wider base. There is nothing wrong in the State of Haryana having chosen to subscribe to the national movement of population control by enacting a legislation which would go a long way in ameliorating health, social and economic conditions of rural population, and thereby contribute to the development of the nation which in its turn would benefit the entire citizenry.

. . .

The disqualification if violates Article 21?

[I]t was forcefully urged that the fundamental right to life and personal liberty emanating from art 21 of the Constitution should be allowed to stretch its span to its optimum so as to include in the compendious term of the article all the varieties of right which go to make up the personal liberty of man including the right to enjoy all the materialistic pleasures and to procreate as many children as one pleases.

The test of reasonableness is not a wholly subjective test and its contours are fairly indicated by the Constitution. The requirement of reasonableness runs like a golden thread through the entire fabric of fundamental rights. The lofty ideals of social and economic justice, the advancement of the nation as a whole and the philosophy of distributive justice—economic, social and political—cannot be given a go-by in the name of undue stress on fundamental rights and individual liberty. Reasonableness and rationality, legally as well a philosophically, provide colour to the meaning of fundamental rights.

It is necessary to have a look at the population scenario, of the world and of our own country.

India has the (dis)credit of being second only to China at the top in the list of the 10 most-populous countries of the world....

The torrential increase in the population of the country is one of the major hindrances in the pace of India's socio-economic progress. Everyday, about 50,000 persons are added to the already large base of its population.

In the beginning of this century, the world population crossed six billions, of which India alone accounts for one billion (17 per cent) in a land areas of 2.5 per cent of the world areas. The global annual increase of population is 80 millions. Out of this, India's growth share is over 18 millions (23 per cent) equivalent to the total population of Australia, which has two and a half times the land space of India. In other words, India is growing at the alarming rate of one Australia every year and will be the most densely populous country in the world, out beating China, which ranks first, with a land area thrice this country's.

... China, the most populous country in the world, has been able to control its growth rate by adopting the 'carrot and stick' rule. Attractive incentives in the field of education and employment were provided to the couples following the 'one-child norm'. At the same time drastic disincentives were cast on the couples breaching 'one-child norm' which even included penal action. India being a democratic country has so far not chosen to go beyond casting minimal disincentives and has not embarked upon penalizing pro-creation of children beyond a particular limit. However, it has to be remembered that complacence in controlling population in the name of democracy is too heavy a price to pay, allowing the nation to drift towards disaster.

The above facts and excerpts highlight the problem of population explosion as a national and global issue and provide justification for priority in policy-oriented legislations wherever needed.

. . .

Fundamental rights are not to be read in isolation. They have to be read along with the chapter on Directive Principles of State Policy and the Fundamental Duties enshrined in art 51A. Under art. 38 the state shall strive to promote the welfare of the people and developing a social order empowered at distributive justice—social, economic and political. Under art 47 the state shall promote with special care the educational and economic interests of the weaker sections of the people and in particular the constitutionally down-trodden. Under art 47 the state shall regard the raising of the level of nutrition and the standard of living of its people and the improvement of public health as among its primary duties. None of these lofty ideals can be achieved without controlling the population inasmuch as our materialistic resources are limited and the claimants are many. The concept of sustainable development which emerges as a fundamental duty from the several clauses of art 51A too dictates the expansion of population being kept within reasonable bounds.

. . .

To say the least it is futile to assume or urge that the impugned legislation violates right to life and liberty guaranteed under art 21 in any of the meanings howsoever expanded the meanings may be.

The provision if it violates art 25?

It was then submitted that the personal law of Muslims permits performance of marriage with four women, obviously for the purpose of procreating children and any restriction thereon would be violative of right to freedom of religion enshrined in art 25 of the Constitution.

. . .

Looked at from any angle, the challenge to the constitutional validity of § 175(1)(q) and § 177(1) must fail. The right to contest an election for any office in Panchayat is neither fundamental nor a common law right. It is the creature of a statute and is obviously subject to qualifications and disqualifications enacted by legislation. It may be permissible for Muslims to enter into four marriages with four women and for anyone whether a Muslim or belonging to any other community or religion to procreate as many children as he likes but no religion in India dictates or mandates as an obligation to enter into bigamy or polygamy or to have children more than one. What is permitted or not prohibited by a religion does not become a religious practice or a positive tenet of a religion. A practice does not acquire the sanction of religion simply because it is permitted. Assuming the practice of having more wives than one or procreating more children than one is a practice followed by any community or group of people the same can be regulated or prohibited by legislation in the interest of public order, morality and health or by any law providing for social welfare and reform which the impugned legislation clearly does.

. . .

The challenge to the constitutional validity of §§ 175(1)(q) and 177(1) fails on all the counts. Both the provisions are held, intra vires the Constitution. The provisions are salutary and in public interest. All the petitions which challenge the constitutional validity of the abovesaid provisions are held liable to be dismissed.

Notes

6–4. The Indian Supreme Court noted the "carrot and stick" approach of China's One Child Policy. *See* Therese Hesketh, Li Lu & Zhu Wei Xing, *The Effect of China's One–Child Family Policy after 25 Years*, 353 New Eng. J. Med. 1171, 1171 (2005) ("The[] regulations include restrictions on family size, late marriage and childbearing, and the spacing of children (in cases in which second children are permitted). The State Family Planning Bureau sets the overall targets and policy direction. Family-planning committees at provincial and country levels devise local strategies for implementation.... The policy is underpinned by a system of rewards and penalties, which are largely meted out at the discretion of local officials and hence vary widely. They include economic incentives for compliance and substantial fines, confiscation of belongings, and dismissal from work for noncompliance."); Ching–Ching Ni, *Chinese Activist Gets Jail Sentence*, L.A. Times, August 25, 2006, at A4 ("A blind activist who drew international attention by exposing China's harsh family planning policies was sentenced by a court Thursday to four years and three months in prison, the official New China News Agency reported.... Chen's supporters say he has become a target of retaliation by officials in the eastern Chinese city of Linyi for publicizing information about forced late-term abortions and sterilization campaigns involving tens of thousands of people. China's one-child policy has become less coercive in recent years, and such draconian family planning measures are no longer common practice. But that hasn't stopped some local officials from continuing with the abuse in order to meet certain quotas."). Would either a carrot or stick approach to restricting childbearing be constitutional if democratically enacted nationally or by one of the U.S. states?

6–5.   A consequence of government efforts to restrict population growth, as well as of easier and cheaper access to sex-predicting ultrasonography, is an increasing ratio of boys to girls. According to a recent study of the effects of China's One Child Policy:

> Since the onset of the one-child policy, there has been a steady increase in the reported sex ratio, from 1.06 in 1979, to 1.11 in 1988, to 1.17 in 2001....

> Many other Asian countries with declining fertility rates and a traditional preference for males are also seeing sex-ratio imbalances—Taiwan, 1.19; Singapore, 1.18; South Korea, 1.12; and parts of northern India, 1.20—largely because of sex-selective abortion."

Hesketh, *supra* page 136, at 1172–73. *See also* Prabhat Jha, et al., *Low Male-to-Female Sex Ratio of Children Born in India: National Survey of 1.1 Million Households*, Lancet 217 (Jan. 9, 2006), available at http://download.thelancet.com/pdfs/journals/0140–6736/PIIS014067 3606679300.pdf (close to 10 million female fetuses aborted in India over the past 20 years). Selective abandonment is common as well in countries with policies to reduce the birthrate. Close to 95% of the babies in Chinese orphanages are girls. Office of Immigration Statistics, U.S. Dept. of Homeland Security, 2005 Yearbook of Immigration Statistics 35 (2006), available at http://www.dhs.gov/xlibrary/assets/statistics/yearbook/2005/OIS_2005_Yearbook.pdf. Do these practices, encouraged by government policy, raise other constitutional concerns? Both China and India have laws prohibiting the disclosure of the sex of a fetus after prenatal tests, although, of course, such prohibitions are notoriously difficult to enforce. Would the U.S. Supreme Court uphold such a law aimed at prohibiting sex-selective abortion?

B. ABORTION

Abortion laws around the world range from the few that prohibit abortion entirely, even when it is necessary to save the life of the mother (Chile, El Salvador and Nicaragua), to the many that permit abortion only upon a certified showing of certain "indications," which range from protecting a women's life or health to broader socioeconomic reasons, and those which permit abortion without a required showing of a reason, at least within a specified gestational time frame (China, Canada and the U.S., as well as most of the countries in Western and Central Europe). Most abortion laws contain some combination of the "indications" and "time frame" approaches. Because of the U.S. Supreme Court's interpretation in *Roe v. Wade,* 410 U.S. 113, 93 S.Ct. 705, 35 L.Ed.2d 147 (1973) and subsequent cases, the U.S. Constitution limits government discretion to regulate abortion. Since *Roe,* limits to legislative discretion to regulate abortion have appeared in other world constitutions, either through judicial interpretation or through explicit drafting or amendment.

FIRST ABORTION CASE

39 BverfGE 1 (1975) (F.R.G. Fed. Const. Ct.)
Translated in Robert E. Joras & John D. Gorby, *West German Abortion Decision: A Contrast to Roe v. Wade,* 9 J. Marshall J. of Prac. & Proc. 605, 638–663 (1978)

[Until the mid–1970's, German law followed a restrictive indications approach, criminalizing abortion absent a certified danger to the pregnant woman's life or health. After the victory of the Social Democratic Party in the 1972 elections, the German Bundestag, in a very close vote, enacted the Abortion Reform Act of 1974. The new law liberalized access to abortion in several respects, most controversially adopting a time frame approach that permitted abortion without a required showing of reason during the first 12 weeks of pregnancy. Members of the Christian Democratic Party, who had argued strenuously against the law's enactment, challenged it immediately.]

C.

. . .

I.

. . .

[1][b]In construing Article 2, Paragraph 2, Sentence 1, of the Basic Law, one should begin with its language: "Everyone has a right to life . . .". Life, in the sense of historical existence of a human individual, exists according to definite biological-physiologi-

cal knowledge, in any case, from the 14th day after conception. . . .
The process of development which has begun at that point is a
continuing process which exhibits no sharp demarcation and does
not allow a precise division of the various steps of development of
the human life. The process does not end even with birth; the
phenomena of consciousness which are specific to the human personality, for example, appear for the first time a rather long time
after birth. Therefore, the protection of Article 2, Paragraph 2,
Sentence 1, of the Basic Law cannot be limited either to the
"completed" human being after birth or to the child about to be
born which is independently capable of living. The right to life is
guaranteed to everyone who "lives"; no distinction can be made
here between various stages of the life developing itself before
birth, or between unborn and born life. "Everyone" in the sense of
Article 2, Paragraph 2, Sentence 1, of the Basic Law is "everyone
living"; expressed in another way: every life possessing human
individuality; "everyone" also includes the yet unborn human
being.

II.

1.   The duty of the state to protect is comprehensive. It forbids
not only—self-evidently—direct state attacks on the life developing
itself but also requires the state to take a position protecting and
promoting this life, that is to say, it must, above all, preserve it
even against illegal attacks by others. It is for the individual areas
of the legal order, each according to its special function, to effectu-
ate this requirement. The degree of seriousness with which the
state must take its obligation to protect increases as the rank of the
legal value in question increases in importance within the order of
values of the Basic Law. Human life represents, within the order of
the Basic Law, an ultimate value, the particulars of which need not
be established; it is the living foundation of human dignity and the
prerequisite for all other fundamental rights.

2.   The obligation of the state to take the life developing itself
under protection exists, as a matter of principle, even against the
mother. Without doubt, the natural connection of unborn life with
that of the mother establishes an especially unique relationship, for
which there is no parallel in other circumstances of life. Pregnancy
belongs to the sphere of intimacy of the woman, the protection of
which is constitutionally guaranteed through Article 2, Paragraph 1
["Everyone has the right to free development of his personality
insofar as he does not violate the rights of others or offend against
the constitutional order or the moral law."], in connection with
Article 1, Paragraph 1, of the Basic Law. Were the embryo to be
considered only as a part of the maternal organism the interruption
of pregnancy would remain in the area of the private structuring of

one's life, where the legislature is forbidden to encroach. Since, however, the one about to be born is an independent human being who stands under the protection of the constitution, there is a social dimension to the interruption of pregnancy which makes it amenable to and in need of regulation by the state. The right of the woman to the free development of her personality, which has as its content the freedom of behavior in a comprehensive sense and accordingly embraces the personal responsibility of the woman to decide against parenthood and the responsibilities flowing from it, can also, it is true, likewise demand recognition and protection. This right, however, is not guaranteed without limits—the rights of others, the constitutional order, and the moral law limit it. *A priori,* this right can never include the authorization to intrude upon the protected sphere of right of another without justifying reason or much less to destroy that sphere along with the life itself; this is even less so, if, according to the nature of the case, a special responsibility exists precisely for this life.

A compromise which guarantees the protection of the life of the one about to be born and permits the pregnant woman the freedom of abortion is not possible since the interruption of pregnancy always means the destruction of the unborn life. In the required balancing, "both constitutional values are to be viewed in their relationship to human dignity, the center of the value system of the constitution." ... A decision oriented to Article 1, Paragraph 1, of the Basic Law must come down in favor of the precedence of the protection of life for the child *en ventre sa mere* over the right of the pregnant woman to self-determination. Regarding many opportunities for development of personality, she can be adversely affected through pregnancy, birth and the education of her children. On the other hand, the unborn life is destroyed through the interruption of pregnancy. According to the principle of the balance which preserves most of competing constitutionally protected positions in view of the fundamental idea of Article 19, Paragraph 2, of the Basic Law; precedence must be given to the protection of the life of the child about to be born. This precedence exists as a matter of principle for the entire duration of pregnancy and may not be placed in question for any particular time. The opinion expressed in the Federal Parliament during the third deliberation on the Statute to Reform the Penal Law, the effect of which is to propose the precedence for a particular time "of the right to self-determination of the woman which flows from human dignity vis-a-vis all others, including the child's right to life", is not reconcilable with the value ordering of the Basic Law.

3. From this point, the fundamental attitude of the legal order which is required by the constitution with regard to the interruption of pregnancy becomes clear: the legal order may not

make the woman's right to self-determination the sole guide-line of its rulemaking. The state must proceed, as a matter of principle, from a duty to carry the pregnancy to term and therefore to view, as a matter of principle, its interruption as an injustice. The condemnation of abortion must be clearly expressed in the legal order. The false impression must be avoided that the interruption of pregnancy is the same social process as, for example, approaching a physician for healing an illness or indeed a legally irrelevant alternative for the prevention of conception. The state may not abdicate its responsibility even through the recognition of a "legally free area," by which the state abstains from the value judgment and abandons this judgment to the decision of the individual to be made on the basis of his own sense of responsibility.

III.

How the state fulfills its obligation for an effective protection of developing life is, in the first instance, to be decided by the legislature. It determines which measures of protection are required and which serve the purpose of guaranteeing an effective protection of life.

. . .

2. The question of the extent to which the state is obligated under the constitution to employ, even for the protection of unborn life, the penal law, the sharpest weapon standing at its disposal, cannot be answered by the simplified posing of the question whether the state must punish certain acts. A total consideration is necessary which, on the one hand, takes into account the worth of the injured legal value and the extent of the social harm of the injurious act—in comparison with other acts which socio-ethically are perhaps similarly assessed and which are subject to punishment—and which, on the other hand, takes into account the traditional legal regulation of this area of life as well as the development of concepts of the role of the penal law in modern society; and, finally, does not leave out of consideration the practical effectiveness of penal sanctions and the possibility of their replacement through other legal sanctions.

The legislature is not obligated, as a matter of principle, to employ the same penal measures for the protection of the unborn life as it considers required and expedient for born life.

. . .

3. The obligation of the state to protect the developing life exists—as shown—against the mother as well. Here, however, the employment of the penal law may give rise to special problems which result from the unique situation of the pregnant woman. [In

cases where a pregnancy puts an "extraordinary" burden on the woman, the legislature may choose not to employ the criminal law.]

. . .

Even in these cases the state may not be content merely to examine, and if the occasion arises, to certify that the statutory prerequisites for an abortion free of punishment are present. Rather, the state will also be expected to offer counseling and assistance with the goal of reminding pregnant women of the fundamental duty to respect the right to life of the unborn, to encourage her to continue the pregnancy and—especially in cases of social need—to support her through practical measures of assistance.

In all other cases the interruption of pregnancy remains a wrong deserving punishment since, in these cases, the destruction of a value of the law of the highest rank is subjected to the unrestricted pleasure of another and is not motivated by an emergency. If the legislature wants to dispense (even in this case) with penal law punishment, this would be compatible with the requirement to protect of Article 2, Paragraph 2, Sentence 1, of the Basic Law, only on the condition that another equally effective legal sanction stands at its command which would clearly bring out the unjust character of the act (the condemnation by the legal order) and likewise prevent the interruptions of pregnancy as effectively as a penal provision.

. . .

D.

. . .

IV.

The regulation encountered in the Fifth Statute to Reform the Penal Law at times is defended with the argument that in other democratic countries of the Western World in recent times the penal provisions regulating the interruption of pregnancy have been "liberalized" or "modernized" in a similar or an even more extensive fashion; this would be, as the argument goes, an indication that the new regulation corresponds, in any case, to the general development of theories in this area and is not inconsistent with fundamental socio-ethical and legal principles.

These considerations cannot influence the decision to be made here. Disregarding the fact that all of these foreign laws in their respective countries are sharply controverted, the legal standards which are applicable there for the acts of the legislature are essentially different from those of the Federal Republic of Germany.

Underlying the Basic Law are principles for the structuring of the state that may be understood only in light of the historical experience and the spiritual-moral confrontation with the previous system of National Socialism. In opposition to the omnipotence of the totalitarian state which claimed for itself limitless dominion over all areas of social life and which, in the prosecution of its goals of state, consideration for the life of the individual fundamentally meant nothing, the Basic Law of the Federal Republic of Germany has erected an order bound together by values which places the individual human being and his dignity at the focal point of all of its ordinances. At its basis lies the concept, as the Federal Constitutional Court previously pronounced . . ., that human beings possess an inherent worth as individuals in order of creation which uncompromisingly demands unconditional respect for the life of every individual human being, even for the apparently socially "worthless," and which therefore excludes the destruction of such life without legally justifiable grounds. This fundamental constitutional decision determines the structure and the interpretation of the entire legal order. Even the legislature is bound by it; considerations of socio-political expediency, even necessities of state, cannot overcome this constitutional limitation. Even a general change of the viewpoints dominant in the populace on this subject—if such a change could be established at all—would change nothing. The Federal Constitutional Court, which is charged by the constitution with overseeing the observance of its fundamental principles by all organs of the state and, if necessary, with giving them effect, can orient its decisions only on those principles to the development of which this Court has decisively contributed in its judicial utterances. Therefore, no adverse judgment is being passed about other legal orders "which have not had these experiences with a system of injustice and which, on the basis of an historical development which has taken a different course and other political conditions and fundamental views of the philosophy of state, have not made such a decision for themselves."

E.

On the basis of these considerations, § 218a of the Penal Code in the version of the Fifth Statute to Reform the Penal Law 1976 is inconsistent with Article 2, Paragraph 2, Sentence 1, in conjunction with Article 1, Paragraph 1, of the Basic Law to the extent that it excepts interruption of pregnancy from punishability if no reasons are present which, according to the present opinion, have standing under the ordering of values of the Basic Law.

[Two dissenting justices strenuously argued that, although the Basic Law obligates the State to protect fetal life, the Court had usurped the role of the legislature, which has the primary responsibility to decide how to fulfill its obligation.]

Notes

6–6. *Roe* and Germany's *First Abortion Case* were rendered only two years apart. What explains the many differences between them—differences in constitutional text, drafters' intent, national history, the nature of judicial review? How does the test and standard of review used by the German court compare to U.S. doctrine? Are either or both decisions the product of an "activist" court? Are they legitimate?

6–7. The German Bundestag responded to the *First Abortion Case* by passing a revised Abortion Reform Act, which prohibited abortion except when the indications listed by the Constitutional Court were present (medical, genetic, ethical or serious social reasons). Although consistent with West Germany's post-World War II Basic Law, the revised Abortion Reform Act posed an obstacle to reunification of the two Germanies after the dissolution of the former Soviet Union. East German law followed a time frame approach, permitting abortion without a required showing of "indication" within the first trimester of pregnancy. To address the impasse, the Unification Treaty specified that the abortion rules applicable to the unified Germany would be decided by an all-German parliament after unification. In the face of a wide range of proposals, the new parliament hammered out a compromise that adopted a modified time frame approach under which abortion was "not illegal" if performed within the first trimester and after counseling and a waiting period. West German legislators challenged the compromise, and so the Constitutional Court, like the U.S. Supreme Court in *Planned Parenthood of Southeastern Pennsylvania v. Casey*, 505 U.S. 833, 112 S.Ct. 2791, 120 L.Ed.2d 674 (1992), was called upon to review its prior abortion decision after a passage of time and in a changed and charged political atmosphere. The German Constitutional Court, in its second abortion decision, affirmed the essence of its earlier ruling—that the State must continue to declare abortions without required indications "illegal"—but eased the application, suggesting that first trimester abortions need not be prosecuted so long as the State vigorously counsels women against it. After the decision, the Bundestag passed yet another compromise law, stipulating that any abortion that does not meet certain "indications" is illegal, but that neither the woman nor doctor will be prosecuted for abortion occurring within the first twelve weeks if the abortion follows the required counseling and three-day waiting period, which is how the law stands today. How does the German Constitutional Court's extended encounter with the abortion issue compare to the experience of the U.S. Supreme Court? After both pairs of decisions, how does the availability of abortion compare in the two countries today?

6–8. In 1997, the Polish Supreme Court invalidated a law that permitted abortion for "social" reasons as contrary to its interim

Constitution. Polish Abortion Law Decision, Constitutional Tribunal (Poland), dated 28 May 1997 (K. 26/96). The Court observed that "[t]here are no provisions relating directly to life protection in the constitutional regulations in force in Poland." (Poland's permanent Constitution, which was being drafted as the decision was written, explicitly charges the government with "ensur[ing] the legal protection of the life of every human being.") Nevertheless, the Court continued, "This is not to say, however, that human life is not a constitutional value. The basic provision from which constitutional life protection should be deduced, is Article 1 of the constitutional provisions continued in force, in particular the rule of a democratic state of law. Such a state is realized only as a community of people; so only people can be proper carriers of rights and duties enacted in such a state." After holding that "[h]uman life ... becomes a value protected under the Constitution from the moment it develops," the Court rejected the claim that a constitutional "right to responsibly decide about reproduction" rendered the abortion access law valid: "One cannot decide about having a child, when this child is already evolving in the pre-natal phase and, in this sense, the parents already have it. The right to have a child, therefore, can be interpreted solely in its positive aspect, and not as a right to annihilate a developing human foetus." What explains the many differences between the Polish decision (rendered after both *Roe* and *Casey*) and the U.S. abortion decisions? Do the same factors explain the German and Polish results?

6–9.   The Canadian Charter of Rights and Freedoms guarantees the "right to life, liberty and security of the person." A 1969 Canadian law, which represented a loosening of abortion restrictions at the time it was enacted, followed an "indications" approach, criminalizing abortion unless a special hospital committee certified that one was required to protect the woman's life or health. A Canadian doctor deliberately provoked a constitutional case by illegally opening abortion clinics in a number of provinces. In *R. v. Morgentaler,* [1988] 1 S.C.R. 30 (Can.), five out of seven justices of the Canadian Supreme Court in three separately reasoned opinions held the abortion law unconstitutional. Only one applied reasoning like *Roe,* interpreting the Charter's "liberty" provision as guaranteeing a woman's right to choose to terminate a pregnancy, within a certain time frame. The other four justices relied primarily on the Charter's "security of the person" guarantee to invalidate the certification procedure as too uncertain and slow to protect the right to choose abortion established by the legislature. Although the Canadian Court, like the U.S. Supreme Court, found constitutional limits to legislative discretion to restrict abortion, what is the significance of its different reasoning? No law currently regulates abortion in Canada. Does the Canadian Charter of Rights and Freedoms require this state of affairs?

6–10. Under the Mexican federal structure, abortion regulations are within state jurisdiction. All states criminalize abortion, but waive penalties in certain circumstances. Most waive penalties to save the life of the mother; fewer than half, to protect the pregnant woman's health. The only exception that applies in all states is in the case of rape. In the early 2000's and in response to the national electoral victory of the conservative PAN party and President Vicente Fox, an out-spoken opponent of abortion, several states modified their abortion laws. The reforms from the Federal District, called the "Robles Law" after the government head who proposed it, made its way to the Mexican Supreme Court. In divided opinions, and even as it affirmed that the Mexican Constitution "protects the product of conception as a manifestation of human life," the Court separately upheld the provisions decriminalizing abortions because of fetal abnormalities and those because of rape and nonconsensual artificial insemination. According to the Court, "[t]his ruling does not authorize abortion at will. These abortions are still considered crimes, and those who abort will be committing a crime but will not be punished." Valida SCJN Articulo 334, Fraccion III del Codigo Penal del Distrito Federal, S.C.J.N. Direccion General de Comunicacion Social Comunicados de Prensa, Jan. 29, 2002, quoted in Corene T. Kendrick, *The Illegality of Abortion in Mexico*, 39 Stan. L. Rev. 125, 148 (2003). Is it logical for the German and Mexican Courts to hold that it is constitutionally permissible for the government to choose not to prosecute certain "illegal" abortions? Is it legitimate? What did the courts hope to accomplish through this reasoning? Do they succeed?

6–11. Since *Roe,* a number of countries have drafted or amended their constitutions to include provisions that more explicitly address abortion. No constitution explicitly guarantees a right to choose abortion. Many constitutions guarantee rights to make decisions concerning reproduction and the spacing of children, to control one's body, and to health care services, which proponents can argue support abortion rights. For example, in its Preamble to the 1996 Choice on Termination of Pregnancy Act, which liberalized access to abortion, the South Africa Parliament explicitly referred to the post-Apartheid Constitution's "right of persons to make decisions concerning reproduction and to security in and control over their bodies" as grounding for a law liberalizing access to abortion. (Choice on Termination of Pregnancy Act 92 of 1996, available at http://www.polity.org.za/html/govdocs/legislation/1996/act96–092.html). In dismissing a constitutional challenge to the new law, a High Court rejected the claim that a fetus has a right to life under the South African Constitution that can impinge on rights expressly granted to women. *Christian Lawyers Association v. Minister of Health* 1998 (1) BCLR 1434 (T.) (S. Afr.).

A number of other constitutions, recently enacted or amended in Latin America, Africa and a few Asian–Pacific nations, protect the life of the "unborn," a number of these specifying that the protection attaches at "conception." Reacting to an easing of abortion access in the U.S., Europe and nearby England, in 1983, Irish voters adopted a referendum to amend their constitution to "acknowledge[] the right to life of the unborn" and to commit the State "with due regard to the equal right to life of the mother ... to defend and vindicate that right." Ir. Const., 1937, art. 40.3.3. Globalization pressures, however, have modified the Irish government's permissible enforcement of the guarantee. After the abortion prohibition became part of the Irish Constitution, the Irish government attempted to "defend and vindicate" the right to life of the unborn by forbidding Irish women to travel abroad (most frequently to England) to obtain an abortion and by prohibiting dissemination in Ireland of information relating to abortion services available abroad. In separate cases, the Irish Supreme Court upheld the government's constitutional obligation to prohibit the activities, *Society for the Protection of Unborn Children v. Open Door Counseling*, [1988] I.R. 593 (Ir. H.Ct.), aff'd [1988] I.R. 624 (Ir.) (affirming High Court holding that counseling women about the availability of abortion in England is destruction of the unborn and rights of privacy, association and expression cannot prevail over the unborn's right to life."); *SPUC v. Grogan*, [1989] I.R. 753 (Ir. H.Ct.), aff'd in part, rev'd in part [1989] I.R. 760 (Ir.) (stating that right to travel to procure abortion "services" under the European Economic Community (EEC) Treaty cannot modify right to life guarantee of Irish Constitution), only to have an international court, the European Court on Human Rights in the first case and the Court of Justice of European Communities (ECJ) in the other, determine that international agreements signed by Ireland modify the way in which it can enforce its constitutional obligation to prohibit abortion. *Open Door v. Ireland*, 246 Eur. Ct. H.R. (1992) (restrictions on abortion information violate freedom of speech guarantee contained in Article 10 of the European Convention on Human Rights); *Society for the Protection of Unborn Children Ireland Ltd. v. Grogan*, [1991] E.C.R. 4685, 3 C.M.L.R. 849 (E.C.J.) (holding abortion to be a "service," which member nations cannot restrict under the EEC Treaty, but finding the plaintiffs in the case not to have standing because they did not provide the abortion service). In response to the ECJ decision, Ireland negotiated a protocol to the treaty implementing union among the European Community nations that exempted its constitutional abortion provision from modification by European Union law. Protocol 17 to the Treaty on European Unity and Final Act, Feb. 7, 1992, 31 I.L.M. 247 [Maastricht Treaty]. After these decisions, in a case where a prosecutor sought to prohibit a 14–year old girl from obtaining an abortion after her rape by a family friend, the Irish Supreme Court modified its constitutional interpretation, finding a limited right to travel to obtain an abortion. *Attorney General v. X*, [1992] I.R. 1 (Ir.). Voters ultimately approved referendums that amended the Constitution to guarantee a right to distribute information about abortion and a right to travel to obtain one. What do the series of events and legal decisions in Ireland say about the efficacy of using a constitution to restrict abortion?

6–12. Most of the world's constitutions have been drafted or substantially modified since the U.S. Supreme Court's decision in *Roe*. Why do so few explicitly address abortion? Nations that have amended their constitutions to explicitly protect fetal rights have large Catholic populations. Nations governed by Islamic law tend also to have very restrictive abortion laws, but do not incorporate fetal rights in their constitution. For example, neither the recently drafted constitution of Afghanistan or of Iraq addresses abortion. Why would that be?

III. USE OF FOREIGN AND INTERNATIONAL LAW IN INTERPRETATION OF CONSTITUTIONAL RIGHTS

In *Lawrence v. Texas*, 539 U.S. 558, 123 S.Ct. 2472, 156 L.Ed.2d 508 (2003), the U.S. Supreme Court held that a state statute criminalizing homosexual sexual relations violated the fourteenth amendment's due process guarantee. The majority opinion, authored by Justice Kennedy, cited English statutory law and a decision by the European Court of Human Rights invalidating a similar North Ireland criminal prohibition. In the prior term, a majority of the Court had also cited foreign law as persuasive in interpreting the "evolving standards of decency" that it uses to interpret the eighth amendment's limits on imposition of the death penalty. In his dissents in both cases, Justice Scalia criticized the Court's references to foreign law as irrelevant and even dangerous in U.S. constitutional decisions. Later that year, Justice Scalia and Justice Breyer, who had joined the controversial decisions, met for a formal conversation about the appropriate uses in constitutional decisions of foreign law.

THE RELEVANCE OF FOREIGN LEGAL MATERIALS IN U.S. CONSTITUTIONAL CASES: A CONVERSATION BETWEEN JUSTICE ANTONIN SCALIA AND JUSTICE STEPHEN BREYER

3 Int'l. J. Const. L. 519, 520–37 (2005)

[Question]: [I]s it appropriate for our judges to use and cite to foreign materials in the course of deciding constitutional cases? If so, does the practice tend to undermine the uniqueness of the American constitutional experience? Or does it deepen the sources for constitutional decision making and thereby strengthen it?

.   .   .

Scalia: Well, most of those questions should be addressed to Justice Breyer because I do not use foreign law in the interpretation of the United States Constitution. [Laughter.] I will use it in the interpretation of a treaty. . . .

But you are talking about using foreign law to determine the content of American constitutional law-to be sure that we're on the right track, that we have the same moral and legal framework as the rest of the world. But we don't have the same moral and legal framework as the rest of the world, and never have. If you told the framers of the Constitution that we're to be just like Europe, they would have been appalled. If you read the Federalist Papers, they are full of statements that make very clear the framers didn't have a whole lot of respect for many of the rules in European countries. . . .

. . . [T]ake our abortion jurisprudence: we are one of only six countries in the world that allows abortion on demand at any time prior to viability. Should we change that because other countries feel differently? Or, maybe a more pertinent question: Why haven't we changed that, if indeed the Court thinks we should be persuaded by foreign law? Or do we just use foreign law selectively? When it agrees with what the justices would like the case to say, we use the foreign law, and when it doesn't agree we don't use it. Thus, we cited foreign law in Lawrence, the case on homosexual sodomy (though not all foreign law, just the foreign law of countries that agreed with the disposition of the case). But we said not a whisper about foreign law in the series of abortion cases.

What's going on here? Do you want it to be authoritative? I doubt whether anybody would say, 'Yes, we want to be governed by the views of foreigners.' Well if you don't want it to be authoritative, then what is the criterion for citing it? That it agrees with you? I don't know any other criterion to bring forward.

. . .

Breyer: . . . [W]hen I refer to foreign law in cases involving a constitutional issue, I realize full well that the decisions of foreign courts do not bind American courts. Of course they do not. But those cases sometimes involve a human being working as a judge concerned with a legal problem, often similar to problems that arise here, which problem involves the application of a legal text, often similar to the text of our own Constitution, seeking to protect certain basic human rights, often similar to the rights that our own Constitution seeks to protect. To an ever greater extent, foreign nations have become democratic; to an ever greater extent, they have sought to protect basic human rights; to an ever greater extent they have embodied that protection in legal documents enforced through judicial decision making. Judges abroad thus face not only legal questions with obvious answers, e.g., is torture an affront to human dignity, but also difficult questions without obvious answers, where much is to be said on both sides of the issue.

. . .

Of course, I hope that I, or any other judge, would refer to materials that support positions that the judge disfavors as well as those that he favors.... The practice involves opening your eyes to what is going on elsewhere, taking what you learn for what it is worth, and using it as a point of comparison where doing so will prove helpful.

. . .

Scalia: I don't know what it means to express confidence that judges will do what they ought to do after having read the foreign law. My problem is I don't know what they ought to do. What is it that they ought to do? Why is it that foreign law would be relevant to what an American judge does when he interprets—interprets, not writes—the Constitution? Of course the founders used a lot of foreign law. If you read the Federalist Papers, it's full of discussions of the Swiss system, the German system, etc. It's full of that because comparison with the practices of other countries is very useful in devising a constitution. But why is it useful in interpreting one? Now, my theory of what to do when interpreting the American Constitution is to try to understand what it meant, what it was understood by the society to mean when it was adopted. And I don't think it has changed since then....

It should be easy to understand why, for someone who has my theory of interpretation, why foreign law is irrelevant....

. . .

[W]hat does the opinion of a wise Zimbabwe judge or a wise member of a House of Lords law committee—what does that have to do with what Americans believe? It is irrelevant unless you really think it's been given to you to make this moral judgement, a very difficult moral judgement. And so in making it for yourself and for the whole country, you consult whatever authorities you want. Unless you have that philosophy, I don't see how it's relevant at all.

Breyer: Well, it's relevant in the sense I described. A similar kind of person, a judge, with similar training, tries to apply a similar document with similar language ('cruel and unusual punishment' or the like), in a society that is somewhat similarly democratic and protective of basic human rights. England is not the moon, nor is India ...... [T]he fact that everyone in the world thinks one thing is at least worth finding out, for I doubt that Americans are so very different from people elsewhere in the world in respect to such matters. And, if my having the legal power to do so adds some uncertainty to the law, I believe the legal system can adjust. That is because the law is filled with uncertainty. Its answers in difficult cases can rarely be deduced only by means of legal logic from clear legal rules and a history book. Were the latter possible, I would be more tempted to agree with your view that a system without reference to foreign law would better control subjective judicial tendencies. But it is not.

[Question]: Is it a fair criticism that there's a certain selectivity that is result-oriented in the way foreign references are considered by you and those who agree with you?

Breyer: Yes, it is a fair criticism. We have referred to opinions of India's Supreme Court. But I confess that fewer opinions from other Asian nations come to our attention. That is one reason why it is important that we understand decisions of foreign courts are not binding. I would rather have this general 'take it for what it is worth' rule than to try to develop a jurisprudence about just when American judges should, and when they should not, take account of a foreign decision. I would avoid the natural tendency of the legal mind, the tendency to make distinctions and then create rules. Foreign decisions in this respect are a little like legislative history. And criticism of their uses is the same.

. . . .

Scalia: That can't be the only explanation for not using other foreign sources—that we don't know what the other countries say. In my dissent in Lawrence, the homosexual sodomy case, I observed that the court cited only European law; it pointed out that every European country has said you cannot prohibit homosexual sodomy.

Of course, they said it not as a consequence of some democratic ballot but by decree of the European Court of Human Rights, which was using the same theory that we lawyers and judges and law students know what's moral and what isn't. It had not been done democratically. Nonetheless, it was true that throughout Europe, it was unlawful to prohibit homosexual sodomy. The court did not cite the rest of the world. It was easy to find out what the rest of the world thought about it. I cited it in my dissent. The rest of the world was equally divided.

Breyer: But the reason that the majority referred to foreign cases in Lawrence is that the Court, in its earlier decision of Bowers v. Hardwick, had said that homosexual sodomy is almost universally forbidden. And I think that Lawrence, through its references, simply wanted to show that this was wrong.

Scalia: Well, I understand. For whatever reason, we said universally, yes, it's not universally. But don't just talk about Europe; let's look at the rest of the world.

. . . .

I mean, it lends itself to manipulation. It invites manipulation. You know, I want to do this thing; I have to think of some reason for it. I have to write something that—you know, that sounds like a lawyer.

. . .

[Question]: The question I have is this—rather than looking at foreign courts, to say for example that Greece decided our way, the United Kingdom decided our way, X country decided a different way, rather than thinking about these courts and cases in terms of the results, to think about them in terms of the persuasiveness of the opinions, just as a New York court might look at a Montana decision and be influenced not by the result of the Montana court but by the cogency of the arguments, by the depth of the reasoning, by the logic. And if our courts look at another country's courts and they're able to find opinions that are persuasive on the merits, why couldn't that be a way of informing our judges in a positive way?

Scalia: Well, you're begging the question. I mean, your question assumes that it is up to the judge to find THE correct answer. And I deny that. I think it is up to the judge to say what the Constitution provided, even if what it provided is not the best answer, even if you think it should be amended. If that's what it says, that's what it says.

But even if you disagree with me, and if you think, well, no, that shouldn't be the test; the Constitution should keep up to date. Fine. But it should keep up to date with the views of the American people. And on these constitutional questions, you're not going to come up with a right or wrong answer; most of them involve moral sentiments. You can have arguments on one side and on the other, but what you have to ask yourself is what does American society think? And the best way, the only way to determine that is certainly not to ask a very thin segment of American society-judges, lawyers, and law students—what they think but rather to look at the legislation that exists in states, democratically adopted by the American people. I'm sure that intelligent men and women abroad can make very intelligent arguments, but that's not the issue, because it should not be up to me to make those moral determinations.

. . .

Breyer: I believe that I am interpreting the Constitution of the United States. If, for example, a foreign court, in a particular decision, had shown that a particular interpretation of similar language in a similar document had had an adverse effect on free expression, to read that decision might help me to apply the American Constitution. That is what is at issue. To what extent will learning what happens in other courts help a judge apply the

Constitution of the United States. As I have said, in today's world where similar relevant experience becomes more and more common we are more likely to learn from other countries. I doubt that Franklin or Hamilton or Jefferson or Madison or even George Washington would have thought we cannot learn anything of value from abroad.

Notes

6–13. Justice Scalia, in his *Lawrence* dissent, called the Court's references to foreign law "[d]angerous dicta, ... since 'this Court . . . should not impose foreign moods, fads, or fashions on Americans.' ") *Lawrence*, 539 U.S. at 598, 123 S.Ct. at 2495. Legislators expressed similar points of view. Representative John Shimkus explained his co-sponsorship of the Constitution Restoration Act of 2005:

'This legislation removes from the jurisdiction of the federal court system any case involving the acknowledgement of God by a public official.'

[The proposed statute] also prohibits a court of the United States from relying upon any law, policy, or other action of a foreign state or international organization in interpreting and applying the Constitution, other than English constitutional and common law up to the time of the adoption of the U.S. Constitution.

'Liberal judges have admitted using laws and decisions from foreign nations in making judgments that should only be based on our own laws and traditions. . . . This is, in effect, turning over our sovereignty and is an outrageous abuse of judicial interpretation.'

Under the Constitution Restoration Act of 2005, any Supreme Court justice or federal court judge who exceeds the jurisdictional limitations of this Act shall be subject to removal from office.

Press Release, John Shimkus, Shimkus Cosponsoring Constitution Restoration Act (Sept. 26, 2005), http://www. house.gov/shimkus/press/cosponso ringhr1070.htm. Is such legislative action necessary to "restore the balance of power among the branches of government and restore the fundamental precepts on which our Constitution is based," as its sponsor suggests? Would the statute, if enacted, pass constitutional review?

6–14. Justice Scalia elaborated, in a speech to the American Enterprise Institute, on his criticism of the Court's selectivity in citing foreign law.

[I]n *Lawrence*, the Court cited European laws to strike down sodomy laws. But of course, Europe is not representative of the whole world. Zero out of fifty countries in Europe prohibit sodomy—not necessarily, by the way, because of the democratic preferences of those fifty countries, but because of the uniformity imposed by the European Court of Human Rights—*but* thirty-three out of fifty-one countries in Africa prohibit it. Eight of forty-three countries in the Americas. Twenty-seven out of forty-seven Asia–Pacific countries. And eleven out of fourteen countries in the middle east. Thus, the rest of the world, aside from Europe, is about evenly split on the issue.

Antonin Scalia, Remarks at the America Enterprise Institute (Feb. 21, 2006), http://www.aei.org/events/filter.all,eventID.1256/transcript.asp. Does this undercut the Court's use of foreign law?

6–15. Justice Breyer claims to "agree with Justice Scalia about the proper role of a judge." According to Justice Breyer, their disagreement is

> about the importance of explicit rules. Some believe that too few rules and too few clear approaches may mean judges with too much power ... it may permit judges to substitute their own subjective views for the views of a legislature. And that substitution runs counter to the principles of democracy. Nonetheless, a legal rule, or a decision-making practice, that is not at all open-ended can produce a cure that is worse than the disease. Legal rules that are inflexible, that do not adjust adequately to changing circumstances, produce law that is divorced from life.

Relevance of Foreign Legal Materials, *supra* page 148, at 539. Who has the better of the argument from democracy? Is a rule against reference to foreign law sources necessary to prevent judges from making, rather than interpreting the Constitution?

6–16. Beyond comparative use in individual rights cases, there are other, less controversial uses in constitutional interpretation of foreign and international law, as the following explains.

> Many participants in the debate over the Court's use of international and foreign sources appear to share a common assumption: that the invocation of such sources is new.
>
> . . .
>
> The present controversy over resort to international and foreign sources has focused on the Court's recent due process and death penalty jurisprudence. A broader view of U.S. constitutional history, however, indicates that international law has always played a substantial, even dominant, role in broad segments of U.S. constitutional jurisprudence.
>
> . . .
>
> [T]he Court traditionally has understood our constitutional design as inviting consideration of international law in three fundamental ways. First, in its strongest form, the Constitution directly invokes international law or concepts of international law in clauses ranging from the treaty and war powers to commerce and citizenship. Second, the Court has employed international law as a background principle of constitutional construction, invoking

international legal principles to limit the Constitution's territorial application, to define powers "inherent" in national sovereignty, and to inform principles of federalism. Finally, the Court has looked to international law to construe individual rights provisions, including in cases in which international law establishes governmental interests implicating constitutional rights, and in cases involving rights under the Just Compensation Clause, involuntary servitude, "cruel and unusual punishments," and substantive and procedural due process, which the Court has read as incorporating common values regarding the basic rights of the person.... Lawrence ... fall[s] into this final category of cases.

Sarah H. Cleveland, *Our International Constitution*, 31 Yale J. Int'l L. 1, 5–7 (2006).

6–17.   Other constitutions and national high courts accord a more authoritative role to international law in constitutional interpretation, particularly with respect to human rights, as the following explains.

[N]ational constitutional systems afford a variety of accommodations to the international human rights regime. Some constitutions elevate human rights treaty norms to the level of constitutional rights; others expressly make international human rights norms a source of guidance in constitutional interpretation. Even without such instructions, constitutional courts may voluntarily take international interpretations of human rights into consideration in construing constitutional rights. Some constitutional courts adopt this method as part of a deliberate strategy of institutional coordination with the international regime, for the mutual strengthening of both. For constitutional courts in none of the preceding categories, a minimal form of accommodation remains: to treat international interpretations as a relevant source of insight on the human rights issues they address.

1.   Giving constitutional status to human rights treaties.

National constitutions often address the relationship of treaties to the domestic legal order. The Supremacy Clause of the U.S. Constitution expressly made treaties supreme over the constitutions and laws of the several states, but left ambiguous their status at the federal level; subsequent interpretation has clarified that treaties are inferior to the Constitution but equal in rank to federal statutes. Some national constitutions go further by giving treaties supremacy over all statutes in the national legal system. Ordinarily, however, treaties remain inferior to the constitution in the domestic legal order.

Some constitutions that do not make treaties in general supreme over statutes nonetheless make special provisions for human rights treaties, or for particular human rights treaties. For example, the Czech Constitution of 1992 made all treaties on human rights and fundamental freedoms ratified by the Czech Republic superior to legislation. In 1994, Sweden adopted a constitutional amendment requiring laws to comply with the European Convention.

An even stronger accommodation ... is to accord a human rights treaty the same status as national constitutional rights. The constitution of Argentina, as amended in 1994, in addition to making treaties in general supreme over statutes, gave constitutional rank (jerarquia constitucional) to eleven named human rights instruments, and authorized the addition of other human rights treaties with constitutional rank by supermajority vote in the legislature. These treaties were incorporated into the constitution alongside other express rights, and the provision specified that the treaties with constitutional rank "do not repeal [other enumerated rights] and must be understood as complementary of the rights and guarantees recognized therein." As a result, human rights protected by these instruments are not displaced by other constitutional provisions, but rather they should be construed in harmony with each other.

On a more limited scale, Austria has given constitutional status to the European Human Rights Convention, using a constitutional procedure by which treaties can become part of the constitution when ratified by the same supermajority required for a constitutional amendment.

Of course, formal elevation of a human rights treaty to constitutional status does not necessarily have any consequences. In a society where the constitution is routinely violated, it may be an empty gesture. The effects depend on many other factors, both social and legal. Among the legal factors, one relevant question is how constitutionalization affects the available remedies. Another is whether the right becomes directly applicable (or self-executing).

. . .

2. Mandatory interpretive direction

A different method for accommodating international human rights within the domestic constitutional system is for a constitutional provision to command that the enumerated constitutional rights be interpreted in accordance with the corresponding international human rights. The Spanish Constitution of 1978 provides one model: "The norms relative to basic rights and liberties which are recognized by the Constitution, shall be interpreted in conformity with the Universal Declaration of Human Rights and the international treaties and agreements on those matters ratified by Spain." Note that the benchmarks are the Universal Declaration—a nonbinding instrument most of whose content has been operationalized in later treaties—and agreements already binding on Spain.

Coordinating interpretation may provide some of the same benefits as giving treaty norms constitutional status, at least with regard to those human rights with analogues already present in the constitution. For new democracies, the availability of external precedents offers guidance in interpreting constitutional rights, and may bolster the authority of the reviewing court against other political forces. In established constitutional systems, coordination enables the procedures for constitutional review to assist in the implementation of international human rights obligations that might otherwise lie outside their jurisdiction. That may provide a particularly strong vehicle for national enforcement of international norms that would be weakly protected by overburdened international courts or by tribunals lacking remedial powers.

Coordinated interpretation may not always function smoothly, however. First of all, there is not one uniform international human rights system with which to coordinate. The international system includes global and regional human rights treaties, and general and particular treaties with overlapping content. If interpreting "in conformity with" a treaty means interpreting as identical to the treaty, then multiple references give constitutional courts inconsistent directions. Perhaps then, such clauses should be understood as making the treaties the minimum level of constitutional protection. In one notable case, however, the Spanish constitutional court used article 10(2) restrictively, to borrow a ground of limitation of free expression not expressly contained in the Spanish constitution from the European Convention.

In fact, multiple references may free the court from the need to equate a constitutional right with a specified treaty norm, and allow the court to choose among or compromise varying treaty norms. Directing the court to interpret a constitutional right in accordance with the authoritative interpretations of a single treaty, such as the European or American Convention, could create problems similar to those caused by incorporating the international right in the constitution.

Greater interpretive freedom results from another mandatory interpretive rule, the requirement to consider international interpretations in construing a constitutional right. The well-known provision of the South Africa constitution exhibits a version of this technique:

When interpreting the Bill of Rights, a court, tribunal or forum—

    (a) must promote the values that underlie an open and democratic society based on human dignity, equality and freedom;

    (b) must consider international law; and

    (c) may consider foreign law.

The South African constitutional court has viewed this direction as requiring it to consider international norms, including interpretations thereof, regardless of whether they are binding on South Africa or whether they come from other regional systems. The court noted that "the weight to be attached to any particular principle or rule of international law will vary."

A "must consider" rule gives particularly strong consent to the influence of international human rights norms, and facilitates their critique of local practices. At the same time, it affords ample room for examination of consensual, suprapositive, and institutional factors that may justify a different interpretation within the context of the national constitution.

If the constitution instead provided that the court "may consider" international law in interpreting constitutional rights, it would provide adequate consent, and equally ample leeway. It would give less assurance, however, that critical capacities would be brought to bear.

Strictly speaking, there is another possibility: The constitution could expressly forbid the court to consider international law in construing constitutional rights. I know of no constitution that contains such a clause.

3. Voluntary consideration

In the absence of express textual direction, a constitutional court may nonetheless choose to include international human rights norms in its interpretive deliberations. Different constitutions may afford different justifications for doing so.

Some constitutions express a positive attitude toward international cooperation, through their rhetoric or their operational provisions or both. Several provisions of the postwar German constitution, for example, have led the German constitutional court to speak of a principle of "openness to international law," and the constitution authorizes participation in regional integration. Although the German constitutional court is influential and self-confident, it has also accepted the principle that interpretations of the European Convention should be taken into consideration in construing constitutional rights, to the extent that the level of protection would not be decreased. A prominent example has been the elaboration of the presumption of innocence, a convention right not mentioned in the German constitution but read into its guarantee of the rule of law.

Gerald L. Neuman, *Human Rights and Constitutional Rights: Harmony and Dissonance*, 55 Stan. L. Rev. 1863, 1890–98 (2003). Into which model does U.S. Supreme Court constitutional interpretation fall? Are there reasons why referring to international human rights law as an aid to constitutional interpretation is less appropriate in the United States than in other countries?

Chapter Seven

FREE SPEECH

Freedom of expression is a core constitutional right, at least for governments that aspire to call themselves democracies. What follows are selected topics in comparative free speech rights.

I. DANGEROUS SPEECH

All nations must draw a line between free speech and speech that unacceptably endangers national security. In the following excerpt, the European Court of Human Rights addresses a Turkish citizen's claim that his criminal conviction for criticizing mandatory military service violated the free expression guarantee of the European Convention on Human Rights.

ERGIN v. TURKEY

[2006] Eur. Ct. H. R. 47533/99

available at http://cmiskp.echr.coe.int/tkp197/view.asp?item=38portal=hbkm&
action=html&highlight=ergin&sessionid=9625577&skin=hudoc-en

PANEL: JUDGE BRATZA (PRESIDENT), JUDGES BONELLO, TURMEN, PELLONPAA, TRAJA, GARLICKI, AND MIJOVIC, AND MR M O'BOYLE (SECTION REGISTRAR)

THE FACTS

. . . .

6. The applicant was born in 1973 and lives in Istanbul.

7. On 1 September 1997, as editor of the newspaper Gunluk Emek (Everyday Work), the applicant published in issue number 297 an article entitled "Giving the conscripts a send-off, and collective memory" signed by Baris Avsar.

8. On 4 December 1997 the public prosecutor at the Military Court of the General Staff ("the General Staff Court"), acting

under art 58 of the Military Penal Code and art 155 of the Criminal Code, charged the applicant with incitement, by publication of the above article, to evade military service.

. . .

11. In its judgment the General Staff Court referred to the following passage from the offending article:

"This last week in bus stations has been a time for sending the August conscripts on their way ... The novice soldiers setting off—"but you'll soon be back", people tell them to console them—already seemed during these ritual send-offs to be plunging into war by donning "invisible khaki". It was a time when war seemed rather attractive; the congratulations and praises made it seem like a warm nest, almost as warm as a mother's arms, into whose embrace they would have liked to run. What we saw at each of these ceremonies shows that the thing has become a collective hysteria and that this hysteria has also spawned its own indispensable attributes: the traditional drum and clarinet, the famous three-crescented flag, sometimes accompanied by the corn-ear flag of the RP [Welfare Party] or the rose-bearing flag of the BBP [Great Union Party] ... Warm-up ceremonies are organised for those setting off for the war, the exaltation felt on killing a man is the exaltation of winning a match and, what is more, the killer justifies his act by speaking of the love he has for his fatherland and his nation. In short, it can't be said that what we're doing is right ... Those verses, written by a fallen soldier, are carved on his own tombstone. He will no longer see those who gather to give the conscripts a send-off, no longer hear the drum, the clarinet or the gunfire, not be able to read the verses written on his tombstone, on seeing which he would perhaps have felt repelled by the determinism they convey. Because from now on he is reduced to a title: a martyr ... It is because the State does not recognise as such the war which is etched deeply into the collective life and the collective memory that, apart from a small minority, those who return from it after losing an arm, a leg or an eye receive no allowance. These people who are no longer capable of meeting their own needs are being deceived by talk of fictitious jobs. 'There is a war, but not officially; you are war-wounded, but you count for nothing.' "

In its considerations the General Staff Court pointed out that military service was a constitutional duty and that the applicant, by denigrating military service had also denigrated the struggle against the PKK, a terrorist organisation which killed soldiers, police officers, teachers and civil servants. It held that the offending article contained terms contrary to morality and public order.

14. In a final judgment of 10 February 1999 the Military Court of Cassation upheld the first-instance judgment....

16. Article 155 of the Criminal Code provides:

"It shall be an offence, punishable by two months' to two years' imprisonment and a fine ... to publish articles inciting the population to break the law or weakening national security, to issue publications intended to incite others to evade military service...."

THE LAW ...

26. The applicant alleged that his criminal conviction had infringed his right to freedom of expression as guaranteed by art 10 of the Convention, the relevant parts of which provide:

1. Everyone has the right to freedom of expression. This right shall include freedom to hold opinions and to receive and impart information and ideas without interference by public authority and regardless of frontiers. ...

2. The exercise of these freedoms, since it carries with it duties and responsibilities, may be subject to such formalities, conditions, restrictions or penalties as are prescribed by law and are necessary in a democratic society, in the interests of national security, territorial integrity or public safety, for the prevention of disorder or crime....

28. The Court notes that it is not disputed between the parties that the applicant's conviction constituted an interference with his right to freedom of expression, protected by art 10(1). Nor is it disputed that the interference was prescribed by law and pursued a legitimate aim for the purposes of art 10(2), namely the prevention of disorder.... The Court agrees with that assessment. In the present case the dispute concerns the question whether the interference was "necessary in a democratic society".

29. The Government submitted that the applicant's conviction was necessary in a democratic society because the article was offensive to the wounded and the families of conscripts who had been killed during their military service, and that the criticisms of military service were contrary to morality and the public interest.

. . . .

31. After examining the present case in the light of its case law, the Court considers that the Government have not submitted any fact or argument capable of leading it to a different conclusion. It has paid particular attention to the terms used in the article and the context in which it was published. In that connection, it has taken into account the circumstances surrounding the case submit-

ted to it, and in particular the difficulties linked to the prevention
of terrorism. . . .

32. The offending article was a critique of the now-traditional
ceremony to mark conscripts' departure for military service. In
literary language the author explained that the enthusiasm surrounding these departures was a denial of the tragic end suffered
by some of the conscripts concerned, namely death and mutilation.

33. The Court notes the General Staff Court ruled that the
offending article contained terms contrary to morality and public
order.

34. The Court has examined the grounds given in the decisions of the domestic courts, which cannot as they stand be regarded as sufficient to justify the interference with the applicant's right
to freedom of expression. . . . It observes in particular that although
the words used in the offending article give it a connotation hostile
to military service, they do not exhort the use of violence or incite
armed resistance or rebellion, and they do not constitute hate-
speech, which, in the Court's view, is the essential element to be
taken into consideration. . . . Moreover, the context in which the
opinions were expressed can be distinguished, as regards their
potential impact, from that of the Arrowsmith v UK case, in which
the applicant, a pacifist activist, had distributed a leaflet inciting
servicemen to desert at a military camp occupied by troops who
were shortly to be posted to Northern Ireland. . . . In the present
case the offending article was published in a newspaper on sale to
the general public. It did not seek, either in its form or in its
content, to precipitate immediate desertion.

35. The Court reiterates that the adjective "necessary", within the meaning of art 10(2), implies the existence of a "pressing
social need". The Contracting States have a certain margin of
appreciation in assessing whether such a need exists, but it goes
hand in hand with a European supervision, embracing both the law
and the decisions applying it, even those given by independent
courts. The Court is therefore empowered to give the final ruling on
whether a "restriction" is reconcilable with freedom of expression
as protected by art 10.

The Court considers that the applicant's criminal conviction
did not correspond to a pressing social need. The interference was
accordingly not "necessary in a democratic society". There has
therefore been a violation of art 10 of the Convention.

Notes

7-1. Turkish fiction writers have also faced criminal charges
under Article 301 of the Criminal Code, which criminalizes criticism of

the state or Turkish identity. *See* Sebnem Arsu, *Istanbul Court Clears Author of Insulting Turkish Identity*, N.Y. Times, Sept. 2, 2006, at A6 ("An Istanbul court on Thursday dropped charges against the writer Elif Shafak of insulting Turkish identity in dialogues by the characters in her latest novel. . . . European Union nations have warned Turkey that putting writers and intellectuals on trial for their statements could prevent it from becoming a member. . . . The acclaimed Turkish writer Orhan Pamuk [who subsequently received the 2006 Nobel Prize in Literature] has faced prosecution under the article, which carries a maximum penalty of three years in prison. The charges against him were dropped after international opposition to his prosecution. Ms. Shafak was accused by nationalistic lawyers of insulting Turkish identity because an Armenian character in her novel, "The Bastard of Istanbul," speaks of "Turkish butchers" who killed his ancestors in 1915. The character uses the term 'genocide.' Turkey refuses to accept the word 'genocide' to describe the killings of Armenians during that period. . . . Lawyers who defend the decision to try her say presenting opinions through fictitious characters should not be an excuse to assault the state."). Would the U.S. Supreme Court uphold the conviction of a fiction writer under a statute that criminalizes speech that endangers national security?

7–2.   Laws that criminalize criticizing the government or its officials are also being used to silence journalists in Iraq. *See* Paul von Zielbauer et al., *Iraqi Journalists Add Laws to List of War Dangers*, N.Y. Times, Sept. 29, 2006, at A12 ("Under a broad new set of laws criminalizing speech that ridicules the government or its officials, some resurrected verbatim from Saddam Hussein's penal code, roughly a dozen Iraqi journalists have been charged with offending public officials in the past year. Currently, three journalists for a small newspaper in southeastern Iraq are being tried here for articles last year that accused a provincial governor, local judges and police officials of corruption. The journalists were accused of violating Paragraph 226 of the penal code, which makes anyone who 'publicly insults' the government or public officials subject to up to seven years in prison.").

7–3.   In response to the 2005 terrorist bombings of the London subways, which killed 52 people, the English Parliament amended its terrorism laws with a provision it had rejected months before, which criminalizes statements that "glorif[y] the commission or preparation (whether in the past, in the future or generally) of such [terrorist] acts . . . and . . . from which those members of the public could reasonably be expected to infer that what is being glorified is being glorified as conduct that should be emulated by them in existing circumstances." According to the law, "It is irrelevant . . . whether any person is in fact encouraged or induced by the statement to commit, prepare or instigate any such act or offence." Terrorism Act 2006, c. 11, § 1(5)(b) (U.K.). A London newspaper reports that the new anti-terrorism provisions have been applied to smash a suspected attempt to recruit and brainwash a cell of British suicide bombers:

Some of the 14 men arrested in London at the weekend-including a group detained while dining in a Chinese restaurant-could become the first to be charged with offences of encouraging terrorism and giving or receiving terrorist training. . . .

Counter-terrorist sources told The Times that those detained included suspected ringleaders and young men who were being groomed as potential recruits to the jihad.

The group had been under surveillance by intelligence agencies for several months.

It used the school grounds, which include a lake and an area of woodland, for survivalist exercises.

Young recruits had to listen to extremist lectures on religion and politics. Police are believed to have intervened after intelligence reports indicated a discernible change in the nature of the rhetoric and language of the alleged recruiters.

Detectives believe that while the group was still being radicalised, no targets had been identified and any possible terrorist attack was a long way off.

One source said: "This is not a case of disrupting an imminent attack. What we are looking at is training and recruitment and encouraging others to take part.

This operation was aimed at the process of radicalisation, at using the new powers we have to tackle glorification of terror and indoctrination of young people."

Counter-terrorist agencies believe that they now have the power to thwart the radicalisation process before there is any threat to public safety.

Sean O'Neill, *New Terror Laws Used to Arrest Men 'Recruiting Suicide Cell'*, Times (London), Sept. 4, 2006, available at http://www.times online.co.uk/article/0,,200–2341858,00.html. Would the "glorification" crime pass constitutional muster in the United States?

7–4. The Chinese Constitution states that Chinese citizens "enjoy freedom of speech, of the press, of assembly." However, another article qualifies the many listed individuals rights with the proviso that the rights of the people "may not infringe upon the interests of the state, of society and of the collective," which include the security interests of the state. Consider the following news report.

China imposed broad new restrictions Sunday on the distribution of foreign news in the country, beefing up state regulations on the news media. . . . President Hu Jintao has intensified a crackdown on all kinds of news media in recent months, arresting and harassing journalists, tightening regulation of Web sites and online forums, hiring tens of thousands of people to screen and block Web content deemed offensive and firing editors of state-run publications that resist official controls. . . . Among the categories of news that will be banned is anything that may 'endanger China's national security, reputation and interests.' China will also censor news articles that violate religious policies, promote cults or superstition, or 'incite hatred and discrimination among ethnic groups'.").

Joseph Kahn, *China Puts Stricter Limits on Distribution of Foreign News*, N.Y. Times, Sept. 11, 2006 at A3. Why does China have a free speech guarantee in its constitution?

II. DEFAMATION

In *New York Times v. Sullivan*, 376 U.S. 254, 84 S.Ct. 710, 11 L.Ed.2d 686 (1964), and subsequent cases, the Supreme Court interpreted the U.S. Constitution's free speech guarantee to set speech-protective limits on state law actions for damage to reputation, which have not been followed by most of the world.

HILL v. CHURCH OF SCIENTOLOGY

[1995] 2 S.C.R. 1130 (Can.)

[At a widely reported press conference, a lawyer for the Church of Scientology, Morris Manning, falsely accused a prosecutor, Casey Hill, of misleading a court and improperly obtaining access to sealed court documents. After contempt charges against him were dismissed, Hill sued Manning and the Church of Scientology, seeking damages for defamation. Defendants argued that the free speech guarantee of the Canadian Charter of rights and Freedoms should limit the scope of the common law defamation action.]

Judgment by: CORY J.:

. . .

(i) Freedom of Expression

101. Much has been written of the great importance of free speech....

102. However, freedom of expression has never been recognized as an absolute right....

103. ... Although a *Charter* right is defined broadly, generally without internal limits, the *Charter* recognizes, under s. 1, that social values will at times conflict and that some limits must be placed even on fundamental rights. [T]his Court has adopted a flexible approach to measuring the constitutionality of impugned provisions wherein "the underlying values [of the *Charter*] are sensitively weighed in a particular context against other values of a free and democratic society . . .".

106. Certainly, defamatory statements are very tenuously related to the core values which underlie s. 2(*b*). They are inimical to

the search for truth. False and injurious statement cannot enhance self-development. Nor can it ever be said that they lead to healthy participation in the affairs of the community. Indeed, they are detrimental to the advancement of these values and harmful to the interests of a free and democratic society. . . .

(ii) The Reputation of the Individual

107.   The other value to be balanced in a defamation action is the protection of the reputation of the individual. Although much has very properly been said and written about the importance of freedom of expression, little has been written of the importance of reputation. Yet, to most people, their good reputation is to be cherished above all. A good reputation is closely related to the innate worthiness and dignity of the individual. It is an attribute that must, just as much as freedom of expression, be protected by society's laws. In order to undertake the balancing required by this case, something must be said about the value of reputation.

108.   Democracy has always recognized and cherished the fundamental importance of an individual. That importance must, in turn, be based upon the good repute of a person. It is that good repute which enhances an individual's sense of worth and value. False allegations can so very quickly and completely destroy a good reputation. A reputation tarnished by libel can seldom regain its former lustre. A democratic society, therefore, has an interest in ensuring that its members can enjoy and protect their good reputation so long as it is merited.

. . .

118.   In the present case, consideration must be given to the particular significance reputation has for a lawyer. The reputation of a lawyer is of paramount importance to clients, to other members of the profession and to the judiciary. A lawyer's practice is founded and maintained upon the basis of a good reputation for professional integrity and trustworthiness. It is the cornerstone of a lawyer's professional life. Even if endowed with outstanding talent and indefatigable diligence, a lawyer cannot survive without a good reputation.

. . .

120.   Although it is not specifically mentioned in the *Charter*, the good reputation of the individual represents and reflects the innate dignity of the individual, a concept which underlies all the *Charter* rights. It follows that the protection of the good reputation of an individual is of fundamental importance to our democratic society.

121. Further, reputation is intimately related to the right to privacy which has been accorded constitutional protection.

. . .

123. At the outset, it is important to understand the social and political context of the times which undoubtedly influenced the decision in New York Times v. Sullivan .. The impugned publication was an editorial advertisement, placed in the appellant's newspaper, entitled "Heed Their Rising Voices". It criticized the widespread segregation which continued to dominate life in the southern states in the late 1950s and early 1960s. Prominent and well respected individuals, including Mrs. Eleanor Roosevelt, lent their name to the advertisement. It communicated information, recited grievances, protested abuses and sought financial support. The group or movement sponsoring the advertisement was characterized by Brennan J. as one "whose existence and objective are matters of the highest public interest and concern" (p. 266).

124. The advertisement did not mention by name the plaintiff, who was a white elected commissioner from Montgomery, Alabama. Only 35 copies of the edition of the *New York Times* which carried that advertisement were circulated in Montgomery, and only 394 were circulated in the entire state of Alabama. The trial took place in 1960, in a segregated court room in Montgomery, before a white judge and all-white jury. Damages of $500,000U.S. were awarded. This would be the current equivalent in Canada of approximately $3.5 million.

125. The Supreme Court, in overturning the verdict, clearly perceived the libel action as a very serious attack not only on the freedom of the press but, more particularly, on those who favoured desegregation in the southern United States. It was concerned that such a large damage award could threaten the very existence of, in Black J.'s words, "an American press virile enough to publish unpopular views on public affairs and bold enough to criticize the conduct of public officials" (p. 294). This concern was intensified by the fact that a second libel verdict of $500,000U.S. had already been awarded to another Montgomery commissioner against the *New York Times*. In addition, 11 other libel suits, arising out of the same advertisement, were pending against the newspaper.

(d) *Critiques of the "Actual Malice" Rule*

(i) Comments on the Decision in the United States

127. The "actual malice" rule has been severely criticized by American judges and academic writers. It has been suggested that the decision was overly influenced by the dramatic facts underlying the dispute and has not stood the test of time. . . .

128. Perhaps most importantly, it has been argued the decision has shifted the focus of defamation suits away from their original, essential purpose. Rather than deciding upon the truth of the impugned statement, courts in the U.S. now determine whether the defendant was negligent. Several unfortunate results flow from this shift in focus. First, it may deny the plaintiff the opportunity to establish the falsity of the defamatory statements and to determine the consequent reputational harm. This is particularly true in cases where the falsity is not seriously contested. . . .

129. Second, it necessitates a detailed inquiry into matters of media procedure. This, in turn, increases the length of discoveries and of the trial which may actually increase, rather than decrease, the threat to speech interests. . . .

130. Third, it dramatically increases the cost of litigation. This will often leave a plaintiff who has limited funds without legal recourse. . . .

131. Fourth, the fact that the dissemination of falsehoods is protected is said to exact a major social cost by deprecating truth in public discourse. . . .

137. The New York Times v. Sullivan decision has been criticized by judges and academic writers in the United States and elsewhere. It has not been followed in the United Kingdom or Australia. I can see no reason for adopting it in Canada in an action between private litigants. The law of defamation is essentially aimed at the prohibition of the publication of injurious false statements. It is the means by which the individual may protect his or her reputation which may well be the most distinguishing feature of his or her character, personality and, perhaps, identity. I simply cannot see that the law of defamation is unduly restrictive or inhibiting. Surely it is not requiring too much of individuals that they ascertain the truth of the allegations they publish. The law of defamation provides for the defences of fair comment and of qualified privilege in appropriate cases. Those who publish statements should assume a reasonable level of responsibility.

. . .

139. None of the factors which prompted the United States Supreme Court to rewrite the law of defamation in America are present in the case at bar. First, this appeal does not involve the media or political commentary about government policies. Thus the issues considered by the High Court of Australia in *Theophanous*, *supra*, are also not raised in this case and need not be considered.

140. Second, a review of jury verdicts in Canada reveals that there is no danger of numerous large awards threatening the viability of media organizations. Finally, in Canada there is no

broad privilege accorded to the public statements of government officials which needs to be counterbalanced by a similar right for private individuals.

141.   In conclusion, in its application to the parties in this action, the common law of defamation complies with the underlying values of the *Charter* and there is no need to amend or alter it.

Notes

7–5.   What explains the higher value placed by the U.S. Supreme Court on freedom of speech as against an individual's interest in reputation? Is it the particular facts of *New York Times v. Sullivan*, as the Canadian court suggests? *See* Sarah Lyall, *High Court in Britain Loosens Strict Libel Law*, N.Y. Times, Oct. 12, 2006 at A10 ("Britain's highest court on Wednesday ruled for the first time that journalists have the right to publish allegations about public figures, as long as their reporting is responsible and in the public interest. The ruling, a unanimous judgment by the Law Lords, is a huge shift in British law and significantly improves journalists' chances of winning libel cases in a court system that until now has been stacked against them.").

7–6.   The Constitutional Court of Germany, like the courts cited by the Canadian court, has declined to place such a high value on free speech as well, instead balancing free speech claims against the individual right to dignity contained in Article 1 of its Basic Law. *See The Boll Case*, 54 BVerfGe 208 (1980) (F.R.G. Fed. Const. Ct.), translated in Donald P. Kommers, *The Constitutional Jurisprudence of the Federal Republic of Germany* 420 (1997) (upholding award of damages for violation of honor to author Heinrich Boll against a television commentator, who had quoted him falsely and in a way that implied that he supported terrorism: "The attacks upon the complainant in the commentary were of such a nature as to impair his constitutionally guaranteed general right to an intimate sphere. Among other things this right includes personal honor and the right to one's own words; it also protects the bearer of these rights against having statements attributed to him which he did not make and which impair his self-defined claim to social recognition.... The use of a direct quotation as proof of a critical evaluation is, as indicated, a particularly sharp weapon in the battle of opinions and very effective in undermining the personality right of the person being criticized.... To rule out any possibility of invading the personality right in these situations, the person quoting someone else is duty-bound to make clear that he is employing his own interpretation of a statement open to several interpretations. The statement would then be placed in proper context: namely, out of the realm of fact and into that of opinion, where it belongs."). What explains the difference between United States and European free speech jurisprudence? Consider the following.

Differences in cultural tradition [in Europe and the United States with respect to privacy], . . . have made for palpable differences in law. The differences are most striking, and most categorical, where the values of free speech are involved. . . .

Oliver Sipple . . . was the unfortunate man who thwarted the attempt of Sara Jane Moore to assassinate President Gerald Ford. He was homosexual—a fact that he very much wanted kept out of the press. This proved to be impossible under the American law of "public figures." Of course, in any democracy the private doings of at least some public figures are a matter of legitimate public interest, and every democratic system recognizes that. Since the 1960s, though, the American "newsworthiness" exception has grown mightily, and peculiarly, in scope. Freedom of expression is a value of constitutional magnitude in the United States, whereas the protection of personal honor is not, which means that freedom of expression almost always wins out. That is what doomed Oliver Sipple's effort to keep his homosexuality out of the papers. Although Sipple's entry into the public eye was the result only of his heroism in a moment of danger, the California Court of Appeal held that there was a legitimate public interest in his private life. In any case, the court held, "he did not make a secret" of his sexual orientation, at least in San Francisco. Sipple (whose family in the Midwest had known nothing of his California life) eventually committed suicide.

It is precisely cases like this that Europeans see differently. The right of free expression that protects the press is always balanced in continental Europe against an individual right to "dignity," "honor," or "personality," which implies a right to personal privacy—as was shown by a 1985 French case. . . . The case involved a man who attended a gay pride parade in Paris, dressed in a way that made it clear that he was himself gay. His image was captured in a news photo. Continental law has long held that persons appearing in public may be photographed, but that no photograph may be published that focuses on them as individuals, unless they consent. Moreover, to the French way of thinking, the fact that one has revealed oneself to a restricted public—say, the gay community of Paris—does not imply that one has lost all protections before the larger public. These principles matter, and the French court accordingly acknowledged the plaintiff's right to oppose publication of his image.

The contrast between the treatment of Sipple and the treatment of this French victim of publicity is typical of a much deeper contrast in attitude. . . .

In Europe, by contrast [to the United States], personal honor very often wins out. As one German author put it in 1959—a time when Germans began to reassert their own distinctive national traditions—there is simply an inevitable tension between the worldview of a Goethe, for whom the development of "personality" was "the greatest blessing of the children of the earth," and the worldview of a Jefferson, for whom press liberty was the indispensable foundation of a free society.

James Q. Whitman, *The Two Western Cultures of Privacy: Dignity Versus Liberty*, 113 Yale L.J. 1151, 1196–98 (2004).

III. HIGHLY OFFENSIVE SPEECH

U.S. Supreme Court constitutional interpretations also stand out with respect to highly offensive speech. Most European nations interpret their constitutional free speech guarantees to permit broader criminalization of so-called hate speech.

HOLOCAUST DENIAL CASE

90 BVerfGE 241 (1994) (F.R.G. Fed. Const. Ct.)
Translated in Donald P. Kommers, *The Constitutional Jurisprudence of the Federal Republic of Germany* 382 (2nd ed. 1997)

[In 1991, a regional association of the far-right National Democratic Party of Germany (NPD) issued invitations to a meeting intended to discuss "Germany's future in the shadow of political blackmail?" The featured speaker was to be David Irving, a revisionist historian who argued that the mass extermination of Jews during the Third Reich never happened. The state government in Munich made it a condition of the meeting's being held that the "Auschwitz Hoax" thesis not be promoted there. The government took this action on the authority of the Public Assembly Act, one provision of which allows the prohibition of meetings when the likelihood exists that things said there will themselves constitute criminal violations. In this case the likely violations were denigration of the memory of the dead, criminal agitation, and, most important, criminal insult, all of which are prohibited by the Criminal Code. The NPD argued that the state's condition was an unconstitutional intrusion on its right to free expression (although the meeting itself took place). The complaint was rejected by the lower courts before being heard by the Federal Constitutional Court.]

Judgment of the First Senate

. . .

B. II. The challenged decisions do not violate Article 5 (1), first sentence, of the Basic Law, which guarantees the right to freedom of expression and dissemination of opinion.

. . .

(b) Article 5 (1) of the Basic Law protects opinion; free expression and dissemination relates to opinion. Opinion is defined by the individual's subjective relationship to the content of his utterance. Comment and appraisal are elements of opinion. To this extent, demonstrating the truth or untruth [of opinions] is impossible. [Opinions] enjoy the protection of basic rights regardless of whether they are well-founded or deemed emotional or rational, valuable or worthless, dangerous or harmless. The protection of the basic right extends as well to the form of the utterance. An expression of opinion does not lose its protection as a basic right by being sharply or hurtfully worded.... [T]he question is only whether, and to what extent, limitations on freedom of expression comport with Article 5 (2) of the Basic Law.

Strictly speaking, representations of fact are not expressions of opinion. In the case of statements of fact it is the objective relationship of the utterance to reality that comes to the fore. Thus, representations of fact are amenable to examination of their truth. But this does not mean that representations of fact are outside the scope of Article 5 (1). Since opinions are usually based on assumptions about facts, or they comment on factual circumstances, [statements of fact] are protected by the basic right to the extent that they are the foundation for opinions, which Article 5 (1) protects as a whole.

Consequently, protection of a representation of fact stops only when [the so-called fact] contributes nothing to the constitutionally protected formation of opinion. From this point of view, incorrect information does not constitute an interest worthy of protection. Thus the Federal Constitutional Court has consistently ruled that a deliberate, demonstrably untrue representation of fact is not protected by the guarantee of free expression....

Distinguishing expressions of opinion from representations of fact can certainly be difficult, because the two are linked and only together give sense to utterances. In this situation, severing the factual from the evaluative elements [of an utterance] is permissible only if in doing so it does not falsify its meaning. Otherwise, in the interest of effectively protecting the basic right, the utterance as a whole must be viewed as an expression of opinion, and thus within the scope of the protection afforded to freedom of expression; to do otherwise would threaten to curtail a basic right.

(c) Freedom of expression, however, is not unconditionally guaranteed. Article 5 (2) limits [such freedom] through general laws and statutory provisions protecting youth and personal honor. We must nevertheless consider the significance of free expression in interpreting and applying laws that limit it. This usually requires balancing the limit on the basic right against the legal interest served by the statute that limits it, in the light of pertinent norms and the [facts of the individual case].

In [achieving this balance], the Federal Constitutional Court has developed rules by which freedom of expression does not always take precedence over the protection of personality, as the complainant thinks. On the contrary, when expressions of opinion are seen as a formal insult or vilification, protection of the personality normally comes before freedom of expression. When expressions of opinion are linked to representations of fact, the [degree of] protection merited depends on the truth of the assumed fact on which [the opinions] are based. If the [assumed facts] are demonstrably untrue, freedom of expression usually gives way to the protection of personality. In general, one must determine which legal interest deserves preference. Here, however, it must be remembered that in questions of importance to the public there is a presumption in favor of free speech. Hence, we must constantly consider this presumption when balancing the legal positions of the parties.

2.   Seen in these terms, a breach of Article 5 (1) of the Basic Law manifestly has not been committed. The condition imposed on the complainant as organizer of the meeting (namely, to see to it that there would be no denial of or doubt cast on [the fact of] the persecution of the Jews during the Third Reich) is compatible with the basic right.

(a) The complainant does not dispute the danger foreseen by the authority overseeing the meeting and affirmed by the administrative courts: namely, that utterances of this kind would be made during the meeting. On the contrary, the complainant argues that he should be able to make such statements.

(b) The prohibited utterance (that there was no persecution of the Jews during the Third Reich) is a representation of fact that is demonstrably untrue in the light of innumerable eyewitness accounts, documents, findings of courts in numerous criminal cases, and historical analysis. Taken on its own, therefore, a statement with this content does not enjoy protection of freedom of expression. There is an important difference between denying the Third Reich's persecution of the Jews and denying German guilt in the outbreak of World War II, the subject of the decision of the Federal Constitutional Court on January 11, 1994. Utterances about guilt and responsibility for historical events are always complex evaluations not reducible to representations of fact, while denial of the very existence of an event will normally be a representation of fact.

. . .

There are doubts about the constitutionality of the criminal provisions on which the condition [i.e., the Auschwitz Hoax thesis not be promoted] was based. The laws against defamation protect personal honor, which is expressly mentioned in Article 5 (2) of the Basic Law as a legal interest that justifies limits to freedom of expression. Section 130 of the Criminal Code is a general law within the meaning of Article 5 (2) serving to protect humanity, ultimately founded on Article 1 (1) [mandating the inviolability of human dignity]....

(1) The administrative authorities and courts based their decisions on the ordinary courts' interpretations of the criminal norm. According to this [interpretation], the Jews living in Germany form an insultable *[beleidigungsfähige]* group in view of their fate under National Socialist rule; denial of the persecution of the Jews is regarded as an insult to Jews as a group. On this point, the Federal Court of Justice had this to say:

> The historical fact itself, that human beings were singled out according to the criteria of the so-called "Nuremberg Laws" and robbed of their individuality for the purpose of extermination, puts Jews living in the Federal Republic in a special, personal relationship vis-à-vis their fellow citizens; what happened [then] is also present in this relationship today. It is part of their personal self-perception to be understood as part of a group of people who stand out by virtue of their fate and in relation to whom there is a special moral responsibility on the part of all others, and that this is part of their dignity. Respect for this self-perception, for each individual, is one of the guarantees against repetition of this kind of discrimination and forms a basic condition of their lives in the Federal Republic. Whoever seeks to deny these events denies vis-à-vis each individual the personal worth of [Jewish persons]. For the person concerned, this is continuing discrimination against the group to which he belongs and, as part of the group, against him.

In the light of this court's jurisprudence, there can be no denial of the fact that these decisions bear witness to a glaring violation of the right of personality where the persecution of the Jews is denied. Constitutionally, there is no flaw in the Federal Court of Justice's logical connection between the racially motivated extermination of Jews during the Third Reich and a [current-day] attack on the right to respect and human dignity of today's Jews. In this way, there is also a distinction between denying the persecution of the Jews and denying German war guilt. At any rate, the latter opinion does not injure the interests of third persons, regardless of its historical questionability....

(2) Balancing defamation, on one hand, against limits on freedom of expression, on the other, does not reveal any constitutional errors. It is the gravity of the injury in each case that is decisive.

When insulting opinions that contain representations of fact are voiced, it is crucial whether the representations of fact are true or untrue. Demonstrably incorrect representations of fact do not merit protection. If they are inseparably connected to opinions, they will enjoy the protection of Article 5 (1) of the Basic Law; but from the outset, limits [on demonstrably untrue assertions] are less serious than in cases where the representations of fact have not been proven untrue.

That is the case here. Even if one considers the utterance that the complainant was forbidden to voice an expression of opinion within the context of the meeting, its factual content has been proven false. Hence, interfering with it is not particularly serious. In view of the weight of the insult, there can be no objection to the precedence given the contested decisions' protection of personality over freedom of expression.

[It does not matter] if one sees Germany's attitude toward its National Socialist past and its political consequences (which were the subject of the meeting) as a question concerning the public in an important way. True, in this case there is a presumption in favor of free speech, but this does not apply if the utterance constitutes a formal insult or vilification [of the Jewish people, nor does [the presumption] apply if the offensive utterance rests on demonstrably untrue representations of fact.

Notes

7–7.   The position of the United States with respect to the constitutionality of criminalizing hate speech impacts the increasingly global marketplace of ideas, as explained below.

> With respect to racism and xenophobia, one of the specific challenges arises from the fundamental clash between the U.S. and Europe. The same speech might indeed be allowed on one side of the Atlantic while, at the same time, being firmly prohibited on the other side.

> . . .

> The strong European view is spreading in the common law world if one considers two recent cases dealing with revisionist propaganda. In Canada, the Human Rights Tribunal decided on January 18, 2002, in the famous *Zundel case*, that the Holocaust denial site hosted in the U.S. but maintained in Canada by Ernest Zundel was unlawful. In the same line stands a decision held in Australia on September 17, 20022. The Federal Court of Australia enjoined Mr. Toben, the director of an important revisionist research and publishing centre, the Adelaide Institute, to remove offensive material posted on the Web.

It is not long ago that, *de facto*, the Internet was escaping from any anti-racist regulation. The hate sites, for the most part hosted in the U.S., were considered as unreachable and the general policy was to put up with the situation....

At the same time, European authorities, as well as national governments and NGOs fighting racism and discrimination have been confronted with the dramatic growth of the hate business online....

. . .

National States have accordingly tried to apply their own legislations to the Internet, upon the principle "what is illegal off-line is illegal online". Then again, there is a huge gap between the national scope of States' sovereignty and the universality of cyber-space where national borders have been until now of little rele-vance. In this respect, the *Yahoo! case* is a major instance. In 2000, a French judge ordered Yahoo! Inc. to take all appropriate meas-ures in order to prevent people located on the French territory from accessing its auction sales of Nazi paraphernalia and, more broadly, from accessing any pro-Nazi site hosted on its servers (mainly, on *Geocities*). In November 2001, at the request of Yahoo! Inc., a U.S. federal District Court declared that the First Amend-ment precludes enforcement within the U.S. of the French rul-ing.... When considering the *Yahoo! case*, it is quite patent that the coexistence of conflicting forums leads to a legal chaos and a jurisdiction dead-end....

. . .

A logical way to escape this jurisdiction dead-end would be to agree on international standards regarding racist and xenophobic speech. As a matter of fact, international law provides such stan-dards....

However, these international provisions do not bind the Unit-ed States of America, which have consistently made constitutional reservations regarding the obligation to outlaw racist speech....

A last solution is to ask the Internet Services Providers (ISPs) to self-regulate racist and xenophobic material posted on-line or to co-regulate such content in collaboration with public authori-ties....

The combination of the E.U. Directive provisions, on the one hand, [which immunize ISPs from liability if they remove offensive content once they receive notice] and the U.S. "Good Samaritan" provision, on the other hand, [which immunizes ISPs whether they choose to remove or retain offensive content] allows the Europeans to play behind the back of the Constitution of the United States of America. It strongly incites U.S. based ISPs operating internation-ally to apply an anti-hate speech policy consistent with the stan-dards of international law.

Up to now, we have seen that the e-commerce Directive induces two strategies for the Member States to get rid of racist material online : either, they ask the European-based access providers to filter the illegal content, or they manage to convince the U.S.-based hosting provider to remove the illegal content from the Net altogether.

But there is a third possible strategy, which consists neither to block access nor to urge for a take down but to target and to pressure the search engines (like Google, Altavista, *etc.*). [T]his strategy seems quite straightforward to implement, as there are only a handful of powerful search engines in use amongst Internet surfers around the world, and especially in Europe. Therefore, search engines are increasingly becoming the key-players in the regulation of illegal content online.

A report from the Berkman Center for Internet and Society of Harvard University, released on October 24, 2002, shows that the famous California based company Google has **quietly** excluded 65 sites from listings available at Google.de. and 113 from listings available at Google.fr. Most of these sites are anti-Semitic, pro-Nazi or related to white supremacy (e.g. *stormfront.org*). Has also been banned *"Jesus-is-lord.com"*, a fundamentalist Christian site that is adamantly opposed to abortion. In a press interview, Google spokesman, Nate Tyler, said : *"To avoid legal liability, we removed sites from Google.de search results pages that may conflict with German law"*. He indicated that each site that was de-listed came after a specific complaint from a foreign government, but he refused to hand down a list of the targeted websites.

Isabelle Rorive, *Strategies to Tackle Racism and Xenophobia on the Internet—Where are We in Europe?*, Int'l J. Comm. L. & Policy 1–9 (2002/2003), http://www.ijclp.org/7_2003/pdf/rorive-ijclp-artikel.pdf. Are there substantial free speech dangers in the strategies the commentator suggests? How can the United States respond to preserve its constitutional interpretation of the broad range of free speech on a global medium such as the Internet? Should the United States take action to preserve its concept of the appropriate balance between free and highly offensive speech when most of the world balances the competing interests differently?

7–8. What are the consequences of responding to broad claims of group-based offense? Joel Simon, *Of Hate and Genocide: In Africa, Exploiting the Past*, 44 Colum. Journalism Rev. 9 (Jan/Feb 2006) ("During the 1994 genocide in Rwanda, media outlets linked to the Hutu-backed government helped lay the groundwork for the slaughter of Tutsis by routinely vilifying them. One radio station, Radio Television Libre de Mille Collines (RTLM), went so far as to identify targets for the Hutu militias that carried out most of the killing. In December 2003, the International Criminal Tribunal for Rwanda convicted three Rwandan media executives—two from RTLM and one from a newspaper called *Kangura*—for their role in the genocide. The convictions represented a small measure of justice for the victims of the Rwandan genocide, but they were not necessarily good news for journalists in Africa. Many governments there have exploited the perception that the violence in Rwanda was fueled by the media to impose legal restrictions on the press in their own countries. The practice of casting the suppression of critical media as a legitimate effort to fight hate speech and incitement is now distressingly common, so much so that it has become a major impediment to independent journalism in many countries in Africa. In fact, the misuse of hate-speech laws by repressive African governments may well be a greater threat right now than hate speech itself.'').

7–9. Although the U.S. Supreme Court has held that the government may not protect the flag as a symbol of national unity, such laws protecting the "dignity of the nation" abound around the world. *See* Caslon Analytics Note, *Flag Burning*, June 2006, http://www.caslon.com.au/flagfiresnote2.htm (detailing flag desecration and protection of state honor provisions in Europe, the Middle East, India and China); Susan Ferriss, *Band Hits Sour Note with Mexico*, Atlanta Journal–Constitution, October 9, 2005, at B1 ("[In addition to threatening legal action against a Mexican–American musician who appeared on an American television show with a Mexican flag sticker on his guitar,] [t]he Mexican government has taken on Mexican artists, . . . for alleged abuse of national symbols. Pop star Luis Miguel was told to remove a flag design from a CD cover, and a mariachi singer was fined $45 last year for muffing the national anthem at a soccer game. A Mexican poet could face jail because he's been accused of violating the honor of the flag for writing a poem about cleaning up urine with it.'').

Chapter Eight

RELIGION

World constitutions vary widely in how they address the relationship of government and religion. Most do not employ the non-establishment and free exercise categories of U.S. constitutional jurisprudence, and, even here, issues that arise under the two separate guarantees often tend to merge. Nevertheless, for ease of comparison, the selections below are divided according to these two general topics.

I. STATE SUPPORT/ESTABLISHMENT

In the first excerpt, the author presents one way of modeling the world's government/religion relationships. The second excerpt, a decision of the German Constitutional Court, illustrates the generally greater constitutional tolerance in European countries for religious education and practice in public schools.

Shimon Shetreet

State and Religion: Funding of Religious Institutions—The Case of Israel in Comparative Perspective

13 Notre Dame J. L. Ethics & Pub. Pol'y 421, 424–27 (1999)

The relationship between state and religion can be ... divided into five models: the theocratic model, the absolute-secular model, the separation of state and religion model, the established church model, and the recognized religion model. Two of these models are non-democratic: the theocratic model and the absolute secular model, which are the most extreme models. The theocratic model suggests that the religion will dominate the state. This theory means that there is one officially recognized religion, and other religions are forbidden. The ruler of the state is a representative of this religion, and the state's law is religious law. This model is held as non-democratic because it maintains a system that causes the deprivation of freedom of religion (and freedom from religion). In the contemporary world we may find theocratic elements in the Middle East countries such as Saudi–Arabia and the Chumenistic Islamic Republic of Iran. The other non-democratic model, the absolute secular model, is the rejection of any religion, and adherence to formal atheism by the state. The law forbids any religious act, and freedom of religion is deprived. Examples of this model could be found in communist regimes, as in the former Soviet Union.

. . .

There are . . . three models of the relationship between state and religion which maintain the[] important principles of democracy. The first model is the separation of state and religion model. The idea is that there is a distinction between the government and religion. The legislation, in its nature, is secular, its purposes are non-religious, and there is no preference for any religion. The separation of state and religion is expressed in the principle that the state does not interfere with religious organizations and these organizations do not interfere in the matters of the state. This separation can be created in different ways: the state can declare itself expressly as a secular or non-religious state (as declared in the constitutions of France, India, and post-communist Russia) or as "neutral" concerning matters of religion (such as in the constitutions of Australia, Ireland, and Spain). Another way is an explicit declaration of the separation of state and religion (as declared in the constitution of Catholic Poland, or the First Amendment of the Constitution of the United States as interpreted by the Supreme Court). A regime of separation of religion and state does not indicate the state's approach toward religion. The separation may be a result of a favorable attitude toward religion and a commitment to a respectful approach to religion (as in the case of the United States) or of a less favorable attitude towards religion (as in the case of France).

The second model is the established church model, which means that the state recognizes a certain religion and a certain church as the state's national church. This recognition does not mean that other religions are prohibited or that a person must be a member of the established church, but that the state formally prefers a certain religion and gives it a priority over other religions. It can be expressed in a constitutional provision, in the state's financial support to institutions of this religion, and in benefits given to the members of this religion. The difference between this model and the theocratic model is in the approach towards other religions and non-religious people. While the state in the theocratic model does not tolerate other religions and non-religious groups, the state in the established church model is a democratic state (or at least it has democratic characteristics in the matter of freedom of religion). Examples of states that adopted this model are: England (the Anglican Church is the Church of England), Denmark, Norway, Iceland, Finland (the Anglo–Lutheran Church),Greece, and Bulgaria (the Eastern Orthodox Church). There are states in which the recognition of one formal church is only a symbolic-declarative one (such as the recognition of the Catholic Church in Liechtenstein, Monaco, and Malta). This is the endorsed church sub-model. In other states, the recognition of the established church has operative implications.

Another model is the recognized religions model. The state in this model does not recognize one formal religion; a formal national state church does not exist. Rather, the state's approach in the matters of state and religion is a neutral approach. This model is reminiscent of the separation model, because the state does not interfere in the internal matters of the religion, such as the appointment of the priests. The difference between these two models is that in the recognized religions model, the churches are recognized by the state as special corporations, and the state is responsible for supplying religious-services and for financing the foundation and maintenance of the churches. There is a cooperation of the state with all the recognized churches, without preferring one to the other. This is the model adopted in Germany, which accepts as "recognized religions" the Catholic, the Protestant, the Anglican, the Jewish and the Muslim communities. Another country which adopted this model is post-communist Hungary, which implements this model in a more liberal way.

SCHOOL PRAYER CASE

52 BVerfGE 223 (1979) (F.R.G. Fed. Const. Ct.)
Translated in Donald P. Kommers, *The Constitutional Jurisprudence of the Federal Republic of Germany* 461 (2nd ed. 1997)

Judgment of the First Senate. . . .

Article 6 (2) [1] of the Basic Law accords parents the right and duty to freely determine the care and education of their children. [Paragraphs] 1 and 2 of Article 4 encompass parents' right to teach their children those religious and ideological convictions which they believe to be true. On the other hand, Article 7 (1) of the Basic Law confers a constitutional mandate upon the state to establish schools. [The state's constitutional] mandate to establish a school system is autonomous and stands on the same footing as parents' right to control the education and upbringing of their children; neither has an absolute priority over the other.

2.   The problem of school prayer must first be seen in the broader framework of whether religious references are ever permissible in (compulsory) interdenominational state schools, or whether the state within its authority to structure the school system is confined to making religious or ideological references in religion classes, which are expressly guaranteed in Article 7 *(3)* of the Basic Law.

The Federal Constitutional Court considered this question in depth in its decisions of December 17, 1975, concerning Baden's interdenominational schools as well as the Bavarian interdenominational schools. [Pursuant] to those decisions, the incorporation of Christian references is not absolutely forbidden when establishing public schools, even though a minority of parents may not desire religious instruction for their children and may have no choice but to send their children to the school in question. However, the school may not be a missionary school and may not demand commitment to articles of Christian faith. [State] schools also must be open to other ideological and religious ideas and values. They may not limit their educational goals to those belonging to a Christian denomination except in religion classes, which no one can be forced to attend. Affirming Christianity within the context of secular disciplines refers primarily to the recognition of Christianity as a formative cultural and educational factor which has developed in Western history. It does not refer to the truth of the belief. With respect to non-Christians, this affirmation obtains legitimacy as a progression of historical fact. Christianity's educational and cultural aspects include not insignificantly the notion of tolerance for those holding other [beliefs].

3.   If religious references are permissible in compulsory state schools within the principles and guidelines developed by the Federal Constitutional Court, then praying in school is not fundamentally and constitutionally objectionable. However, the performance of the prayer also must comply with the limits of the states' right to establish school systems under Article 7 (1) of the Basic Law and not violate other constitutional precepts, in particular the individual rights of participants derived from Article 4 of the Basic Law.

(a) School prayer, in the sense in which it is the subject matter of this constitutional complaint, represents a supradenominational (ecumenical) invocation of God based upon Christian beliefs.

As an act of religious avowal made outside religion class, school prayer is not part of the general school curriculum taught within the framework of the states' mandate to establish an educational system for children. . . .

(b) Because school prayer is not a part of teaching a class in the sense of scholastic instruction, it cannot be a component of a binding lesson plan. Its performance must be completely voluntary. [The] state does not issue an order in this case; it makes an offer which the school class may accept.

(c) If the state, in the sense described, permits school prayer outside religion classes as a religious exercise and as a "school event," then certainly it is encouraging belief in Christianity and thus encouraging a religious element in the school which exceeds religious references flowing from the recognition of the formative factor of Christianity upon culture and education. Even in its transdenominational form, prayer is connected to the truth of a belief; specifically, that God can grant that which is requested. Nonetheless, permitting this religious element in (compulsory) interdenominational schools with the safeguard of voluntary participation still remains within the scope of creative freedom granted to the states as bearers of supreme authority in school matters pursuant to Article 7 (1) of the Basic Law.

Article 4 of the Basic Law grants not only freedom of belief but also the external freedom publicly to acknowledge one's belief. In this sense Articles 4 (1) and 4 (2) of the Basic Law guarantee a sphere in which to express these convictions actively. If the state permits school prayer in interdenominational state schools, then it does nothing more than exercise its right to establish a school system pursuant to Article 7 (1) of the Basic Law, so that pupils who wish to do so may acknowledge their religious beliefs, even if only in the limited form of a universal and transdenominational appeal to God.

To be sure, the state must balance this affirmative freedom to worship as expressed by permitting school prayer with the negative freedom of confession of other parents and pupils opposed to school prayer. Basically, [schools] may achieve this balance by guaranteeing that participation be voluntary for pupils and teachers.

. . .

3. The objection of a pupil holding other beliefs or of his parents or guardians could lead to the prohibition of school prayer only if the [school] did not guarantee the dissenting pupil's right to decide freely and without compulsion whether to participate in the prayer. As a rule, however, a pupil can find an acceptable way to avoid participating in the prayer so as to decide with complete freedom not to participate.

(a) Pupils can avoid praying in the following ways. The pupil can stay out of the classroom while the prayer is being said; for example, he or she can enter the room only after the end of the prayer or leave the room at the end of class, before the closing prayer is spoken. The pupil holding other beliefs may also remain in the classroom during the prayer but not say the prayer along with the others; he may then remain seated at his desk, unlike his fellow pupils saying the prayer.

(b) Admittedly, whenever the class prays, each of these alternatives will have the effect of distinguishing the pupil in question from the praying pupils—especially if only one pupil professes other beliefs. His behavior is visibly different from that of the other pupils. This distinction could be unbearable for the person concerned if it should place him in the role of an outsider and serve to discriminate against him as opposed to the rest of the class. Indeed, the pupil in a classroom is in a different, much more difficult position than an adult who publicly discloses his dissenting conviction by not participating in certain events. This is especially true of the younger schoolchild, who is hardly capable of critically asserting himself against his [environment].

4. Nonetheless, one cannot assume that abstaining from school prayer will generally or even in a substantial number of cases force a dissenting pupil into an unbearable position as an outsider. An assessment of the conditions under which the prayer is to occur, the function that the teacher has in connection with this exercise, and the actual conditions in the school leads us to conclude that we need not fear discrimination against a pupil who does not participate in the prayer. . . .

Notes

8–1. In 1995, Germany's Constitutional Court surprised the nation by accepting claim of parents that a Bavarian ordinance, which required the display of a crucifix, a cross bearing the figure of Christ, in every elementary school classroom, violated their constitutional religious liberty right. Professor Kommers explains the aftermath:

> . . . [The] case triggered a storm of protest throughout Germany. Chancellor Helmut Kohl called the decision "incomprehensible." Conservative newspapers bashed the Constitutional Court for overriding the popular will. Church leaders uniformly condemned the decision, calling it a threat to Germany's Christian culture. Many constitutional lawyers, including a former president of the Constitutional Court, chastised the justices for their infirm reasoning. The decision produced the strongest denunciation in Bavaria. Holding crucifixes aloft, demonstrators in Munich and other communities marched in defiance of the Karlsruhe court as their political leaders called on state officials not to enforce the decision. It was the most negative reaction to a judicial decision in the history of the Federal Republic and the only instance of clear and open defiance of a ruling by the Federal Constitutional Court.

> The duration and intensity of the protest worried Germany's judicial establishment. The German Judges' Association warned that the rule of law was at stake and that any refusal to obey the

... ruling would endanger the Federal Republic's constitutional democracy. Justice Dieter Grimm, one of the five justices in the majority, was prompted to answer the court's critics in the *Frankfurter Allgemeine Zeitung,* Germany's newspaper of record. Grimm's prominently displayed letter was published under the caption "Why a Judicial Ruling Merits Respect" ...

Kommers, *supra* page 181, at 482–83.

Since then, a lower federal court has upheld Bavarian legislation that mandated that crucifixes appear in classrooms, but allowed parents to object for "understandable reasons," finding that an assertion by parents that they are atheists was sufficient to require the crucifix removed from their child's classroom. *See* Internationaler Bund der Konfessionslosen und Atheisten e.v., *Religion in Europe,* http://ibka. org/en/infos/europe.html (last visited Nov. 29, 2006).

What is the difference between the display of the crucifix in a classroom and prayer?

... Inasmuch as schools heed the Constitution, leaving room for religious instruction, school prayer, and other religious events, all of these activities must be conducted on a voluntary basis and the school must ensure that students who do not wish to participate in these activities are excused from them and suffer no discrimination because of their decision not to participate. The situation is different with respect to the display of the cross. Students who do not share the same faith are unable to remove themselves from its presence and message. Finally, it would be incompatible with the principle of practical concordance to suppress completely the feelings of people of different beliefs in order to enable the pupils of Christian belief not only to have religious instruction and voluntary prayer in the public schools, but also to learn under the symbol of their faith even when instructed in secular subjects.

Classroom Crucifix II Case, 93 BverfG 1 (1995) (F.R.G. Fed. Const. Ct.), translated in Kommers, *supra* page 181, at 478. Do you agree with the German Constitutional Court's reasoning? Why did the German Constitutional Court reach a different result with respect to school prayer than the U.S. Supreme Court?

Many European countries permit government aid to go to the teaching of religion in public and/or private schools. *See* Gulnoza Saidazimove and Golnaz Esfandiari, *The Role of Religion in the Classroom,* RadioFreeEurope: Radio Liberty (2005), http://www.rferl. org/specials/religion/archive/education1.asp ("In Austria, Germany, and Finland, as well as parts of Eastern and Southern Europe, children attend separate religion classes according to their denomination. Elsewhere, for instance in Italy, Spain, Belgium, and Portugal, there are alternative classes for those not wishing to take religion, dealing with general ethics and philosophy. But France, which zealously guards the separation of church and state, does not even allow religious symbols to be displayed in schools."). The same is true in Latin America. *See* Paul

Sigmund, *Education and Religious Freedom in Latin America*, http://www.iarf. net/REBooklet/ LatinAmerica.htm (last visited Nov. 29, 2006) ("Instruction in Catholicism had been an integral part of the curriculum in the public schools of some of the more Catholic countries of Latin America, such as Colombia and Argentina. However, in recent years, it has been offered on a voluntary basis. Provision has been made in some countries, Colombia and Chile for example, to offer instruction in Protestantism as well. A particularly strict separation of church and state is still observed in Mexico. Conversely, in many countries, government money still provides significant support to Catholic universities. In the case of Chile, government funds are provided to non-profit schools of all kinds on the primary and secondary level.").

8–2. A number of predominantly Muslim countries "establish" religion in their constitutions, by providing, in various ways, that Islam is to be the guiding principle of law and constitutional meaning, as explained below.

The global Muslim population is estimated at over 1.3 billion. Of this figure, approximately 1 billion Muslims live in forty-four predominantly Muslim countries where Muslims constitute more than half of the population. Of the 1 billion Muslims living in predominantly Muslim countries, 28% live in ten countries that, according to the constitution, declare themselves to be Islamic states. [Afghanistan, Bahrain, Brunei, Iran, Maldives, Mauritania, Pakistan, Qatar, Saudi Arabia, and Yemen.] Generally, a country with a constitutional provision declaring itself to be an Islamic state distinguishes itself by seeking to promote a broader, more significant role for Islam within that country. This role can manifest itself in a number of ways, and the practical ramifications of a constitution declaring an Islamic state are not uniform.

. . .

The constitutions of several countries where Islam is the state religion, including Egypt and the Gulf states, establish Islamic law, principles, or jurisprudence as "the basis for," "the principal source of," "a principal source of," or "the source of" legislation. This practice of declaring Islamic law as a basis for legislation also occurs in countries such as Syria and Sudan, which do not have a declared state religion.

. . .

. . . [H]uman rights ramifications of establishing a constitutionally-mandated role for Islam vary from country to country. As the 2004 Arab Human Development Report points out:

Does [sharia] mean those Islamic schools of thought that promote justice, equality, reason and respect for human dignity? Or does it refer to the doctrines of Islamic jurisprudence, which may be understood only within their cultural and historical context and which give rise to various forms of conflict between them and present-day human rights principles?

Tad Stahnke & Robert C. Blitt, *The Religion–State Relationship and the Right to Freedom of Religion or Belief: A Comparative Textual Analysis of the Constitutions of Predominantly Muslim Countries*, 36 Geo. J. Int'l L. 947, 953–60 (2005).

Afghanistan presents an example of an Islamic state where constitutional ambiguities as to the scope of religious liberty remain. Consider the following news report.

Abdul Rahman, the man now on trial in Kabul for having abandoned the religion of his birth for Christianity, will be invited to reconvert to Islam, Judge Ansarullah Mawlawizadah told the BBC on March 20. And, if Abdul Rahman agrees, "we will forgive him," Mawlawizadah said, "because the religion of Islam is one of tolerance."

If he does not, he will be judged according to Islamic law. And under the Hanafi school of jurisprudence adhered to by Afghanistan's Sunni majority and privileged by the Afghan Constitution, apostasy—the rejection of Islam in favor of another religion—is a crime punishable by death.

In establishing the sovereignty of the people—and not the sovereignty of God—the constitution enables a reform-minded judge to interpret it as a fundamentally secular document. That is a possibility that has prompted open criticism from abroad, with critics questioning how anyone in a democratic state can be executed for their beliefs.

Other international reactions have been cautiously optimistic.

. . .

They have some reason to be optimistic. But so too do advocates of the death penalty, because, on this and other issues of religious freedom, Afghanistan's Constitution is inherently contradictory.

Islam is central to the constitution. Indeed, the document begins with the statement: "With firm faith in God Almighty . . . and believing in the sacred religion of Islam." The constitution also identifies Afghanistan as "an Islamic Republic."

The constitution also provides little legal guidance about how other faiths can live or operate in this Islamic republic.

While followers of other religions enjoy the right to freely exercise "their faith and perform their religious rites within the limits and the provisions of law," neither the constitution nor the country's law set those limits. For example, there is no law that makes it clear whether a church can operate in the country. The unstated understanding seems to be that churches can operate inside diplomatic missions or in military bases but not publicly.

The constitution also states that in "Afghanistan, no law can be contrary to the beliefs and provisions of the sacred religion of Islam." This confers extraordinary power on those interpreting the laws. And so, if an Afghan court decides that it is against the "beliefs" of Islam to have a church in the country, the constitution would—if applied literally—support such a decision.

But despite labeling the country "an Islamic Republic," Afghanistan's Constitution can also be read as a secular document. Pakistan's Constitution proclaims that "sovereignty over the entire Universe belongs to Almighty Allah alone." Iran's Constitution links the foundation of the Islamic republican regime to the "exclusive sovereignty of Allah." By contrast, the Afghan Constitution stipulates that "national sovereignty in Afghanistan belongs to the nation." In establishing the sovereignty of the people—and not the sovereignty of God—the constitution enables a reform-minded judge to interpret it as a fundamentally secular document.

And, in a clause of particular relevance to the Abdul Rahman case, the constitution stipulates that Afghanistan "shall abide" by the United Nations Universal Declaration of Human Rights— which states that "everyone has the right to freedom of thought, conscience and religion; this right includes freedom to change his religion or belief."

In other words, the case against Abdul Rahman could be unconstitutional or constitutional depending whether the judges are conservative or reformers.

. . .

Unfortunately for Abdul Rahman, at the moment, the judiciary is overwhelmingly in the hands of men from conservative religious circles. They view the judiciary as their prerogative and tend to view any encroachment on their turf, whatever the reason, as a challenge to their power.

Ever since the demise of the Taliban regime, conservative judges have used their power base—which includes a large, strong section of the National Assembly—to challenge Afghanistan's reform-minded government.

. . .

The main source of the conservatives' legitimacy is that they are guardians of Islamic values and the country's interpreters of Islam, and they will presumably be determined to protect that legitimacy. Nor has there been any debate on the issue of apostasy that would at least have questioned the conservatives' position and, possibly, have undermined it. It is a position that is open to question by religious scholars because the Koran contains numerous passages that could be read as supporting freedom of religious choice. One verse (Surah 2:226) states, "let there be no compulsion in religion." In another (in Surah 16:82) Prophet Muhammad is instructed that his "duty is only to preach the clear message" for those who "turn away" from Islam.

Amin Tarzi, *Afghanistan: Apostacy Case Reveals Constitutional Contradictions*, Radio Free Europe: Radio Liberty (2006), http://www.rferl.org/featuresarticle/2006/03/ad051c73–2777–4497–9f13–1293c2293380.html. After an international outcry, the Afghan court found Rahman mentally incompetent to stand trial and he left the country. *Abdul Rahman,* the Afghan convert to Christianity who was not a poster child for interfaith dialogue in his native country has been granted asylum in Italy, National Reviews April 24, 2006, at 10.

8–3. Consider the extent of "establishment" in England:

[T]he Established Church organizes the formal state ceremonies, such as the monarch's coronation ceremony or requiem ceremonies for soldiers who died in a war; twenty-six of the senior bishops, including the archbishops of York and Canterbury, sit in the House of Lords as "Lords Spiritual"; all the measures of the Established Church, which are accepted by the General Synod (the general assembly of the church) must get the confirmation of the Parliament; the Book of Common Prayer is confirmed by the Parliament; and the monarch appoints the archbishops and bishops at the recommendation of the Prime Minister.... [T]he Law of Blasphemy ... holds that "to reproach the Christian Religion is to speak in subversion of the law." In the schools, a daily act of collective worship is accustomed, and the prayers in most of the country schools in England and Wales are of a Christian nature and reflect the basic principles of the Christian tradition (without referring a specific church). In addition, religious lessons are carried out in the public schools, but the parents may forbid their children's participation in those lessons and in the daily conduct of collective worship.

Shimon Shetreet, *supra* page 179, at 431.

II. FREE EXERCISE

A. MANDATORY ACCOMMODATION

Jehovah's Witnesses have been plaintiffs in U.S. cases establishing free exercise and free speech rights. In the following excerpt a modern plaintiff makes the same types of claims in Singapore.

CHIAN HIANG LENG COLIN & ORS
v. PUBLIC PROSECUTOR

[1994] 3 S.L.R. 662 (Sing. H.Ct.).

Judgment by: YONG PUNG HOW, CJ

This was an appeal brought by the appellants against their convictions in the district court for being in possession of publications published by the Watch Tower Bible & Tract Society

(WTBTS), which are prohibited by gazette notification No 123 dated 14 January 1972 (Order 123), made pursuant to s 3 of the Undesirable Publications Act (Cap 358) (the UPA).... The appellants were adherents of the sect known as the Jehovah's Witnesses. [O]n 14 January 1972 the Singapore Government de-registered the Singapore Congregation of Jehovah's Witnesses. In a press statement from the Ministry of Home Affairs, it was stated that:

> ... its [the Jehovah's Witnesses] continued existence is prejudicial to public welfare and good order in Singapore. The doctrine of the sect and nature of its propaganda are based on its claim that Satan and its dispensation are responsible for all organized Government and religion. The result of the impending 'Armageddon' will be the destruction of everyone except Jehovah's Witnesses who will inherit the earth. By virtue of this doctrine the sect claims a neutral position for its members in wartime. This has led to a number of Jehovah's Witnesses in the National Service to refuse to do any military duty. Some of them even refuse to wear uniforms.

The dissolution of the Singapore Congregation of Jehovah's Witnesses as a society was ordered by the Minister for Home Affairs pursuant to his powers under s 24(1) of the Societies Act (Cap 311) and via gazette notification No 179 (Order 179). At the same time, the Minister for Culture (now MITA) by Order 123 banned all publications by WTBTS, the parent body of the Jehovah's Witnesses, pursuant to his powers under the UPA.

The appellants did not dispute that they were caught in possession of the prohibited publications. Instead, they raised before me through their counsel the same issues which were canvassed before the district judge ...:

> (1) whether Order 123 was ultra vires the UPA; and

> (2) whether Order 123 was ultra vires art 15 of the Constitution of the Republic of Singapore.

The relevant provisions of art 15 of the Constitution are as follows:

> (1) Every person has the right to profess and practise his religion and to propagate it.

> . . .

In the course of the hearing of this appeal, Mr How referred me to various judicial pronouncements in the United States on the right to freedom of religion. There is a fundamental difference between the right to freedom of religion under the First Amendment to the United States Constitution and art 15. Significantly, the Singapore Constitution does not prohibit the 'establishment' of any religion. The social conditions in Singapore are, of course, markedly different from those in the United States. On this basis alone, I am not influenced by the various views as enunciated in the American cases cited to me but instead must restrict my analysis of the issues here with reference to the local context. Mr How's submissions centered upon the concept of broad unreasonableness, and little legal argument was presented in support of this allegation. However, if I understood him correctly, one of the challenges he was making was with respect to whether the minister had exercised his discretion based upon the correct criteria as stipulated under the relevant empowering sections. He attacked the dissolution of the Jehovah's Witnesses in Singapore as impinging on the affected individuals' right of religious freedom, and referred to art 15(4), which provides that the right of freedom of religion can only be constrained if public order, public health or morality is affected, and § 24(1)(a) of the Societies Act, which states that registered organizations can be dissolved on the ground that they are a threat to public peace, welfare or good order.

It was then contended that there was nothing which showed that the activities of the Jehovah's Witnesses, being a small, non-violent Christian group, were in any way against public order. Mr How contended that the membership of the Jehovah's Witnesses in Singapore was small and the alleged prejudice to public welfare was therefore insignificant. Further, he submitted that there needed to be a clear and immediate danger to public order before the right of freedom of religion could be curtailed, and, in this case, the de-registration orders could not have been justified since there was no such threat at all. In my view, Mr How's submission that it must be shown that there was a clear and immediate danger was misplaced for one simple reason. It cannot be said that beliefs, especially those propagated in the name of 'religion', should not be put to a stop until such a scenario exists. If not, it would in all probability be too late as the damage sought to be prevented would have transpired. In my opinion, any administration which perceives the possibility of trouble over religious beliefs and yet prefers to wait until trouble is just about to break out before taking action must be not only pathetically naive but also grossly incompetent.

I am of the view that religious beliefs ought to have proper protection, but actions undertaken or flowing from such beliefs must conform with the general law relating to public order and social protection. The right of freedom of religion must be reconciled with 'the right of the State to employ the sovereign power to ensure peace, security and orderly living without which constitutional guarantee of civil liberty would be a mockery'. The sovereignty, integrity and unity of Singapore are undoubtedly the paramount mandate of the Constitution and anything, including religious beliefs and practices, which tend to run counter to these objectives must be restrained.

I think it is useful to consider parts of the additional evidence submitted by the prosecution. The Assistant Director of Manpower of the Ministry of Defence had stated in his affidavit that from 1972 until May 1994, 108 persons, who claimed to be Jehovah's Witnesses and who were liable to serve national service, had been disciplined under s 17 of the Singapore Armed Forces Act (Cap 259) for wilfully refusing to comply with orders to put on military uniforms. Their reasons were that they were unable to render any form of military service, including obeying military orders or even saluting the flag, because their religion forbade them from doing so. The Assistant Director expressed the concern that such wilful disobedience of orders would affect the motivation of the Singapore Armed Forces and noted that 'the beliefs subscribed to by persons who profess to be Jehovah's Witnesses would, if recognized, mean that persons who enjoy the social and economic benefits of Singapore citizenship and permanent residence are excused from the responsibility of defending the very social and political institutions and structure which enable them to do so'. This concern was in fact reflected in arts 128 and 131 of the Constitution under which a citizen may not renounce his citizenship unless he has discharged his liability for national service.

In many Western European countries, they would count as conscientious objectors. But the idea of conscientious objection does not apply in Singapore. There is no such tradition in Singapore. If we try to introduce the practice here, the whole system of universal National Service will come unstuck. Many other people will ask: why should I also not decide to have conscientious objections and therefore exempt myself from National Service? And of course, even in Western Europe, not all countries acknowledge conscientious objectors. In Switzerland, those who do not do National Service also go to jail. Therefore, the Enlistment Act in Singapore does not recognize conscientious objection. National Service is a secular issue, subject to government laws. Everybody accepts this, including all the other religious groups. In this case, the line between religion and politics is drawn clearly. But it is not drawn in the same place as in other countries.

In my view, it was not for this court to substitute its view for the minister's as to whether the Jehovah's Witnesses constituted a threat to national security. Therefore, Order 179 could not have contravened art 15(1) or been ultra vires § 24(1)(a).

. . .

The final submission made by the appellants was that the orders were disproportionate to the interests of the State and operated unfairly.

As I understood it, the respective ministers were clearly of the view that the continued existence of the Jehovah's Witnesses was prejudicial to the national interest. The basis for the de-registration clearly flowed from the danger of allowing absolute freedom of religion which might create a complete denial of a government's authority and ability to govern individuals or groups asserting a religious affiliation. The Jehovah's Witnesses were not mere conscientious objectors to national service but were engaging in conduct which was prejudicial to national security. The activities of the Jehovah's Witnesses were therefore restricted on the basis that they were against the 'public order'. Equally, the prohibition on their publications was a natural consequence and was therefore in the 'public interest'. In my view, the respective decisions were not irrational or disproportionate.

For the reasons indicated, I found no merit in the appeal and dismissed it accordingly.

Appeal dismissed.

Notes

8–4. The International Religious Freedom Report 2005 summarizes the current state of religion/state relationships in Singapore:

All religious groups are subject to government scrutiny and must be registered legally under the Societies Act. . . .

The Government plays an active but limited role in religious affairs. For example, the Government seeks to ensure that citizens, most of whom live in publicly subsidized housing, have ready access to religious organizations traditionally associated with their ethnic groups by helping such institutions find space in these housing complexes. The Government maintains a semi-official relationship with the Muslim community through the Islamic Religious Council (MUIS), which was set up under the Administration of Muslim Law Act. The MUIS advises the Government on concerns of the Muslim community, drafts the approved weekly sermon, regulates some Muslim religious matters, and oversees a mosque-building fund financed by voluntary payroll deductions. The Constitution acknowledges Malay/Muslims as "the indigenous people of Singapore" and charges the Government specifically to promote their political, educational, religious, economic, social, cultural, and language interests.

. . .

The Government does not permit religious instruction in public schools.

There is one or more official holiday for each major religion in the country: Hari Raya Haji and Hari Raya Puasa for Muslims,

Christmas and Good Friday for Christians, Deepavali for Hindus, and Vesak Day for Buddhists.

. . .

The Government restricts certain religions by application of the Societies Act. . . .

The Government can also influence religious practice through the Maintenance of Religious Harmony Act. The act was passed in 1990, and revised in 2001, in response to actions that the Government viewed as threats to religious harmony. This includes aggressive and "insensitive" proselytizing and "the mixing of religion and politics." The act established the Presidential Council on Religious Harmony, which reports to the Minister of Home Affairs and is empowered to issue restraining orders against leaders and members of religious groups to prevent them from carrying out political activities, "exciting disaffection against" the Government, creating "ill will" between religious groups, or carrying out subversive activities. . . .

Bureau of Democracy, Human Rights, and Labor, U.S. Dept. of State, *International Religions Freedom Report 2005* (2005), http://www.state. gov/g/drl/clrl/rls/irf/2005/51529.htm. Is Singapore a country that respects religious liberty? Would the U.S. Constitution compel the federal government to exempt Jehovah's Witnesses from military service?

8–5. Is the right to proselytize appropriately included within the scope of the internationally recognized rights to religious liberty? Consider the following.

[T]he human rights movement is premised on societies being open to new ideas and challenges; even when a creed seeks homogenization, it must be open to persuasion from other traditions. Although I agree with and share this basic ideal of the human rights corpus, I am deeply concerned that the movement's central tenets may support forms of advocacy that negate certain rights and give legitimacy to abusive conduct. In the case of Africa, the arrival of Christianity, for example, was so violent towards indigenous traditions that the possibility of the free exchange of values and a voluntary commingling was non-existent. . . .

. . . I am concerned by those dimensions of messianic religions that claim a right not merely to persuade individuals or groups of people of the 'truth' as they see it but rather actively demonize, systematically discredit, and forcibly destroy and eventually replace non-universalist, non-competitive, indigenous religions. . . .

. . . It is this loss [of the indigenous religions] that I mourn and for which I blame Christianity and Islam. The human rights corpus should outlaw those forms of proselytization used in Africa, because their purpose and effect have been the dehumanization of an entire race of people. It could do so by elaborating a treaty that addresses religious human rights but provides for the protection and mechanisms of redress for forms of proselytization that seek to unfairly assimilate or impose dominant cultures on indigenous religion.

Makau Wa Mutua, *Limitations on Religious Rights: Problematizing Religious Freedom in the African Context in* Religious Human Rights in Global Perspective: Legal Perspectives 417, 439–40 (Johan D. van der Vyver and John Witte, Jr. eds., 1996). Is the above proposal consistent with a free exercise of religion guarantee? If so, how could it be implemented globally? Could such a qualification be appropriate in a national court's interpretation of its constitution's free exercise guarantee? Is it of the same type as the free exercise qualification applied by the Singapore court?

8–6. China's Constitution guarantees the freedom of religious belief. Human Rights Watch summarizes the implementation of this guarantee:

> Beginning with the 1982 Document 19: The Basic Viewpoint and Policy on the Religious Question During Our Country's Socialist Period, the Chinese leadership, through policy guidelines and a series of regulations, has tried to pursue a dual purpose, reining in religious freedom but eliminating arbitrary implementation of the rules by local-level cadres, a common enough practice in China. Every new religious document or regulation tightened restrictions and increased penalties for believers who dared to assert their rights outside the narrow construct of what the government said was "normal" religious activity.

> As a first step, the government declared only five religions legitimate. Step two involved protecting only those religious activities it deemed "normal." Oversight was accomplished through a country-wide system, requiring that every mosque, temple, church, and monastery register with the government. Unregistered religious sites are illegal–the collective and its individual members subject to a range of administrative and criminal punishments. Registration is by no means risk-free. It brings government control of finances, personnel, publications, activities, evangelical activity, and censorship of selected religious tenets.

Human Rights Watch, *China: A Year After New Regulations Rights Still Restricted* (2006), http://hrw.org/english/docs/2006/03/01/china12740.htm.

Which model of government interaction with religion best describes China? Why does a government that does not seek to "establish" a particular religion regulate the practice of all religions so heavily?

8–7. Government officials in Europe have, in various ways, prohibited public employees and students from wearing the head scarves worn by observant Muslim women, as the following explains.

In Dahlab v. Switzerland and Leyla Sahin v. Turkey, the European Court of Human Rights has addressed, respectively, the use of a head scarf by a primary school teacher in Geneva, and the use of a head scarf by Islamic women in Turkish public universities. . . .

[I]n Dahlab v. Switzerland, the European court found that a democratic State should be allowed to limit the right to wear the Islamic head scarf if it found wearing it was incompatible with the protection of rights and freedoms of others, public order and public safety. The court deferred to the Swiss court's holding, according to which the head scarf produced a proselytizing effect, and wearing it appeared to be a requirement imposed upon women by a precept of the Koran difficult to reconcile with the principle of gender equality. In Leyla Sahin v. Turkey, the court considered all the same values, but it also had to face the possibility that use of the veil could pose more difficult questions regarding the protection of women's rights, as well as those of secular and religious minorities. According to Turkish authorities, if the overwhelmingly Muslim majority of Turkish women wore the veil it would be very easy to discriminate against those who did not. But what really became the major obstacle to the full protection of the free use of the head scarf was the fact that, in the context of Turkish religious and political history, the practice had become not only a religious statement, but also a powerful theologico-political symbol of political Islam. This was an ideology that actively sought to establish a political regime based on the Sharia, threatening human rights, equality, democracy and the rule of law; these were all modern values that the present Turkish secular republic, led by Mustafa Kemal Ataturk, wanted to preserve. It was mostly in the face of this reality that the court thought it best to acknowledge a "margin of appreciation," or deference, to Turkish authorities, and accept their decision to prohibit the use of the head scarf.

. . .

In March 2004, following a 2003 report by the Stasi Commission to the President of the Republic, several other reports presented to the National Assembly and the Senate, and public debates . . . the French legislature enacted a law prohibiting students from wearing clothing and insignia that "conspicuously manifest a religious affiliation" in public schools.

The aim of the law was really to address the question of the Islamic head scarf (foulard islamique). However, to make the targeting less discriminatory, the law established a general prohibition for all religious symbols—such as kippas, turbans, monks' or nuns' habits and crucifixes, among others.

. . . The objective of the legislature was to protect the secular nature of the French Republic by conceiving public institutions—including the educational ones—as "religion-free zones."

Jonatas E.M. Machado, *Freedom of Religion: A View From Europe*, 10 Roger Williams U. L. Rev. 451, 488–90 (2005).

The author concludes, with respect to the French head scarf ban,

> In reality the legislation enforces a kind of "civic atheism" that demands people present themselves in public as if God did not exist, regardless of whether the use of religious apparel is actually disruptive," and with respect to the European attitude generally, "The dominant view in the head scarf debate is clearly an exaggerated response to—and thus focuses on the prevention of—the speculative danger that open society will be overthrown by some theocratic republic, where every religious symbol is seen as a clear and present danger.

Id. at 495. Do you agree? How would the French law fare if it were enacted by a school board in the United States? Would the Swiss or Turkish prohibitions be constitutional if implemented in the United States?

The German Constitutional Court invalidated a head scarf ban imposed on an elementary school teacher for only "administrative reasons," but indicated that states could enact substantially grounded and nondiscriminatory religious symbols bans. *Headscarf Case*, 108 BverfGE 282 (2003) (F.R.G. Fed. Const. Ct.). Numerous German states have done so, some exempting the wearing of a cross or the display of crucifixes in classrooms. A German commentator explains the different treatment of the religious symbols:

> According to [the viewpoint that supports different treatment], the crucifix stands for tolerance, freedom, and reconciliation and, as Social Democrat [and president of the German Parliament] Wolfgang Thierse said, is "not a symbol of oppression."
>
> . . .
>
> The head scarf, on the other hand, is perceived as a symbol of intolerance, extremism, female subjugation, and, as Munich's Cardinal Friedrich Wetter put it, a "militant challenge to the values of our Basic Law."

Astrid Holscher, *Germany: A Country with a Christian Character; The Trouble with the Head Scarf*, World Press Review, March 2004, at 12, available at http://www.world press.org/Europe/ 1802.cfm.

B. PERMISSIVE ACCOMMODATION

In the following, Israel's Supreme Court addresses the extent to which, in its "Jewish and democratic state," the government may enact laws that privilege Orthodox Jewish practitioners.

LIOR HOREV v. MINISTER OF COMMU-NICATION/TRANSPORTATION

[1997] IsrLR 149 (S.Ct.)

[Bar Ilan Street is a major thoroughfare through Jerusalem. Responding to pressure and protests by ultra-Orthodox Jews, the government decided to close the approximately one kilometer section that runs through the ultra-Orthodox neighborhood during hours of prayer on the Sabbath and holidays. Those opposed to the closure challenged the constitutionality of the government's decision, invoking Israel's Basic Law: Human Dignity and Liberty (1992), which its Supreme Court has interpreted to contain a religious liberty guarantee.]

President A. Barak

1. In Israeli public discourse, Bar–Ilan Street is no longer simply a street. It has become a social concept reflecting a deep-seated political dispute between the Ultra–Orthodox and the secular populations in this country. This debate is not limited to the matter of freedom of movement on Bar–Ilan Street on Friday evenings and on the Sabbath. It is, in essence, a difficult debate involving the relationship between religion and state in Israel, which pierces through to Israel's very character as a Jewish or a democratic state. It is a bitter debate about the character of Jeruselem, which has found its way to the Court's doorstep....

. . .

54. In the wake of the adoption of the Basic Laws regarding human rights, the accepted criteria for balancing is the standard stipulated in the limitation clause of sec. 8 of the Basic Law: Human Dignity and Liberty:

> There shall be no violation of rights under this Basic Law except by a law befitting the values of the State of Israel, enacted for a proper purpose and to an extent no greater than that is required.

For our purposes, the relevant question is whether the order issued by the Traffic Controller ... is commensurate with the values of the State of Israel, whether it was enacted for a proper purpose and whether the infringement of the freedom of movement does not exceed that which is required....

55. The values of the State of Israel are its values as a "Jewish and democratic state." See the Basic Law: Human Dignity and Liberty, sec. 1. It appears beyond dispute that consideration of religious sensibilities is commensurate with the values of the State of Israel as a Jewish state....

56. Is it consistent with democratic values to restrict human rights for the purpose of protecting religious feelings?

The answer to this question is quite complex. Taking into account human feelings, including religious feelings, as grounds for restricting human rights is particularly problematic under the democratic conception.... [D]emocracy finds itself in a dilemma when broaching the issue of whether the desire to protect human feelings can justify infringing on human rights. Indeed, democratic considerations seem to pull in opposite directions. On the one hand, protecting human feeling is natural to the democratic system, for society exists in order to give expression to these. This is the principle of tolerance, a basic tenet of democratic theory, vital to a pluralistic democracy....

... A democratic society, which is prepared to restrict rights in order to prevent physical injury, must be equally sensitive to the potential need for restricting rights in order to prevent emotional harm, which, at times, may be even more sever than physical injury. A democratic society seeking to protect life, physical integrity and property must also strive to protect feelings.

57. On the other hand, a democratic system prioritizes human rights above all else.... [D]emocracy's need to protect and preserve human rights gives rise to a familiar dilemma, namely, whether it is at all possible to infringe on human rights in order to consider human feelings, themselves being harmed by the exercise of particular human rights. Indeed, the exercise of a right, by its very nature, risks offending another's feelings. However, recognizing offensiveness as grounds for restricting human rights may pave the way for undermining human rights entirely. Consequently, a democratic society must be most careful in recognizing the legitimacy of infringing on human rights for the purpose of protecting feelings.

. . .

58. How can a democratic society escape this dilemma? How do we resolve the complications flowing from the fact that tolerance, which underlies the democratic conception, simultaneously justifies both protecting rights and infringing them? It appears to me that the answer lies in our duty to recognize a certain "threshold of tolerance" regarding hurt feelings, which every member of a democratic society accepts as part of the social contract upon which democracy is predicated....

And so, it is possible to infringe human rights for the purpose of protecting hurt feelings—particularly religious feelings and lifestyle—in a society with democratic values, provided that the harm exceeds the threshold of tolerance accepted in that society. Quite naturally, the "threshold of tolerance" varies from one democratic society to the next. This being the case, while it is possible to learn from the experiences of other democracies, the utility of such comparisons is rather limited. Thus, for instance, the stricter the separation between religion and state under a given system, and the more the rights are set out in more "absolute" terms, the more likely that such a system will prefer human rights to human feelings. Conversely, the more permeable the boundaries between religion and state, and the more a legal culture is predicated on a "relative" conception of human rights, the greater significance it will attach to feelings as a proper ground for limiting human rights.

Our society is unique. Consequently, the solutions that we must seek are undoubtedly equally unique, or "Israeli-style" ...

. . .

78.   ... [T]he proper balance is arrived at through examination of the limitation clause of the Basic Law: Human Dignity and Liberty. The State of Israel's values as a Jewish state require us to consider religious sensibilities, and indeed to attach significant weight to this factor. The essence of the problem is in the State of Israel's values as a democratic state. . . . [I]t is proper to take into account the religious feelings of the religious public residing around Bar–Ilan Street, if the Sabbath traffic arrangements aimed at safeguarding these constitute a substantial social need, if allowing traffic to travel on the Sabbath and festivals offends religious feelings in a manner that is severe, grave and serious, and if the probability of this harm materializing is nearly certain. Then and only then does it become possible to say that the harm to religious sensibilities around Bar–Ilan Street exceeds the threshold of tolerance which is acceptable in a democratic society. Is this the case here?

79.   To my mind, the harm to the Ultra–Orthodox public's religious feelings ensuing from the free-flow of traffic on the Sabbath in the heart of their neighborhood is severe, grave and serious. . . . [T]he observant Jew perceives the Sabbath as a normative framework, intended to create a particular atmosphere. . . . [R]ather than merely a private or family affair, the Sabbath is a community matter. Thus, an observant community's expectation is that the Sabbath rest is not restricted to the private domain of its members, but that it will envelop the public realm as well. . . . A crowded street that traverses the heart of the neighborhood, with the sounds of honking and engines, stands in stark contrast to the Sabbath atmosphere, as the majority of the local residents understand it. In effect, severe, grave and serious harm to a religious Jew observing the Sabbath ensues upon encountering traffic on one's way to synagogue or to a Torah institute. . . .

. . .

81.   The near certainty test is met in this case....

82.   [Although the matter is "borderline," the Traffic Controller could reasonably conclude that closing the street was necessary to address a substantial social need.]

83.   Freedom of movement—the right infringed by Bar–Ilan's closure on Sabbaths—must not be restricted beyond what is strictly necessary. Is this condition met in this instance? This matter is difficult to resolve. This having been said, it appears to me that Bar–Ilan Street's absolute closure throughout the Sabbath, from beginning to end, is excessive. As the harm to religious feelings and lifestyle is inflicted during prayer times, closing the street beyond those times would infringe the freedom of movement more than is necessary. Indeed, it is incumbent on the authorities to opt for the least restrictive means at their disposal....

This having been said, is closing the street to traffic only during prayer hours excessive? To this end, we must distinguish between harm to the interests and values of those secular residents residing outside the Ultra–Orthodox neighborhoods crossed by Bar–Ilan Street, and the harm caused the interests and values of their counterparts, residing within these neighborhoods.

84.   The harm caused to the secular members of the public, residing outside the Ultra–Orthodox neighborhoods ... is not excessive.... [A]ll that is required of them is a detour, taking no more than two extra minutes....

85.   The matter is quite different with regard to the area's secular residents of Bar–Ilan Street, or those secular members of the public looking to visit family or religious friends living in Ultra–Orthodox neighborhoods....

86.   ... Closing Bar–Ilan Street to traffic on the Sabbath causes severe harm to the secular residents living in neighborhoods around Bar–Ilan Street.

... Every effort should be made in order to minimize injury to these secular residents. Consequently, it is only appropriate to consider the possibility of granting special permission to the secular residents to use Bar–Ilan Street even when it is closed ...

. . .

102.   Tolerance is among Israel's values as a democratic state. It is by virtue of tolerance that rights may at times be infringed on in order to protect feelings, including religious sensibilities....

How is one to be tolerant towards those who are not? In the petitions before us, we repeatedly heard the argument that the Ultra–Orthodox residents are not tolerant of their secular counterparts. They are not prepared for any compromise whatsoever, as tolerance would dictate.

. . .

103. It cannot be denied that these contentions do have a certain basis in the facts presented. . . .

What then is the law when certain groups in society are intolerant? Are they then unworthy of tolerance? To my mind, it is incumbent upon us to be consistent in our understanding of democracy. According to the democratic perspective, the tolerance that guides society's members is tolerance of everyone—even towards intolerance. . . .

. . .

106.   . . . [T]he partial closure of the street during prayer times on the Sabbath, as per the Minister's decision, strikes an appropriate balance between freedom of movement and the Ultra–Orthodox local residents' religious sensibilities and observant lifestyle.

. . . Clearly, this presumes that three conditions are met. First, the alternative routes must be open on the Sabbath. Second, Bar–Ilan Street must remain open to traffic on the Sabbath during the hours when traffic is permitted, and the free-flow of traffic must not be hampered by violence. Third, Bar–Ilan Street should remain open to emergency and security vehicles even during prayer times.

. . . There is a problem with the traffic arrangements regarding the local secular residents . . . and all secular residents who visit their religious friends on the Sabbath. The interests of these individuals were not taken into account. . . . I suggest that the court . . . strike down the Minister's order . . . and return the matter to him. In his new decision, the Minister will take into account the interests of the local secular residents and their guests, as this judgment instructs.

Notes

8–8. Is the ideal of a "Jewish and democratic state" achievable or an oxymoron? Compare the view of the Israeli Supreme Court with that of Baruch Kimmerling:

> [I]n order to define Israel as a democracy only the condition of changing of government by free elections is satisfied. Three additional necessary conditions are missing. First, the parliament, or the people, has abandoned the whole private sphere, including marriage, divorce, and burial, to the control of rabbinical and *halakhic* rules, courts, and institutions. This imposed religious rules over all the citizens and subjugates the state to the syna-

gogue. Second, there are different gradations of civil rights: for example, Arabs cannot buy or lease public lands and cannot reunite with their relatives abroad.... Moreover, all the symbols and official holidays of the state are Jewish. Third, the very definition of the state as Jewish, when Jewishness is interpreted as a mixture of religion and nationality, with all the above-mentioned restrictions, represents the tyranny of the majority, which is incompatible with any definition of modern democracy. In addition, a vote for an "Arab party" is in fact lost because generally a law passed with a majority based on such votes, or a government based on their support, is considered illegitimate. This derives from the constitutional definition of the state as "Jewish and democratic," and is a clear violation of the democratic principle of equality of votes.

Baruch Kimmerling, *Israel at the Crossroads: Religion, Nationalism and Democracy in Israel*, 6 Constellations: An Int'l J. of Critical and Democratic Theory 339, 360 (1999).

8–9.　Would an accommodation such as the street closing in *Lior Horev* comport with the U.S. Constitution's religion clauses? *See* Diane B. Henriques, *Religion Trumps Regulation as Legal Exemptions Grow*, N.Y. Times, Oct. 8, 2006, at 11 (listing more than 200 exemptions for religious institutions to generally applicable regulations of land use, employment, and payment of benefits).

*

Index

References are to Pages

205